with such a command. therefore

Resolved that captain Roach be suspended
until the navy board for the eastern department shall have enquired fully into his cha-
racter & report thereon to the marine committee.

Resolved that capt John Paul Jones be appointed
to command the said ship Ranger.

Resolved that William Whipple esq: one
of Congress and one of the marine committee

106692

929.9
MOR

Morris, Robert
Truth about the Betsy Ross story

Lodi Memorial Library
Lodi, New Jersey

RULES

1. Books are due on date indicated under "Date Due" and may not be renewed.

2. A fine of five cents a day will be charged on each book which is not returned according to the above rule. No book will be issued to any person or his immediate family until fines in excess of $2.50 are paid.

3. All injuries to books beyond reasonable wear and all losses shall be made good to the satisfaction of the Librarian.

4. Each borrower is held responsible for all books drawn on his card and for all fines accruing on the same according to Boro Ordinance No. 81-36.

1) Flags, United States,
2) Flags — United States
3) U.S. — History — 1775-1783, Revolution
4) Betsy Ross, genealogical
5) The Free Quakers
6) Flags in portraits

THE TRUTH ABOUT

the

BETSY ROSS STORY

To The Lodi Memorial Library

Robert Morris
1982

GEORGE WASHINGTON AT THE BATTLE OF PRINCETON, Charles Willson Peale, courtesy Princeton University Art Museum.
A Betsy Ross flag flies proudly over Washington at this battle on January 3, 1777. The artist was there as captain of a company of foot. He was known to be historically accurate and he knew Washington and his flags well.

The Truth About the Betsy Ross Story

by

ROBERT MORRIS

Wynnehaven Publishing Co.
212 Ocean Street
Beach Haven, N.J. 08008

The Truth About
the
Betsy Ross Story
by
Robert Morris

Copyright © 1982 Wynnehaven Publishing Co.

All rights reserved. No part of this publication may be reproduced or transmitted without prior written permission of the publisher.

Printed in the United States of America
First Edition

Library of Congress cataloging in publication data:-

Morris, Robert, 1905 -

    The Truth About the Betsy Ross Story / Robert Morris - 1st ed. Beach Haven, N.J. Wynnehaven Publishing Company, c1982

    237 pp. incl. xiv
    Bibliography
    Includes index
    Illustrated

    1. Flags, United States, Revolutionary War.
    2. History, Revolutionary War.
    3. Betsy Ross, genealogical.
    4. The Free Quakers.
    5. Flags in portraits.

I Title, II Flags, United States.

ISBN 0-9601476-3-2

Library of Congress Catalog Card No. 82-70798

DEDICATION

to

FAITH

My Late Beloved Wife, and to Our Sons

and Their Families

Acknowledgments

Obtaining facts to support traditions, and to refute misinformation or faulty conjectures that have been circulated, requires patience and minute research. It is encouraging that prime source research has, in recent years, yielded more information to scholars than was hitherto thought available, and as correct data from many sources are assembled under one cover they become a tool for future scholars. Help in this regard has been received from many able historians.

Ann Hawkes Hutton, an author, playwright and historian of note, has given invaluable assistance; her books on Revolutionary War subjects tell history as it actually was, and are entertaining as well. Harriet McLoone, Assistant Curator of Americana at the Huntington Library, San Marino, California, has provided first hand, original material from their rare manuscripts and rare book departments which has been particularly revealing. Caroline Chisholm, of the San Diego Museum of Art has steered this researcher into many useful sources. Samuel Stelle Smith, by his painstaking references in his historical works listed in this bibliography has assembled much useful material for the employment of others interested in certain events of the Revolutionary War. Edith Hoelle, of the Gloucester County Historical Society, New Jersey, was especially helpful in providing information on the siege of the Delaware River forts and leads for genealogical information.

Colonel John R. Elting has provided facts from his knowledge in depth of historical matters which give the researcher studying his books a well rounded view of the times. The Charles B. Barclays, of Philadelphia, have added greatly to the known facts about Betsy Ross and have generously imparted them to scholars of the subject. The works of Edward West Richardson, Martin P. Snyder and Edwin Wolf 2nd are recommended to students for their detail and historical accuracy.

This researcher has visited the following libraries in quest of documentary and other first hand information. They are mentioned as useful sources for other scholars pursuing Betsy Ross and related subjects: The Library of Congress, National Archives, and the Library of the Daughters of the American Revolution, in Washington, D.C.; the Historical Society of Pennsylvania, The Genealogical

Society of Pennsylvania, The Germantown Historical Society, The American Philosophical Society, records of Christ Church and Gloria Dei Church, in Philadelphia, Pennsylvania; Friends Historical Library of Swarthmore College; The Library of Haverford College; The Bucks County Historical Society and Spruance Library, Doylestown, Pennsylvania; The Gloucester County Historical Society Library, Woodbury, New Jersey; the State Archives of the New Jersey State Library, Trenton, New Jersey; The Huntington Library, San Marino, California; The Peabody Museum, Salem, Massachusetts; the Clements Library, Ann Arbor, Michigan; the Washington Crossing Library of the American Revolution at Washington Crossing Historic Park, Pennsylvania; the libraries of the Rhode Island Historical Society and the State Capitol, Providence, Rhode Island; The Bennington Museum and Library, Bennington, Vermont; The Fort Ticonderoga Museum and Library, Fort Ticonderoga, New York; the National Flag Foundation, Pittsburgh, Pennsylvania; The Hall of Records, Annapolis, and the Enoch Pratt Library, Baltimore, Maryland.

In addition to the above, certain art galleries have been visited for portraits related to this subject and are recommended to those interested in historical findings from that angle. Among them are: The Academy of the Fine Arts, and The Army and Navy Museum, Philadelphia, Pennsylvania; Abbot Hall, Marblehead, Massachusetts; the Rotunda and the Gallery of the Senate Chamber at the United States Capitol, Washington, D.C.; the Art Museum, and the Faculty Room of Nassau Hall, Princeton University; the Governor's Palace of Colonial Williamsburg, Williamsburg, Virginia; the State House, Annapolis, Maryland; and the Yale University Art Gallery.

CONTENTS

	Page
Dedication	v
Acknowledgments	vi
Prologue	xi
Illustrations	xiii

Chapter

I   **EARLY DAYS**   1
- Betsy and John Elope
- Griscom Family
- "Unchaste Intimacy"
- Betsy's Schooling

II   **BETSY DISOWNED**   18
- "Mixing in Marriage"
- The Testimony
- Betsy Read Out of Meeting
- Starting the Upholstery Business

III   **COLONIAL LIFE**   25
- A Prosperous City
- Unrest in the Colonies
- Clouds of War
- John Ross Killed
- Visit of Colonel Ross, Morris and General Washington
- The Grand Union Flag

IV   **A NEW FLAG**   41
- Stars in Our Flag
- The Betsy Ross Story
- War Intensifies
- Independence Declared
- Washington Crossing the Delaware
- Battle of Trenton

V   **THE WAR AROUND BETSY**   64
- Betsy Remains in Philadelphia
- The Pincers - Canada and Pennsylvania
- Fall of Brandywine
- Fall of Germantown
- Fall of Philadelphia
- Betsy in the Occupied Capital
- Fort Mifflin and Fort Mercer

| VI | THE FLAG RESOLUTION OF CONGRESS | 89 |

No Details
No Specifications
Slow to Adopt
Flagmakers Fancies

| VII | WIDOW BETSY'S SUITORS | 98 |

Joseph Ashburn
John Claypoole
Claypoole's Diary
Mill Prison

| VIII | THE FREE QUAKERS | 107 |

The Discipline
A New Meeting House
Lydia Darragh
Claypoole Deceased
Betsy Deceased

| IX | CRITICS AND DOUBTERS | 121 |

William J. Canby's Address
Theodore J. Gottlieb's Criticisms
The Affidavits

| X | EARLY STARS AND STRIPES | 131 |

Five in Existence
Stars and Stripes in Portraits
Charles Willson Peale
Colonel John Trumbull

| XI | SITE OF THE BETSY ROSS HOUSE | 139 |

Three Numbering Systems
Directories
Tax Lists
Affidavits

| XII | MORE CRITICS | 147 |

Whitney Smith
Quaife, Weig and Appleman
The Hopkinson Flag

| XIII | ADDITIONAL FLAGS | 162 |

Frank Earle Schermerhorn
The General Philip Schuyler Flag
The Cowpens Flag - Murfin Criticism

XIV CRITICS UNLIMITED   167
   The Textile Angle
   The Cowpens Story
   Bennington Flag
   Emanuel Leutze

Appendix A Chronology of Important Dates of Flag Changes 179

Appendix B Chronology of Important Dates in Betsy   180
            Ross' Life

Appendix C Affidavits   182

Appendix D Dates the States Entered the Union, Flag Dates, 186
            Number of Stars

Appendix E How to Display Our Flag, Laws, Regulations   188

Appendix F General Greene's Letters   196

Appendix G Betsy's Family - Children   199

Appendix H Biographical Notes on Principal Characters   201

Bibliography   206

Index   213

The Truth About the Betsy Ross Story

Prologue

The story about Betsy Ross making our nation's first flag has been treasured by generations of Americans who first learned it in elementary schools. It strikes a quaint patriotic chord unmatched by any other known flag story. The legend has stood the test of time against the most minute examination, and is so firmly implanted that attacks against it have failed to dislodge it from our hearts. In Philadelphia the Betsy Ross House, where she made our first flag, draws more school children and tourists than any other attraction save Independence Hall and the Liberty Bell.

As with many prominent facets of our national history the story has become a target for those who wish to detract, primarily for publicity value. This author had no intention of delving closely into the controversial items of the story until studies of our national, colonial and Revolutionary War flags induced him to proceed on a detailed quest for facts. The sincerity of the Betsy Ross story soon became apparent, and a re-reading of the arguments of the detractors revealed that they were rather thin, and were for the most part unsupported personal opinions of the doubters, not facts, not history.

Throughout our nation's written records, and back to colonial times, information on who designed flags, who first made them, where, and when they were first flown, was seldom considered important enough to set down for future reference, hence our data is not complete. For instance, we have no record of the American flag flying on the battleship *Missouri* in Tokyo Bay on September 2, 1945 when the Japanese signed the surrender document ending World War II. Of course it was flying, this researcher was there and saw it on that historic day; it was flying as it was on every ship of the navy. However, the deck log of the vessel for that day, now available both at the Naval Academy Library and the Naval Academy Museum, Annapolis, has been examined in vain for any entry that it was hoisted.[1] So it goes, back through events of World War I, the Civil War, and before. Seldom does a flag record remain unless it happened to be mentioned in a letter or report, or some contemporary writing that survived. Few have.

[1] The story goes that the particular American ensign on the *Missouri* was the same one which flew over the Capitol at Washington on December 7, 1941, Pearl Harbor Day. Apparently no records remain to prove it, however.

When William J. Canby wrote down the facts of his grandmother, Betsy Ross, making our first flag he had no way of knowing the story would be treasured as a national tradition that stirs our innermost feelings, nor that it would in later years be disputed line for line, word for word. He remembered his grandmother as a boy, but did not rely on those early recollections. When he was 32 years of age, in 1857, he felt that someone in the family should gather what information was still available from first hand sources, data largely taken for granted by family members and friends.

Canby's notes, taken from daughters and a niece who were close to Betsy and worked in the flag making business with her, were used for the story related by him in 1870, when he was 45, at the behest of the Historical Society of Pennsylvania. Some of the notes are available at the Huntington Library, San Marino, California, in the Rare Book Department, also on microfilm by this author at the Library of Congress, Washington; the American Philosophical Society, and the Historical Society of Pennsylvania, Philadelphia; and several other libraries having Betsy Ross material.

One does not have to research our early flags long to discover that there were many of them, regimental and organizational, as well as national. Since they were all new there was great latitude for art and imagination, and they were created with reverence and patriotic feeling. The absence of any specifications for our national ensign, other than 13 white stars on a blue field and 13 alternate red and white stripes, allowed flag makers to position the stars in the field as they wished; to have any number of points in the stars, and to have seven white and six red stripes or the reverse. They also added eagles, scrolls, the numerals "76" and other heraldic devices. We do not know whether some regiments intended their flags to be national, to represent only their own regiment, or to be national ensigns with minor differences symbolic of their own regiment. Regimental flags were supposed, by General Washington's suggestion, to have a field or banner color similar to the facings of their uniforms, but that was not always so.

Such uncertainty invites flag writers to make their own assumptions and conjectures but ventures of that kind should be avoided, for if every author were to project his private conclusions we would indeed have a confused picture of flag history. It is hoped that the material herein will be studied by scholars and others who seek the truth. Further information comes to light from year to year from unexpected sources and perhaps more and more proof about our heroine, Betsy Ross, may yet be found.

LIST OF ILLUSTRATIONS

"George Washington at the Battle of Princeton" - Charles Willson Peale Portrait	ii
Marriage Bond of John Ross	2
Marriage License of John Ross and Elizabeth Griscom	4
Hugg's Tavern	5
Christ Church in Philadelphia	7
Minutes of Philadelphia Friends Monthly Meeting - Samuel and Rebecca Griscom	11-15
Minutes of Philadelphia Friends Monthly Meeting - Betsy "Read out" of Meeting	20-22
Betsy Ross Pew, Christ Church	24
Second Warning to Delaware River Pilots - tea ship *Polly*	27
Third Warning to Delaware River Pilots - tea ship *Polly*	28
Thomas Holme Map of 1687	32
General Sir William Howe	34
Scull and Heap "Perspective View" of Philadelphia	38
Declaration of Independence, rough draft	45
Council of Safety Broadside	47
House of Decision	52
Washington Crossing the Delaware, Emanuel Leutze portrait	54
The American Crisis	55
Old Ferry Inn, McKonkey's Ferry	56
Colonel Rodney's Journal, December 25, 1776	58
Attack on Trenton, Map I	60
Attack on Trenton, Map II	61
City Tavern	65
London Coffee House	65
Cheveaux de Frise	67

Battle of Germantown, Map	75
Deshler - Morris House	77
British Attack on Delaware Defenses, Map	80
The Fight for the Delaware	82
The Blowing up of the British Frigate *Augusta*	85
British Plan of Attacks on Fort Mifflin, Map	86
Flag Resolution of Congress	91
Lieutenant Digby's Diary	94
Marriage Record, Joseph Ashburn and Elizabeth Ross	100
Free Quakers Meeting House	108
Free Quakers Membership Book	110-113
Loxley Hall	114
Schuyler Flag	133
Dock Ward Tax List, Title Page	142
Dock Ward Tax List, John Ross, Upholsterer	143
Betsy Ross House	144
How to Make a Five-Pointed Star with One Snip of the Scissors	151
"The Spirit of '76" - Archibald M. Willard Painting	152
"The Birth of Our Nation's Flag" - Charles Weisgerber Painting	153
"Washington at the Battle of Princeton" - Charles Willson Peale Painting	154
Bennington Flag	169
Independence Hall, 1876	175
Scull and Heap Plan of Philadelphia and Environs	177
An East Prospect of the City of Philadelphia, Scull and Heap	178
Flags - Color Plates	
Grand Union	134
Betsy Ross	134
Cowpens	135
Bennington	135

CHAPTER I

Early Days

BETSY AND JOHN ELOPE
GRISCOM FAMILY
"UNCHASTE INTIMACY"
BETSY'S SCHOOLING

Crossing the broad Delaware River in November could be hazardous for a small boat but John Ross and Betsy Griscom were determined to make it. Tidal currents run over two knots past Philadelphia and even a moderate wind will whip up nasty waves and chilly spray which break over the bow of an open skiff, but it mattered not to this happy couple for they were in love and were eloping.

The river was nearly a mile wide and they had five miles to go downstream to reach their destination at Hugg's Tavern on the waterfront at Gloucester, New Jersey. Depending on whether the tide was ebbing or flooding would determine whether they rowed all that distance or made a landing straight across and walked. Details on their venture are lost to history, but the day was a working day for both of them so they probably left after dark and after Cooper's crude ferry had stopped running.

John's friend, William Hugg, Junior, proprietor of the tavern had Justice of the Peace, James Bowman, waiting. William had also signed the surety bond for the young couple. Petite Betsy was just 21 years of age, pretty with her sparkling blue eyes, auburn hair, and pink complexion. John was 22. Religious scruples had stood in the way of a regular family wedding because Betsy was a Quaker and John was the son of an Anglican clergyman. Quakers did not

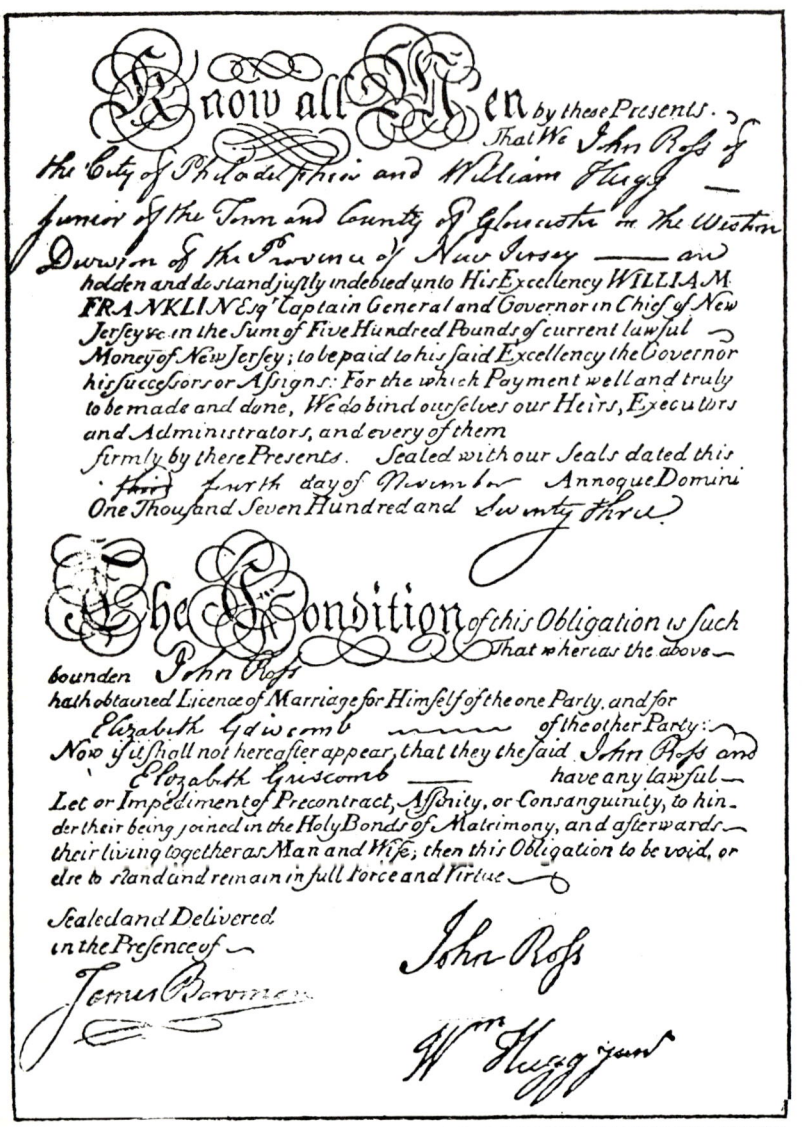

GLOUCESTER COUNTY HISTORICAL SOCIETY

MARRIAGE BOND

Upon issuance of a marriage license, a bond was required in order to satisfy the state that the proposed marriage was lawful and free of impediment, etc. In this case, John Ross and William Hugg bound themselves to the governor under penalty of 500 pounds currency.

The bond was, until recent years, in New Jersey Archives, Colonial Records vol. R, p. 265. It is now missing but an exact copy, from which this photo was taken, is at the Gloucester County Historical Society, Woodbury, New Jersey.

like their members to "marry out of Meeting," and so the Griscoms disapproved the match.

Why would Betsy leave her comfortable bed and board in a modest but substantial and well respected home to elope? Religious differences with her parents and a deep love must have been the reasons. The first we know from facts, and the second was proved by their steadfast devotion to each other — as long as they both did live.

A surety bond, signed and sealed before the ceremony, was required to assure the governor of the colonial province that they were both of age, 21, and legally qualified in all respects for marriage. It stated specifically that, unless the parties were legally qualified, ".... John Rofs of the City of Philadelphia and William Hugg Junior of the Town and County of Gloucester in the Western Division of the Province of New Jersey are holden and do stand juftly indebted unto His Excellency William Franklin Esqr [son of Benjamin Franklin] Captain General and Governor in Chief of New Jersey & c in the sum of Five Hundred Pounds...." Until recent years the bond was located in the State House, Trenton, Colonial Records, Vol. R, p. 265, but it has been torn out and is now missing. Fortunately a photo copy is in the Gloucester County Historical Society Library, Woodbury, N.J.[1] where also reposes the original copy of their marriage license.

The ceremony was performed by Justice James Bowman, who signed both instruments. The license was signed by, and issued in the name of ".... His Excellency William Franklin, Efq. Captain-General and Governor in Chief in and over His Majefty's Province of New-Jersey, and Territories thereon depending in America, & c...." Franklin received one pound and five shillings for the license and James Bowman got ten shillings for performing the ceremony.

The date of those happy proceedings was Thursday, November 4, 1773. Tradition has it that the marriage took place in front of a fireplace in the tavern and a part of the furnishings of the room was a tall grandfathers clock which had only one hand, the hour hand. Hugg's Tavern was demolished in 1929 but the fireplace was saved and was rebuilt in the basement of the Gloucester County Historical Society. There is no record of what became of the marriage certificate or of that precious one-handed clock. A painting depicting the scene was ordered by the late Frank H. Stewart, of the Historical Society, and it now hangs in the Savitz

---

[1] Gloucester County Historical Society Bulletin, Vol. 14, No. 1 Sept. 1973.

By His Excellency WILLIAM FRANKLIN, Esq. Captain-General and Governor in Chief in and over His Majesty's Province of *New-Jersey*, and Territories thereon depending in *America*, &c.

To any Protestant Minister, or Justice of the Peace.

WHEREAS there is a mutual Purpose of Marriage between *John Ross of the City of Philadelphia* of the one Party, and *Elizabeth Griscom the* _____ of the other Party, of which they have desired my Licence, and have given Bond, upon Condition, that neither of them have any lawful Let or Impediment, Pre-Contract, Afinity or Confanguinity, to hinder their being joined in the Holy Bands of Matrimony. These are therefore to authorize and impower you to join the said *John Ross and Elizabeth Griscom* in the Holy Bands of Matrimony, and them to pronounce Man and Wife.

GIVEN under my Hand and the Prerogative Seal, at *Burlington* for the *Majesty* Day of *November* in the *foresaid* Year of the Reign of our Sovereign Lord GEORGE the Third, by the Grace of GOD, of Great-Britain, France and Ireland, King, Defender of the Faith, &c. Annoque Domini, One Thousand Seven Hundred and *Seventy-three*.

Entered in the Registry of the Prerogative Office.

James Bowne

Wm Franklin

GLOUCESTER COUNTY HISTORICAL SOCIETY, NEW JERSEY

MARRIAGE LICENSE OF JOHN ROSS AND ELIZABETH GRISCOM
Note that King George III was considered King of France as well as Great Britain and Ireland.

Library, Glassboro State College. Since the verso of the marriage license bears the endorsement — "John Rofs and Elizabeth Griscomb were married the 4h day of November 1773. (s) James Bowman," it is possible that there was no other marriage certificate.

John Ross was an upholsterer at William Webster's upholstery shop, Philadelphia, where he had been apprenticed in his youth by his devoted, but poor father, a man of the cloth, and therefore one who most likely had little money to call his own. It was in the shop that John met Betsy, who was adept as a seamstress and had been apprenticed there by her Quaker father.

John's father, the Reverend Eneas Ross (variously spelled Oneas, Anaes, Aeneas) immigrated from England in 1741. Christ Church in Philadelphia had a vacancy at that time due to the death of the Reverend Mr. Cummings and Ross became an assistant to the newly appointed Reverend Dr. Jenney. In July 1743 Eneas

GLOUCESTER COUNTY HISTORICAL SOCIETY, NEW JERSEY

HUGG'S TAVERN

Betsy Griscom and John Ross were married here November 4, 1773. Built in 1750, this tavern became headquarters for the Gloucester Fox Hunting Club. Foxes were a bane of farmers in the area. It was later known as the Surf House and when it deteriorated from its original social grandness, it became a hotel. It was demolished in 1929 and only a bronze plaque remains to mark the site.

became rector of the churches of Oxford (Old Trinity), and White-Marsh, which lay north of the city.[2] Trinity was organized by the congregation of Christ Church.[3]

Eneas married Sarah Leech at Christ Church on January 3, 1745.[4] The edifice is an historic Anglican (now Protestant Episcopal) church and is one of the city's treasured colonial structures. It is in active service today.

The Griscom family had been staunch Quakers in America for generations and in those days Quakers objected to their members marrying without the permission of their families and Meetings, and particularly not to those of other faiths. Pretty Betsy had not lacked for suitors, but this one was of the Anglican faith and therefore not a proper match. A somewhat intriguing circumstance in the marriage of her parents 32 years earlier might have caused them to forgive their daughter but there is no record that they did, in fact it appears that she was completely disunited from her family for many years after her marriage. Apparently she was never reconciled to her parents. It is interesting that the exigencies of the war and the caprice of the sea implemented her following marriages to two others of her girlhood suitors, neither of whom was a Quaker.

Elizabeth, daughter of Samuel and Rebecca James Griscom, was born on January 1, 1752.[5] She was of the fourth generation of Griscoms in America. Her great-grandfather, Andrew Griscom, a Quaker carpenter, immigrated from England in 1680 and acquired land in Newton Township (South Camden or Collingswood) in West Jersey. He soon had interests in Pennsylvania because in

[2] Dorr, Reverend Benjamin, D.D. *The History of Christ Church in Philadelphia,* 1841.
[3] *The Story of Christ Church.* Philadelphia: Christ Church publication, 1969, p. 33.
[4] Christ Church, Philadelphia, Marriage Record Book, 1709 - 1800, p. 4120.
[5] This was the first day of the first month of the first year in which the new Gregorian Calendar was adopted in England and her colonies. Hitherto, under the old Julian Calendar, the first month was March and the new year began on March 25th. The new calendar, named for Pope Gregory XIII, brought us in step with Scotland and all of Europe except Russia, where it was not adopted until 1918. The Calendar Act of Parliament, of 1751, which decreed this change, also dropped the 11 days between September 3 and 13 inclusive, 1752, the purpose being to restore the vernal equinox, by which Easter is determined, to March 21. When stating dates, historians and genealogists seldom attempt to adjust the new to the old calendars; they state the dates exactly as they found them on the old records.

However, for precision it sometimes becomes necessary to give double dates, or to show dates between January 1 and March 24, inclusive, prior to 1752, as falling within the year of the new calendar. This applies especially for marriages and births, dates on wills and dates of death. Viz. a marriage might be recorded as of, say April 5, 1750, and the birth of the first child on February 26, 1750. Actually, in 1750 February followed April; April was the second month and February the 12th month of that same year. A genealogist might show the marriage as April 5, 1750 and the birth on February 26, 1750/1, or simply February 26, 1751. In the same way, a person could have signed his own will on November 1, 1750 and died on February 1, 1750, three months later.

CHRIST CHURCH PUBLICATIONS

CHRIST CHURCH IN PHILADELPHIA

Founded in 1695 pursuant to a provision by King Charles II in his Charter for Pennsylvania, which he gave to William Penn. The present structure was begun in 1727. Seven signers of the Declaration of Independence rest in Christ Church burial grounds.

Betsy and John Ross worshiped here. Their pew is still marked.

February, 1684, in the presence of William Penn, he was appointed to the first Grand Jury of the Province of Pennsylvania.[6]

By 1684 Andrew had taken a patent on 495 acres of land just north of Spring Garden Street and with it title to a plot of ground in the City of Philadelphia proper.[7] On February 7, 1685 he married Sara Dole in New Jersey. She was a Quaker, of Newton, New Jersey.

Andrew and Sara's son, Tobias, Betsy's grandfather, married Debora Gabitis, a Quaker of Salem County, New Jersey on January 5, 1711.

Samuel Griscom, son of Tobias and Debora, became Betsy's father.[8]

The Griscoms were among the earliest colonists in William Penn's Quaker settlements. Penn first founded establishments in the Jersies and followed in Pennsylvania after obtaining that vast grant from King Charles II. In the early 1670's East Jersey and West Jersey had been the property of John Lord Berkeley and Sir George Carteret. In 1674 Berkeley sold his holdings, which were in West Jersey, to two Quakers, Edward Billinge (or Billing or Byllynge) and John Fenwick. William Penn, eager to establish settlers, served as arbitrator. In 1677 Penn assembled 250 Quaker colonists and their families, who sailed for America with the grace of King Charles II at their departure.[9] Penn received the grant of the Province of Pennsylvania from the King on March 4, 1680/1[10] and came over in 1682, first setting foot at Upland, now Chester, Pennsylvania on October 28.

All three Griscom fathers were carpenters. Samuel worked on the first belfry of the State House,[11] now known as Independence Hall, and also on the Friends Meeting House. Tobias' and Samuel's names are inscribed in the assembly room of the well known Carpenters' Hall as early members of the Carpenters' Company, an organization still in existence in Philadelphia.

[6] Parry, Edwin S., *Betsy Ross, Quaker Rebel*. Philadelphia: John C. Winston Co., 1930, pp. 3-12.
[7] See William Penn's land distribution plan, in Wm. Alan Ryerson, Penna. Genealogical Magazine, Vo. XXXII, No. 2, 1981.
[8] Yarrington, Robert W., Betsy Ross Genealogical Data. Library of the Gloucester County Historical Society, Woodbury, N.J.
Morris, Robert, *Betsy Ross Papers*. Microfilm in Historical Society of Pennsylvania, American Philosophical Society, Huntington Library, Library of Congress and other repositories for Betsy Ross material. Items G-1, G-20, G-25 & G-29.
[9] Wilson, Robert H., *Philadelphia Quakers*. Philadelphia: Philadelphia Yearly Meeting of the Religious Society of Friends, 1981, pp. 6,7.
[10] Charles II used the double year identification beside his name when he signed the Charter (now in the William Penn Museum, Harrisburg). He considered himself Emperor of France as well as King of England and so noted the preamble of that document. France was using the new Gregorian calendar then and the year was 1681 in France.
[11] The State House was completed about 1748. The first tower was completed by 1753 and the State House bell, now known as the Liberty Bell, was hung there that year. The present tower was erected in 1828.

Samuel married Rebecca James on February 6, 1741. He was 24 and she 20 years of age. Rebecca, also of an old Philadelphia family, was a sister of Abel James, an importer of the trading firm of James and Drinker; she was a daughter of George James according to the marriage license. Both the Griscom and James families had long been staunch believers in peace, sobriety and the strict code of discipline of the Religious Society of Friends, a people who called themselves Quakers. The young Griscoms took up residence in a small house on Mulberry Street, now Arch Street, near Fourth, a home left to Samuel by his father.[12] He continued in the carpenter's trade and both Samuel and Rebecca took active parts in the affairs of the Society of Friends, as indicated by the minutes of their meetings. The intriguing factor in the circumstances of their marriage, mentioned earlier, is revealed in the minute books of their Meeting. The details quoted below provide a good example of Quaker justice in accordance with their discipline.

In the book covering the minutes of 1715 - 1744 of the Philadelphia Monthly Meeting of Friends[13] there is entered under date of 8th mo. (October)[14] 29th, 1742:

"Samuel and Rebecca Griscom brought in a paper condemning their unchaste intimacy before marriage which was read and sent to the Women Friends, which this Meeting directs to be publickly read at the close of one of our First Day Morning Meetings betwixt this and the next Meeting."[15] The minutes of the Philadelphia Monthly Meeting for Women, 1728 - 1756 record under 9th mo. (November) 26, 1742". . . . A joynt acknowledgment from Samuel and Rebekah Griscomb for their disreputable freedoms (and breach of discipline in) their Marriage, was read and accepted."[16]

However, the records for the next men's monthly meeting reveal that the acknowledgment paper was not read at a first day meeting as directed and so a member was appointed, ". . . .to Read it betwixt this and the next [monthly] Meeting at the close of one of our First day [Sunday] Morning Meetings."[17]

---

[12] Thompson, Ray, *Betsy Ross, Last of Philadelphia's Free Quakers*. Fort Washington, Pa: The Bicentennial Press, 1972, p. 16.

[13] Monthly meetings were business meetings. First Day (Sunday) meetings were for worship, meditation, announcements, brief reports, etc. The term Monthly Meeting was also used to describe an organization and/or meeting house; such as, Philadelphia Monthly Meeting, Bank Street Monthly Meeting, etc. Within most Monthly Meetings there were Women's Meetings for business, and Men's Meetings, also for business. Quarterly Meetings, mostly for business purposes, included groups of adjacent Monthly Meetings. Yearly Meetings were established to encompass, for administrative purposes, all the Monthly Meetings within a wide area. Presently the Philadelphia Yearly Meeting embraces 113 Monthly Meetings in parts of Pennsylvania, New Jersey, Delaware and Maryland.

[14] q.v. fn. - supra for calendar transposition.

[15] Microfilm. Minutes of Phila. M.M. 1715 - 1744, pp. 347, 8. Friends Historical Library, Swarthmore College. Morris, Robert, microfilm, op. cit. Items SFL-2 & 3.

[16] Ibid., (Robert Morris microfilm), Item SFL-8

[17] Ibid., Item SFL-4.

By the next monthly meeting it had still not been read at a First Day meeting and so the clerk was then directed to furnish one of their members, Owen Jones, with a copy of the Griscom paper to be read as formerly required.[18]

At the next monthly meeting, January 28, 1742/3[19] it was recorded that the clerk did not furnish a copy to Owen Jones and he was again directed as before. The minutes of the 12th mo. (February) 25, 1742/3[20] record that, "....Owen Jones Reports he published Samuel and Rebecca Griscomb's Paper as directed." No description of what was in that acknowledgment paper has ever been found.

As the matter ended, Samuel and Rebecca did commit some violation of custom. They were dealt with by their Meeting and they jointly admitted their transgression. Their admission was accepted and they were forgiven. They subsequently had 17 children and were respected members of their Quaker Meeting for many years until they both became victims of the great yellow fever epidemic in Philadelphia in 1793. They succumbed to the dread disease and were buried within eight days of each other.[21]

What was meant by "unchaste intimacy before marriage," "disreputable freedoms," and "breach of discipline" must be left to each reader to interpret. It should be borne in mind that usage of such terms has changed considerably over the centuries. There is no record of Samuel and Rebecca having made the required two separate appearances before their Quaker overseers to request permission to marry. However, such negative evidence does not allow us to conclude that none was made. There is also no record of their marriage within the care of the Philadelphia Friends Meeting, nor of any other Quaker meeting, which might explain their "breach of discipline." Their marriage is recorded in New Jersey Archives, No. 37, as: "Samuel Griscom and Rebecca James 6 February 1741."[22] The first proceedings against them, October 29, 1742, would have been eight months later under the old calendar then in effect. The first of their 17 children, Deborah, was born in April, 1743.[23]

[18] Ibid., Item SFL-5.
[19] Ibid., Item SFL-6.
[20] Ibid., Item SFL-7.
[21] Morris, Robert, microfilm, op. cit. Item HSP-4-c.
[22] Their "Licence of Marriage," also dated "Sixth Day of February A.D. 1741," reads: "Samuel Griscom of Philadelphia, in Pennsylvania, hous (sic) Carpenter of the one Party, Rebecca James, Spinster, daughter of George James of Philadelphia Shopkeeper of the other Party. . . ."
[23] Genealogical data for the Griscoms, Rosses, and later related families of Betsy and of her descendants is available in libraries, principally the Gloucester County Historical Society, Woodbury, N.J. and the Huntington library, San Marino, CA. Some is also available in the works cited herein by Edwin S. Parry and Ray Thompson. Most of the library records are also to be found on the Robert Morris microfilm.

COURTESY FRIENDS HISTORICAL LIBRARY, SWARTHMORE COLLEGE

Philadelphia Monthly Meeting (men's) 29th of 8th mo. 1742 (Oct. 29, 1742)

"UNCHASTE INTIMACY" BEFORE MARRIAGE

Minutes of Philadelphia Friends Monthly Meeting, 1715 to 1744, pp. 347-352 reveal the affair of Betsy's parents, Samuel and Rebecca Griscom. A study of this and other items in the minutes gives one a wholesome respect for the Quaker rules of discipline and moral requirements by which their members were bound. The dates of the excerpts range from 8th mo. 29, 1742 to 12th mo. 25, 1742 (October 29, 1742 to the following February 25, 1742/3). Their marriage is recorded in New Jersey archives as on February 6, 1741/2.

The proceedings related herein did not start until eight months after their marriage, although there must have been some prior inquiry. The first two photos, from minutes of 8th mo. 29, 1742, relate that Samuel and Rebecca brought in a paper condemning their unchaste intimacy before marriage, which paper was then directed to be read before all members at the close of a First Day (Sunday) morning meeting prior to the next monthly meeting. However, at the next monthly meetings, 9th, 10th and 11th months, it was still not read, but at the 12th month meeting, last photo, it was recorded that, ". . . .Owen Jones reports he published Samuel and Rebecca Griscombs paper as directed."

Incidentally, another minute on the same page tells in quaint language of the disownment of one Margaret Williams, ". . . .for want of due regard to that holy principle which admits not of any Evil. . . ."

Philadelphia Monthly Meeting (men's) 29th of 8th mo. 1742 (continuation)

Philadelphia Monthly Meeting (men's) 26th of 12th mo. 1742 (the following February - Feb. 26, 1742/3)

Minutes of the Women Friends, Philadelphia Monthly Meeting, 26th of the 9th mo. 1742 (Nov. 26, 1742). From Minute Book, Phila. M.M. for Women, 1728 - 1756, p. 157

One wonders why the Griscoms, after this transgression in their own lives, do not appear to have helped their daughter in her time of need. Was their own infringement a haunting thing that they did not wish to disturb? Did they entreat with her but remain inflexible against her unyielding spirit? Was Betsy's love, as in many similar cases, so strong it could not be denied and was to be pursued at all costs? We shall never know what, if anything, her parents did but we do know she followed the dictates of her heart and carried on against heavy odds.

The Griscom's eighth born, Elizabeth, attended the Quaker school of Rebecca Jones at number 8 Drinker's Alley, near the Delaware River bank and just a short walk from their home.[24] After her elementary education she was sent to the Friends Public School on Fourth Street south of Chestnut, near the State House. This had been chartered by William Penn as a public grammar school and was open to all religious denominations. The children of prominent Philadelphia families, such as Mifflin, Shippen, Morris, Pemberton and Biddle were educated there.[25]

The daily routine of that grammar school[26] was set forth as:
"That the fcholars be kept in the morning two hours at reading, writing, bookkeeping, etc., and two hours at work in that art, myftery or trade that he or fhe moft delighteth in, and then let them have two hours to dine and for recreation, and in the afternoon two hours at reading, writing, etc., and the other two hours at work at their several employments.

"The feventh day of the week the fcholars may come to fchool only in the forenoon, and at a certain hour in the afternoon let a meeting be kept by the fchoolmasters and their fcholars where good inftruction and admonition is given by the mafters to the fcholars and thanks returned to the Lord for his mercies and bleffings that are daily received from Him, then let a ftrict examination be made by the mafters, of the converfations of the fcholars in the week paft, and let reproof, admonition and correction be given to the offenders, according to the quantity and quality of their faults."

It appears then that for five days of each week there were 10 hours of schooling including a two hour midday period for dinner,

[24] Parry, Edwin S., op. cit. pp. 10, 11.
[25] Parry, Edwin S., op. cit., p. 13.
[26] Ibid. p. 14

which would have been at home, and for recreation. That would have taken from seven o'clock in the morning until five in the afternoon, about all the daylight hours of mid-winter time. In addition, a good part of each seventh day, or Saturday, was also spent at school, for the purposes of worship, moral education and discipline.

CHAPTER II

Betsy Disowned

"MIXING IN MARRIAGE"
THE TESTIMONY
BETSY READ OUT OF MEETING
STARTING THE UPHOLSTERY BUSINESS

From descriptions by family members and descendants Betsy must have been a sprightly and pretty girl, who although she had a number of suitors, never participated in the social life of affluent Philadelphia. The fortunes of war and the martinet customs of religion and family dictated a course of life that was not easy, though she surmounted her problems through her exceptional courage. Her marriage apparently did not have the blessings of John's parents either, although, along with her husband, she soon became a parishioner at their former church.

The rule of the Quakers disapproving their members marrying outside the Society of Friends was contained in their Book of Discipline with this admonition:

"Mixing in Marriage with thofe not of our Profefsion is an unequal Yoking which brings ill Confequence to the Parties as well as Grief to their honeft friends and Relatives, and frequently ends in Woe and Ruin of themselves and their children."[1]

Of course there were such marriages; they were dealt with by the overseers, the Monthly Meeting, or an appointed committee. Those who diverged from custom were encouraged to acknowledge their variance and submit a paper of acknowledgment and repen-

---

[1] Parry, Edwin S., op. cit. p. 32.

tance. The Meeting would then decide whether or not to disown the member.

Betsy chose not to repent. The way was left open for her to return but she never did. The records in the minute book reveal:[2]

"The Women Friends reported that a Committee from their Meeting had treated with Elizabeth Rofs late Griscom on Account of her Marriage with a Person of another Religious Persuasion, contrary to the advice of her parents and the good order used amongst us — that she did not appear in a suitable disposition or exprefs any inclination to condemn her breach of Duty to her Parents on her outgoing in Marriage — Thomas Scattergood is desired to afsist the Women Friends in preparing a Testimony to be brought to next Meeting."

The minutes of the next monthly meeting record as follows:

"Monthly Meeting of Friends, Northern District of Philadelphia held at the Bank Meeting House 24th day of 5th mo. 1774.[3]

"A Testimony having been prepared as directed last month in the case of Elizabeth Rofs, John Parrish & John Thomson in company with such Women Friends as may be appointed at their Meeting, are desired to deliver to her a copy of said Testimony and acquaint her with her right of Appealing, it being as follows —

"Elizabeth Rofs, late Griscom of the Northern District of this City, having had her Education and made profefsion with us the People called Quakers, but for want of taking heed to the dictates of Truth in her own Mind, hath so far deviated therefrom as to be Married to a Man of another Religious Persuasion without the consent of her Parents, for which disorderly and undutiful conduct she hath been treated with, but our labors of Love not having the desired effect, we hereby testify that she hath disunited herself from the Religious Fellowship with us, untill by Repentance and amendment of Life, she seeks to make such acknowledgment to this Meeting as the nature of her case requires, which we desire she may be enabled to do through the afsistance of Divine Grace."

While today we may view such proceedings as bigoted or trivial and perhaps a bit humorous, we must remember that a Quaker meeting in colonial times exercised more than spiritual guidance. The general health and welfare of members; their education, and assistance in times of adversity; moral counsel and

---

[2] Haverford College Quaker Collections. Microfilm No. 7, 1772 - 1781, p. 89, part 1. Philadelphia Monthly Meeting, Men's Meeting 26th of 4th mo. 1774.
Morris, Robert, microfilm, op. cit. Item HAV-2a.
[3] Haverford College Quaker Collections. Microfilm No. 7, 1772 - 1781, pp. 89, 90, part 1. Phila. M.M. Men's Meeting 24th of 5th mo. 1774.
Morris, Robert, microfilm, op. cit. Item HAV-2b.

HAVERFORD COLLEGE QUAKER COLLECTIONS

BETSY ROSS READ OUT OF QUAKER MEETING

Minutes of Philadelphia Monthly Meeting of Friends reveal action taken against Elizabeth Ross, late Griscom, for marrying out of Meeting. On April 26, 1774 the Women Friends reported that she had been treated with for her outgoing and she was not disposed to condemn her breach. A month later a testimony was read declaring her disunited from the Meeting.

Three excerpts from the original minutes now on microfilm at the Haverford College Library record the proceedings. 1, Philadelphia Monthly Meeting. Men's Meeting of 26th of 4th mo. 1774. 2 & 3, Do. 24th of 5th mo. 1774.

a prospect of performing to Friends in New England —
Friends here having fully Unity with Samuels proposal, the
Clerk is desired to furnish him with a Copy of this Minute.

A Certificate was brought in from the Womens
Meeting, dated at Chesterfield in New Jersey, from the Monthly
Meeting of Friends there, held the 7. of the 4 mo. last, recom=
=mending Mary Sykes as a Woman of a sober conduct, together
with her son Joseph being in his Minority.

A Testimony having been prepared as directed last
month in the case of Elizabeth Ross, John Parrish & John
Thomson in Company with such Women Friends as may
be appointed at their Meeting, are desired to deliver to her
a Copy of said Testimony and acquaint her with her right
of Appealing, it being as follows —

"Elizabeth Ross, late Grossom of the Northern District of
this

"this City, having had her Education and made profession with us the
"people called Quakers, but for want of taking heed to the dictates
"of Truth in her own Mind, hath so far deviated therefrom as
"to be Married to a Man of another Religious persuasion
"without the consent of her Parents, for which disorderly &
"undutiful conduct she hath been treated with, but our labours
"of Love not having the desired effect, we hereby testify that
"she hath devested herself from Religious Fellowship with us,
"untill by Repentance and amendment of Life, she seeks to
"make such acknowledgment to this Meeting as the nature of
"her Case requires; which we desire she may be enabled to do
"through the assistance of Divine Grace.

The Friends named in the 10 mo: last to the oversight
of the Youth in and about our Religious Meetings, now desiring
to be Released from that Service, Jacob Lindley, Silas Thomson,
William Shipley, William Atkinson, Joseph Yarden & Henry
Drinker are desired to undertake it.

As Peter Brown has omitted to attend these &
some of our late Meetings, the Friends who have his Case

redress from wrongs — all were matters for consideration at monthly business meetings. A close reading of the minutes above indicates their genuine desire and painstaking effort to be helpful according to their discipline.

The newlyweds returned to their jobs at Webster's and did their work very well. John was known to be adept at the manual arts and Betsy had been skillful with the needle from her early teens, hence their apprenticeship at this prestigous establishment. No address has been found for their first residence but Webster's was on Second Street below Chestnut, a few blocks south of Arch Street where Betsy was raised. There is a record showing that John paid taxes in 1775 in the Walnut Ward, which included the shop area. They are also known to have moved to Arch Street and opened their work place that same year; a daring venture for a young couple who could have had little in savings and little or no outside help.

John probably owned his own tools, and since there were no sewing machines in those days Betsy's equipment, principally needles, scissors and the like would not have been costly. However fabrics were not woven in the colony and were expensive to import. Betsy's uncle, Abel James, the importer, may have helped. Her family reputation at their Quaker meeting, and John's family connections at Christ Church doubtless put them in touch with the best known and wealthiest groups in the city and their new business soon prospered. They worshiped in the Anglican faith[4] at Christ Church and their pew, number 12, is still marked with Betsy's name and flag. It is adjacent to the pew in which Martha and George Washington worshiped when in Philadelphia.[5]

---

[4] Christ Church was the first Anglican church in Pennsylvania, founded in 1695 as authorized by King Charles II in his Charter for the Province of Pennsylvania, which he gave to William Penn. The term "Anglican" was changed in America to "Episcopalian" when the separation from Great Britain came.
[5] The Story of Christ Church, op. cit. p. 12.

CHRIST CHURCH PUBLICATIONS

BETSY ROSS PEW, Christ Church

A Betsy Ross Flag now flies evermore at pew number 12, where Betsy worshiped when a member of Christ Church. George and Martha Washington, when in Philadelphia, worshiped in the adjacent pew on the other side of the column.

Benjamin Franklin, Joseph Hewes, George Ross, Francis Hopkinson, Dr. Benjamin Rush, James Wilson and Robert Morris, all signers of the Declaration of Independence, also worshiped here and are buried in the grounds.

CHAPTER III

Colonial Life

A PROSPEROUS CITY
UNREST IN THE COLONIES
CLOUDS OF WAR
JOHN ROSS KILLED
VISIT OF COLONEL ROSS, MORRIS AND WASHINGTON
THE GRAND UNION FLAG

    Philadelphia was a prosperous city, and with a population of 34,000[1] just before the Revolution, it was the largest in all Britain's dominions overseas. Products of the forests and rich farmland nourished a profitable three cornered trade with the West Indies and the mother country; merchants, craftsmen and artisans of the growing, young metropolis were active and thriving. But with all this happy setting there were political difficulties, and they were intensifying.

    The end of the Seven Years War in 1763 found Great Britain victorious over France and Spain. The seas were now free of the threat of Spain over our commerce and the lands were free of the fear of France to the north in Canada, west of the Alleghenies and in the Ohio and Mississippi valleys. To the south there was no more concern of Spanish conquest. The cost of the war had been great, however, and Parliament and King George III wished to help pay for it by tapping the wealth of their maturing colonial possessions on this side of the Atlantic. In so doing Britain instituted taxes, trade limitations, political and legal restrictions intolerable to the

---

[1] Alexander, John K., Penna. Magazine of History and Biography, Philadelphia; Historical Society of Pa. Vol. 98, No. 3, July 1974, p. 324.

colonists. Those burdensome measures and our retaliation were amply delineated in the Suffolk Resolves,[2] adopted by the County of Suffolk, Massachusetts, on September 9, 1774, and endorsed by the First Continental Congress on September 17, 1774. They were again forcefully stated in the Mecklenburg Resolves[3] of North Carolina adopted at Charlotte on May 31, 1775, and were most eloquently blazoned in the Declaration of Independence unanimously approved by the Second Congress under date of July 4, 1776.

The peace treaty freed Britain's vast naval and military forces from the strain of war and, flushed with victory and power, she was in no mood to accept resistance to her measures to collect much needed revenues from her colonial possessions. But the colonists, now enjoying freedom of the seas and secure borders, were in no mood to submit, and because of Britain's victory were less dependent upon the mother country. Furthermore, they were united by common grievances and became bold enough to oppose. So far as this side of the Atlantic was concerned Britain's triumph became, ironically, her misfortune, and eventually her defeat.

The Stamp Act, the Sugar Act and other taxation measures of the Townshend Acts were countered on the part of the colonists by boycotts and non-importation measures. On January 19, 1770 a scuffle in New York City over the enforced quartering of troops and the cutting down of a Liberty Pole caused the serious wounding of Sons of Liberty members. On March 5, 1770 British guards fired into a disturbance in front of the Boston customs house, killing five and wounding six others. That became known as the Boston Massacre. On June 9, 1770 a British armed revenue schooner, the *Gaspee,* became grounded in Narragansett Bay and was attacked by the colonists and burned. In 1773 tea cargoes were impounded, turned back, or destroyed in Boston; New York; Philadelphia; Greenwich, New Jersey; Annapolis; Wilmington, North Carolina; and at Charleston, South Carolina.

The incident in Philadelphia was typical of the seaboard wide unanimity of feeling against the tea tax. Word came that the tea ship *Polly* had sailed from London in September, 1773, bound for Philadelphia. On October 18 a crowd assembled to protest the

[2] The Suffolk Resolves were written by Major General Joseph Warren, a doctor, who was later killed in the Battle of Bunker Hill, and who was the principal subject in Colonel John Trumbull's painting, *The Battle of Bunker's Hill, Charlestown, Massachusetts, 17 June 1775.* The original is now at the Yale University Art Gallery.

[3] The original copy of the Mecklenburg Resolves was destroyed, but in later years a copy with the salient points was drawn from memory by one who had been instrumental in its formulation. Some of the phraseology is identical with that in the Declaration of Independence. An earlier version contained in the North Carolina Gazette of June 16, 1775, has the legal wording of Colonel Thomas Polk as to the new powers to be vested in the Provincial Congress. It was close to a declaration of independence.

ship's arrival.[4] Three sets of hand bills were distributed warning that Captain Ayres, her master, would be tarred and feathered if he attempted to land his cargo in Philadelphia, where it was consigned to James & Drinker, importers. This was the Abel James who was Betsy's uncle. A final notice described the *Polly* and was addressed to Delaware River pilots, asking them not to bring the vessel up to Philadelphia. The text contained ringing phrases, such as:[5]

"Pennsylvanians are to a man, passionately fond of Freedom, the Birthright of Americans, and at all events are determined to enjoy It ... they sincerely believe no Power on the Face of the Earth has a right to tax them without their consent ... You are sent out on a diabolical service, and if you are so foolish and obstinate as to complete your Voyage by bringing your ship to anchor in this Port, you may run such a Gauntlet, as will induce you, in your last Moments, most heartily to curse those who have made you the Dupe of their Avarice and Ambition ..." The notice ended with, "What think you, Captain, of a Halter around your neck ... ten gallons of liquid tar decanted on your pate ... with the feathers of a dozen wild geese laid over that to enliven your appearance! ... Fly without hesitation ... without the formality of a Protest, and above all, Captain Ayres, let us advise you to fly without the Wild Geese Feathers."

The ship came up river but stopped at Chester, Pennsylvania. It was Christmas Day. Captain Ayres was handed the notices and

TO THE
Delaware Pilots.

WE took the Pleasure, some Days since, of kindly admonishing you *to do your Duty*; if perchance you should meet with the *(Tea,)* SHIP POLLY, CAPTAIN AYRES; a THREE DECKER which is hourly expected.

We have now to add, that Matters ripen fast here; and that *much is expected from those Lads who meet with the Tea Ship.*---There is some Talk of A HANDSOME REWARD FOR THE PILOT WHO GIVES THE FIRST GOOD ACCOUNT OF HER.-----How that may be, we cannot *for certain* determine: But ALL agree, that TAR and FEATHERS will be his Portion, who pilots her into this Harbour. And we will answer for ourselves, that, whoever is committed to us, as an Offender against the Rights of *America*, will experience the utmost Exertion of our Abilities; as

THE COMMITTEE FOR TARRING AND FEATHERING.

COURTESY LIBRARY COMPANY OF PHILADELPHIA

Second warning to Delaware River pilots not to bring the tea ship *Polly* to Philadelphia.

[4] Wolf, Edwin, 2nd, *Philadelphia, Portrait of an American City.* Harrisburg: Stackpole Books, 1975, p. 79.
[5] Thompson, Ray, op. cit. p. 20.

TO THE
DELAWARE
PILOTS.

THE Regard we have for your Characters, and our Desire to promote your future Peace and Safety, are the Occasion of this Third Address to you.

In our second Letter we acquainted you, that the Tea Ship was a Three Decker; We are now informed by good Authority, she is not a Three Decker, but an *old black Ship, without a Head,* or *any Ornaments.*

THE *Captain* is a *short fat* Fellow, and a little *obstinate* withal.----So much the worse for him.----For, so sure as he *rides rusty,* We shall heave him Keel out, and see that his Bottom be well fired, scrubb'd and paid.----His Upper-Works too, will have an Overhawling----and as it is said, he has a good deal of *Quick Work* about him, We will take particular Care that such Part of him undergoes a thorough Rummaging.

WE have a still *worse* Account of *his Owner* ;----for it is said, the Ship POLLY was bought by him on Purpose, to make a Penny of us ; and that *he* and Captain *Ayres* were well advised of the Risque they would run, in thus daring to insult and abuse us.

Captain Ayres was here in the Time of the Stamp-Act, and ought to have known our People better, than to have expected we would be so mean as to suffer his *rotten* TEA to be funnel'd down our Throats, with the *Parliament's Duty* mixed with it.

WE know him well, and have calculated to a Gill and a Feather, how much it will require to fit him for an *American Exhibition.* And we hope, not one of your Body will behave so ill, as to oblige us to clap him in the Cart along Side of the *Captain.*

WE must repeat, that the SHIP POLLY is an *old black Ship,* of about Two Hundred and Fifty Tons burthen, *without a Head,* and *without Ornaments,*----and, that CAPTAIN AYRES is a *thick chunky Fellow.*----------As such, TAKE CARE to AVOID THEM.

YOUR OLD FRIENDS,

THE COMMITTEE FOR TARRING AND FEATHERING.

Philadelphia, December 7, 1773.

LIBRARY COMPANY OF PHILADELPHIA

Third warning to Delaware River pilots not to bring the tea ship *Polly* to Philadelphia. She got as close as Gloucester, New Jersey and after Captain Ayres attended a mass meeting on the State House grounds, he sailed her away without unloading that tea.

invited to attend a meeting at the State House, Philadelphia, two days hence at ten o'clock in the morning.[6] The *Polly* then came up to Gloucester, New Jersey, where Hugg's Tavern was situated and which had so lately been the scene of Betsy and John's happy union.

On the 27th of December, 1773, the day of the meeting, a crowd of thousands assembled in the State House yard — as many as 8,000 were reported. James and Drinker put on a bold front of "business as usual" but their attitude was not forgotten two years later when, with the dissolution of the crown authority, they were named as "dangerous enemies" to the cause as Tories and Drinker was arrested and banned to Winchester, Virginia. Captain Ayres agreed to sail his ship away without unloading and did so promptly.[7]

These actions of the colonists, as depicted, were not those of uncontrolled, irresponsible mobs and rabble; they did not destroy for the sake of destruction, as so often happens in revolutions. The proceedings were those of gentlemen, tradesmen, farmers and artisans; their leaders were men of education and culture — men who had the vision to foresee the coming greatness of this land.

The clouds of war soon began to descend on Philadelphia. What had begun with faint rumblings ten years earlier — legal injustices, unpopular taxes, and other grievances best delineated in the Declaration of Independence, had now erupted into armed rebellion. In 1775, the people of Philadelphia, hitherto dominated by Quaker influences, now agreed to associate ".... for the purpose of defending with arms, their lives, their property, and liberty." On 10 May 1775 the Second Continental Congress convened at the State House, Philadelphia. On the same day Fort Ticonderoga, New York, fell to an American force of Green Mountain Boys and others under Ethan Allen and Colonel Benedict Arnold. On the 11th Patriots in Savannah, Georgia, seized powder from the royal magazine, and on the 12th Crown Point, the British post on Lake Champlain, was taken, effectively cutting off the inland waterway between Canada and the middle American colonies.

In June Massachusetts requested the Continental Congress to take over the regulation and direction of the New England Army; men were streaming to Cambridge and besieging Boston, then held by the British. On June 14th 1775 Congress officially

---

[6] Wolf, Edwin, 2nd, op. cit. p. 79.

[7] Returned to England also aboard the *Polly* was a new bronze bell that had been ordered for the tower of Germantown Academy. It was not until 1784, after the war was over, that the bell was returned to America and installed in the school's tower. The building is the oldest in America in continuous use for a school, it predates Nassau Hall of Princeton University - Ray Thompson, op. cit. p. 20.

established an army. That date is held to be the birthday of the United States Army. Before that time the Continental Congress had secretly adopted forces in New England and New York but now did so openly. On June 15th George Washington was appointed General and Commander-in-Chief of the Continental Army, he left immediately for Cambridge, Massachusetts. On the 17th came the Battle of Bunker Hill following patriot fortification of Breed's Hill, in front of Bunker's Hill, overlooking Charlestown. In the engagement about 2,000 ragged patriots fought 2,500 well trained British. There were 441 patriot casualties, including 140 killed; 1,150 British casualties (40% of those engaged), including 251 killed.

Men were now at sea as privateers and with state navies. Patriot forces attacked British ships and shore installations and carried off powder and supplies in raids as far away as Bermuda. On 13 October 1775 Congress authorized the fitting out of vessels for a Continental Navy; the date marks the birth of the United States Navy. On 10 November two marine battalions were directed to be raised, marking the birth of the United States Marine Corps.[8] By December Commodore Esek Hopkins, of Rhode Island, and John Paul Jones, a young naval officer, were aboard the *Alfred,* formerly the *Black Prince,* in the Delaware River at Philadelphia. Hopkins was in command of the new Continental Navy and Jones was First Lieutenant of the ship. The latter claims to have been the first to raise the American flag over a ship of the navy (the Grand Union Flag).[9]

Betsy and John were scarcely affected by all this military activity because business in Philadelphia was carried on in 1775 much the same as before the war efforts were concentrated there, and in fact many citizens passively resisted the rebels. Once that their snug little home and shop on Arch Street were firmly established, and their religious connections at Christ Church were made, Betsy and John were well on their way to a place in the commercial life of the city and were becoming known as substantial trades people. It is easy for us to picture the life of this busy couple from what we know of their surroundings.

An upholstery shop then did not differ very much from one

---

[8] Coakley, Robert W. & Conn, Stetson, *The War of the American Revolution.* Washington: Center of Military History, United States Army, 1975. Many of the foregoing dated events were excerpted from Part Two, An Army Chronology of the American Revolution, pp. 85 - 137.

[9] The exact date on which the Grand Union Flag was first raised on board the recently commissioned flagship *Alfred* has long been in dispute but it is not doubted that it was raised in December 1775. See *Naval Documents of the American Revolution.* Wm. Bell Clark, et al. eds. Washington: Naval History Department, U.S. Navy, 1966, Vol. 2, p. 1307.

today for the craft is mostly skilled hand work. A modern shop would have a power bench saw for required woodwork, and sewing machines with attachments for certain kinds of seaming and piping, but otherwise the tools and hand operations would be the same. Betsy doubtless did other kinds of seamstress work in those early years and her skill was probably used in flag making also. Flags were elaborate and sometimes embroidery was required, as well as the time consuming "fell" seams. The Swiss Mr. Schiffli had not yet produced his multi-needle embroidery frame nor had our Mr. Elias Howe invented his sewing machine. Today fell seams and zig-zag stitching are zipped along in no time but then it was all laborious hand work.

The portraits we have of colonial people dressed in handsome attire and seated comfortably about a cheerful fireplace are doubtless accurate but it is hard for us to imagine their day to day life without running water, central heat, stoves, electricity and sanitary plumbing. For water, most substantial homes had a cistern of some sort, or even a well. At John's house a cistern has now been excavated, so they probably did not have a well. However, there were public wells nearby a few blocks to the west where the city was sparsely settled, also the Delaware River only the same distance to the east had a vast supply of pure, fresh water; the tides seldom brought brackish water north of New Castle, Delaware, 33 miles below.

Markets were just south of Arch along Market (High) Street and there were abundant food shops at the nearby Dock Street area, a victualling district that carried on for nearly two centuries after colonial times. Dock Street was easily accessible to the river so there were ice houses for the abbatoirs, fish and meat shops. Produce from the rich farms of Chester and Bucks counties was plentiful; the same from nearby New Jersey farms and the Reading agricultural center, all converged there. Cabbage and turnips, onions and beans, wheat and corn, beef, pork and lamb, squash and pumpkins, radishes and carrots; milk, butter, eggs, fowl; apples, cider, pears and peaches, all were in copious supply. The good potatoes of Bucks County and other hardy staples came by boat down the Delaware, as well as firewood, hides and grain. Up river came imports from the West Indies of sugar, rum, mahogany and fruit; from England and Europe came manufactured goods, hardware and fabric.

About this time a drover named Jonathan Morris wrote that he brought a drove of pigs from western Pennsylvania to Philadelphia.

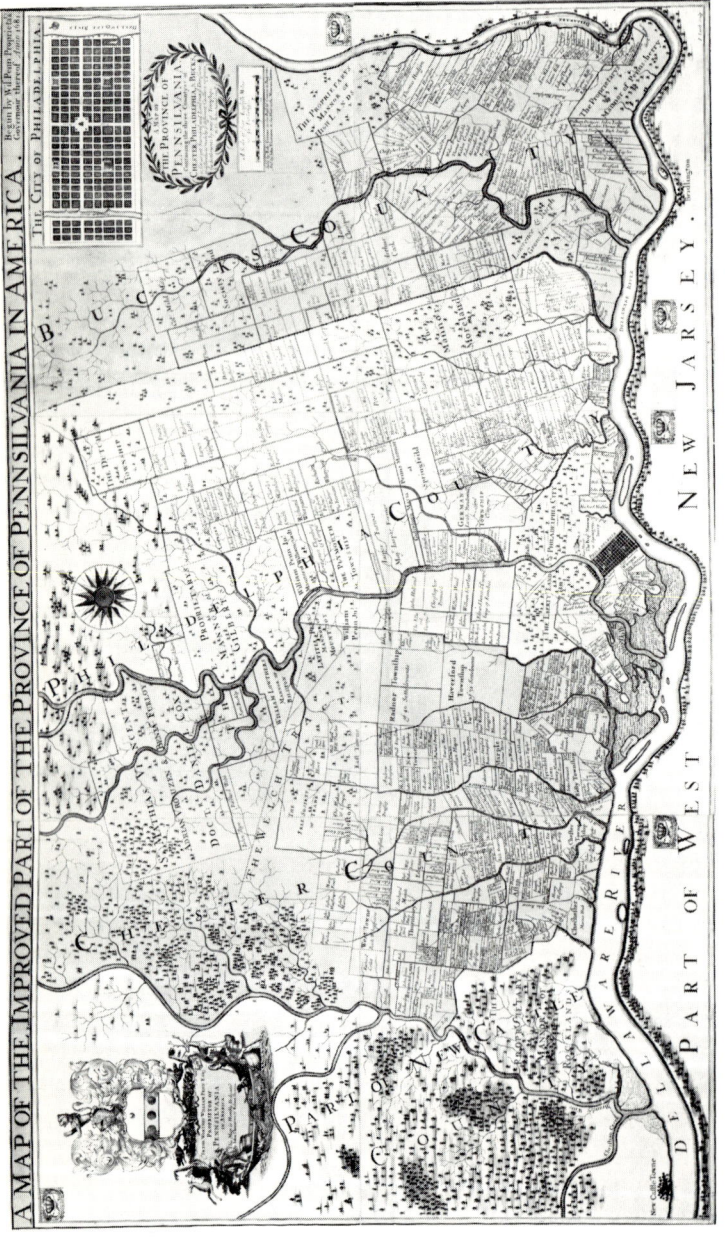

THOMAS HOLME MAP, 1687

Holme was the Surveyor General for the Province of Pennsylvania. This copper engraving was published in London and as advertised in the *London Gazette* of Jan. 9, 1687 contained the names of ". . . . every particular Persons piece or parcels of land taken up there, it contains 7 sheets of Paper, and is Five Foot long, and Three Foot six inches deep. Surveyed by Captain Thomas Holmes, Surveyor General. . . ." It did not attempt to include the patentees of city lots.

Courtesy The Henry Francis duPont Winterthur Museum
Winterthur, Delaware

The pigs were not the subject of his letter as that was apparently a regular enterprise for him, but we wish he had told more as we have often wondered how he got those pigs all the way across the Allegheny Mountains and traveled three hundred miles with them. There was no mention of a cart or dray or a boat. Did he follow streams such as the Schuylkill, Tulpehocken Creek, the Juniata, Conemaugh and other rivers, some of which later became useful during canal building? How did he feed them and how much time did a venture take? All of the details escape us.

The daily life of our young couple was a work routine of six days; half-day Saturdays had not yet been thought of. The city afforded amusements, plays, musicals and elaborate dinner parties for the wealthy, but the social life of John and Betsy was mostly confined to their attendance at Christ Church. Reading aloud was a sabbath afternoon educational pastime then but how much of that either did was not recorded. They had the happiness of the newly wed, togetherness, and the satisfaction of a promising enterprise. Fortunately they did not know it was soon to come to a fatal end.

As a patriotic citizen John took part in civilian volunteer work. One night while guarding military stores he was injured. Betsy nursed him as best she could but as she tended him and worked in the shop day by day she watched him slowly fail. He tried to carry on but his anxious eyes revealed his desperation and struck fear to her heart. She could not allow herself to think about life without him for besides being her husband he was her partner and was all she could claim as family. She stitched fabrics busily but her thoughts were with him in the next room.

Then came that inevitable day she had been dreading ever since the accident. On January 18 or 20, 1776 John passed away. Without her own family her source of strength seemed gone with him and she was desperately alone. His gentleness, understanding, and cheerful conversation while they worked suddenly evaporated from her life. The record at Christ Church states simply:[10]

Jan. 21, 1776 John Ross, upholsterer, buried at CC.

Letters of administration for his estate were granted on January 23, 1776. Her signature on that instrument as administratrix is one of the very few Betsy Ross signatures extant. The document was in

[10] Christ Church. Burial Record Book 1709-1785. p. 3247.
Morris, Robert, microfilm, op. cit. Item CC-1.
The notation "CC" was because at that time there was a single vestry for both Christ Church and St. Peter's, a few blocks to the south. Each had its respective congregation and ministers but otherwise they were administered together. There was one burial book for both churches and it showed whether the burials were at CC or St. P. In 1832 St. Peter's became a separate corporation and remains so today.

City Hall archives, Philadelphia, until recent years but is now missing. Fortunately a photocopy is at the Historical Society of Pennsylvania in the manuscript department.

Betsy became a widow at 24 years of age. She did not go back to her family but continued in the upholstery business. She could have retreated, could have gone back to Webster's shop, or a similar one; her Quaker Meeting would have taken her back and probably her family as well, but her fortitude and independence carried her on and she was soon able to turn adversity to better fortune.

The war situation intensified in early 1776. In Canada our campaign had not been going well and was about to end in disaster; by April Washington had assembled his army in the New York area in anticipation of the arrival of British General Sir William Howe with a large force by sea. On May 23 the Commander-in-Chief came to Philadelphia, joined Mrs. Washington who had arrived from Virginia the day before, and spent nearly two weeks in conferences with the Continental Congress, numerous committees and military leaders.

One of Washington's many interests was his concern over flags for identification purposes and, as he said, ". . . . for the . . .better discipline among the troops." He wrote at least two letters during

GENERAL SIR WILLIAM HOWE
Fifth Viscount Howe, knighted after the Battle of Bunker Hill and promoted from Lieutenant General to "General In America," Howe commanded the British forces here until 1778 when they evacuated Philadelphia. A huge and extravagant party called a Meschianza was held on May 18, 1778 and Howe, having relinquished his command to General Sir Henry Clinton, departed Philadelphia on May 25. Philadelphia was left a shambles of disorder and disrepair; 3,000 loyalists departed for Arcadia, never to set foot in the city again, and 10,000 troops under Clinton marched overland for New York on June 18, 1778.

FREE LIBRARY OF PHILADELPHIA

this time about their importance.[11] And so, for Betsy in bereavement over the loss of her young husband and struggling alone to make a success of her upholstery and seamstress business, a great event occurred at this time.

One day a knock on the door of her shop signalled the arrival of three distinguished gentlemen; General George Washington, Colonel George Ross and Robert Morris. Ross had been an uncle of Betsy's late husband, John, and was well known to Washington, hence it was natural that he would be there. Colonel Ross had been a delegate to the Continental Congress from Lancaster, Pennsylvania and presently served on various committees. He also served on the Council of Safety of Pennsylvania, was about to begin another term as a delegate to Congress and would become a signer of the Declaration of Independence. Robert Morris had extensive shipping and financial interests, was vitally interested in flags for proper identification of his ships at sea, had served as a delegate and would also become a signer, as well as the financier of the Revolution. Betsy had done needlework for the Washingtons, and since the pew where she and John worshiped at Christ Church was adjacent to the one the Washingtons used when in Philadelphia there must have been at least brief conversations with Betsy; doubtless she was known to them. It is not surprising then, that these particular men had planned to ask the patriotic young widow Ross to make a flag from the rough sketch which Washington showed her when they became seated at her shop.

There had been no official flag to represent our united colonies at sea or on land. Of course there were many flags but they were mostly regimental to identify the various military organizations and there was the Grand Union (or Cambridge) Flag. This was our own adaptation of the British Red Ensign, already familiar to the colonists, especially near seaports. It had a banner of red, and in the upper left corner, next to the staff, was the British Union Jack, which was a blue field charged with the red Cross of St. George for England, and the white saltire (X-shaped) Cross of St. Andrew for Scotland. It was the same flag as the red ensign flown today on most British merchant ships — except that the red saltire Cross of St. Patrick for Ireland was added at the beginning of the 19th century. The adaptation for our use was simply the placing of six white stripes across the red banner, making 13 red and white stripes altogether and standing for the union of the 13 colonies. The British crosses in the upper left still remained and signified our allegiance to the crown.

11 q.v. Washington's order to regimental colonels of Feb. 20, 1776, and letter of May 28, 1776 to Gen. Putnam.

Admiral Preble,[12] relating the outfitting of the first ships of the Continental Navy during the latter part of 1775 said, "Notwithstanding the equipping of this fleet, the necessity of a common national flag seems not to have been thought of, until Dr. Franklin, Mr. Lynch and Mr. Harrison were appointed to consider the subject and assembled at the camp at Cambridge [Massachusetts]. The result was the retention of the king's colors or union jack representing the yet recognized sovereignty of England, but coupled to thirteen stripes alternate red and white emblematic of the union of the thirteen colonies against its tyranny and oppression, in place of the hitherto loyal red ensign." Preble did not attempt to place a date for its adoption but Washington took charge at Cambridge on July 3, 1775 and he may have flown it at that time, or soon afterward.[13]

In further reference to this Grand Union Flag Preble said,[14] "The flag adopted closely resembled, if it was not exactly like the flag of the English East India Company then in use, and which continued to be the flag of that company with but trifling variation, until its sovereign sway and empire of the east, exercised for over 200 years, was in 1834 merged in that of Great Britain."

On January 1, 1776 the American forces besieging Boston, which was then held by the British, reorganized in accordance with a Congressional resolution of the preceding November to place them within the Continental Army. On that day Washington had the Grand Union Flag raised on Prospect Hill near Charlestown, now part of Somerville, Massachusetts and overlooking Boston.[15] The British, seeing their Union Jack in the flag, at first thought it an act of submission.[16]

In Philadelphia ships of the new Continental Navy being commissioned in the Delaware in November and December of 1775 raised the Grand Union and it was accurately described by a

---

[12] Preble, George Henry, U.S.N., *The Story of the United States Flag*, Albany: Joel Munsell, Printer, 1872. p. 151.
[13] The history of the Grand Union Flag during the last half of 1775 is far from clear, however, because we have from Lossing's Pictorial Field Book of the Revolution, q.v. vol. 1, p. 575 fn. 3: ".... the ensign [for the floating batteries on the Charles River] was the pine tree flag, according to Colonel Reed, who, in a letter from Cambridge to Colonels Glover and Moylan, dated October 20th, 1775, said, 'Please to fix some particular color for a flag and a signal by which our vessels may know one another. What do you think of a flag with a white ground, a tree in the middle, the motto 'Appeal to Heaven'?'...."
   A note of passing interest, though not relevant to flags stated: "The rations at the camp at Cambridge: Corned beef and pork four days in the week, salt fish one day, and fresh beef two days. Each man had a pound and a half of beef, or eighteen ounces of pork a day; one quart of strong beer [for each man], or nine gallons of molasses, to one hundred men per week; six ounces of butter, or nine ounces of hogs' lard per week; three pints of pease, per man, a week, or vegetables equivalent; one pound of flour per day, and hard bread to be dealt out one day in the week."
[14] Preble, supra. p. 154.
[15] Coakley, Robert W. & Conn, Stetson, op. cit. p. 96.
[16] Evidence that Washington became aware that the Grand Union would be confusing as a national flag to represent a united America is revealed in Lossing, Benson John, *Pictorial Field Book of the Revolution*, vol. II, p. 9 fn. in which he

British observer reporting on our new fleet.[17] Although the Grand Union was never made official nor was anything ever written down about it by the Continental Congress or any colony, it nevertheless was unquestionably regarded for a short time as our first American flag and it represented our united forces on land and at sea.[18]

Those British crosses in the upper left were becoming more and more inappropriate, however, and needed to be changed to something else. Moreover, as pointed out by Admiral Preble, our Grand Union was discovered to be identical with the house flag flown by ships of the British East India Company and our sea captains did not like it for fear of being mistaken for a British vessel.

The visit of the three prominent gentlemen at Betsy's shop was timely indeed; especially with Washington wanting something new which had no British connection; and Robert Morris with his vast shipping interests was vitally concerned. In this connection, Washington had issued an order on February 20, 1776 to colonels of regiments to ".... fix upon colours for regiments and grand divisions [battalions] ... for the identification of units and the better discipline among the troops." Only a few days before Betsy was requested to make the flag, Washington sent a message, May 28, 1776, to General Putnam desiring him in the ".... most preffing terms to give pofitive orders to all colonels to have colors immediately completed for their refpective regiments." At that same time, Colonel Ritzema, addressing members of the New York Provincial Congress, stated that Washington's instructions were that the

---

quotes a letter from General Washington to Joseph Reed, under date of January 4, 1776:

"The speech [of the king] I send you. A volume of them was sent out by the Boston gentry, and, farcical enough, we gave great joy to them without knowing or intending it; for on that day, the day which gave being to the new Army, but before the proclamation [of the king] had come to hand, we had hoisted the union flag in compliment of the United Colonies But behold! it was received in Boston as a token of the deep impression the speech had made upon us, and as a signal of submission...By this time, I presume, they begin to think it strange we have not made a formal surrender of our lines."

The Annual Register, 1776 says, "So great was the rage and indignation, [of the Americans] that they burned the speech, changed their colors from a plain red ground which they had hitherto used, to a flag of thirteen stripes as a symbol of the number and the union of the colonies." Lossing continuing, —"The blue field in one corner, with thirteen stars, was soon after adopted; and by resolution of the Continental Congress, already referred to, passed on June 14, 1777, this was made the national flag of the United States."

[17] Morris, Robert, *The Truth About the American Flag*. Beach Haven, NJ: Wynnehaven Publishing Co., 1976, pp. 5, 6, 9fn.

A letter describing the flags flying over the ships of the new Continental Navy was written by Gilbert Barkly, a British observer who sent an express post on Jan. 10, 1776 to Sir Gray Cooper in New York. He described the ships in detail and said, ".... they have hoisted what they call the American Flag, viz., The British Union, with thirteen stripes red and white, for its field, representing the 13 colonies."

[18] Ibid., pp. 9, 10.

It was flown on the first ships of our new Continental Navy authorized by Congress on October 13, 1775. They departed the Delaware estuary February 18, 1776 for a successful raid on New Providence, Bahamas, under command of Commodore Esek Hopkins of Rhode Island. *Naval Documents of the American Revolution*, op. cit., Vol. III, pp. 636, 637, Vol. II, p. 1307.

Miller, Nathan, *U.S. Navy, An Illustrated History*. Annapolis: U.S. Naval Institute Press, 1977, p. 11.

1. Christ Church (The "Philadelphia Tower")
2. State House
3. Academy (later University of Pennsylvania)
4. Presbyterian Church
5. Dutch Calvinist Church
6. Court House
7. Philadelphia Friends Meeting House
8. High Street Wharf
9. Mulberry Street
10. Sassafras Street
11. Vine Street
12. Chestnut Street
13. Draw Bridge (at Dock Street)

"Perspective View" of Philadelphia from the New Jersey shore. A drawing after George Heap and Nicholas Scull. 1754 engraving of the City of Philadelphia. Note the Grand Union Flag (as of 1752) on stern of vessel in left foreground.

banners be "... of fuch colour and with fuch devices as fhall be deemed proper by the [Provincial] Congress."[19] Apparently at this time regimental flags were meant, but there is no doubt that Washington felt the importance of standards and was eager to have a suitable national ensign.

At this juncture it may be well to inject an enigma which exists as to the Grand Union Flag. Although that banner has been assumed to have been invented some time during the latter half of 1775 there is a further complication which should be recognized.

In 1752 one George Heap, a surveyor, produced an engraving which he entitled, *"Perspective View" of Philadelphia*. He died before it could be printed in London as planned, but it was produced in 1754 under the direction of Nicholas Scull, Surveyor General of the Province of Pennsylvania.[20] Lo and behold — a Grand Union streamed prominently from a ship in the left foreground! That was in 1752 when we were a placid colony, a proprietorship under the king; the Seven Years War had not yet been fought, there were no Townshend Acts, no oppressive tea taxes. It has been said the flag was not a Grand Union but was the exactly similar house flag of the British East India Company, but that could hardly be so because it was not flown from the main or foremast where the house flag belonged. Instead it was worn on her taffrail staff astern where the national ensign belonged, and forward on the jackstaff was the union jack, where it belonged. She was unmistakably a provincial vessel. To add to the enigma — Heap showed less than 13 stripes, however he may not have had room for more, also Georgia did not become a royal province until 1754 so a lesser number was acceptable.

We flag historians should thus learn not to jump to conclusions but to realize we don't know it all and to allow that there are enigmas which remain unsolved.

---

[19] Morris, Robert, *The Truth About the American Flag,* op. cit. p. 39.
[20] Snyder, Martin P., *City of Independence*. New York: Praeger Publishers, 1975, pp. 42-47.

CHAPTER IV

A New Flag

STARS IN OUR FLAG
THE BETSY ROSS STORY
WAR INTENSIFIES
INDEPENDENCE DECLARED
WASHINGTON CROSSING THE DELAWARE
BATTLE OF TRENTON

There is no record of why it was stars that were selected to replace the British crosses. Some say they were suggested by the three heraldic molets, or mullets (stars), in Washington's family coat of arms, or from the 13 six-pointed stars in Washington's (so called) Headquarters Flag; but there is no early tradition, nor documentary foundation for either contention. There were precedents of stars in other flags of the time, however. The flag of the Green Mountain Boys contained 13 five-pointed stars, as did the flags of the First and Second Rhode Island Regiments.[1] Colonel John Stark led the Green Mountain Boys at Bunker's Hill on June 17, 1775. In the State House at Providence, Rhode Island, and at the Rhode Island Historical Society are the original flags of the Rhode Island regiments mentioned.

Thomas G. Brennan, Registrar of the Society, showed this author the flag of the United Company of the Train of Artillery of Providence. It has 13 five-pointed stars and is of great heraldic beauty.[2] He said the flag may date as early as 1774, though the company was officially formed in 1775. Historian E. Andrew

---
[1] Chapin, Howard M., *The Artistic Motives in the United States Flag*. Providence: Roger Williams Press, 1930.
[2] Morris, Robert, *The Truth About the American Flag*, op. cit. pp. 21-23.

Mowbray of the Company of Military Historians has competently researched the flag.³ Moreover, there is ample confirmation that the First and Second Regiments had their 13 star flags by 1775. The United Company took part in the siege of Boston in 1775 resulting in the evacuation of the British under General Sir William Howe on March 16 and 17, 1776 to Halifax.

Additionally, there is an early reference to stars in a verse published in the March 10, 1774 issue of the Massachusetts Spy, or Thomas's Boston Journal:

> A ray of bright glory
> Now gleams from afar;
> The American Enfign
> Now fparkles a ftar.

What that particular flag was may never be known. Apparently it was one of the many that have disappeared forever.

According to the family story the sketch which Washington, Ross and Morris brought on the visit of those three distinguished gentlemen to Betsy's shop contained six-pointed stars and Betsy made the suggestion that they be five-pointed because the latter could be cut with a single snip of the scissors from fabric properly folded; such a time saver being important in view of the large number of hand made flags that would be required. She is also said to have suggested that it be of rectangular shape instead of square. Most regimental flags of the time were square for ease in parading, but others, particularly marine, were longer on the fly than on the hoist because they streamed more beautifully in a breeze. Betsy was asked to make a flag as soon as possible. She did so and it was accepted at the State House. She was then asked to make many more. That was the start of her flag making business and it continued throughout her life and beyond. To Betsy the important thing was the visit of General Washington, not the fact that she made our nation's first stars and stripes flag.

That is the Betsy Ross Story. It is very simple, direct and logical. She never wrote it down, nor did she record the exact date; though she told of it many times to family and friends and always placed the time at the end of May or the first days of June, 1776. No other contemporary person ever claimed to have made our first flag nor disputed Betsy.

Washington departed Philadelphia June 4th or 5th 1776 for New York.⁴ On the 25th British General Sir William Howe arrived

3 Ibid., p. 23.
4 Freeman, Douglas Southall, *George Washington*, New York: Charles Scribner's Sons, 1951. Freeman quotes sources giving June 4; some sources give the date as June 5.

off Sandy Hook, New Jersey with over 100 ships. Eventually 32,000 men were disembarked on Staten Island in perhaps the greatest amphibious operation in all history up to that time. In Canada, General Benedict Arnold evacuated his patriot forces from Montreal on June 9 and at the same time our men met defeat at Three Rivers, between Montreal and Quebec. On June 14, General John Sullivan retired his American forces southward toward Lake Champlain and then to Crown Point, New York; ending our unsuccessful Canadian campaign.

France and Spain were in armed conflict with England[5] and had begun sending us munitions valued at two million livres; this month France supplied Hortalez et Cie. a million livres in gold to finance armament for our operations. Also in June of 1776, British naval forces were repulsed at Charleston, South Carolina, ending their efforts to invade the South for nearly three years.[6]

There had been a gradual build-up over the months to declare independence,[7] although an exact transcript of the minutes of Congress makes the proceedings sound almost like any other routine business. On Wednesday, July 3, 1776 some of the many items of the day were:

"Refolved, That this Congress will to-morrow again refolve itself into a committee of the whole, to take into their farther confideration, the declaration of independence."

"Adjourned to nine o'clock to-morrow."

On Thursday, July 4, 1776 the day began with such business as:

"Refolved, That application be made to the committee of fafety of Pennsylvania for a fupply of flints for the troops of New York."

Another minute was:

"Agreeable to the order of the day, the Congrefs refolved itself into a committee of the whole, to take into farther confideration the declaration. . .[of independence]."

"The declaration being read, was agreed to as follows:

"A declaration by reprefentatives of the United States of America in Congrefs Affembled."

---

[5] France declared war on Great Britain in February of 1778. Spain did likewise in 1779. In 1780 Russia declared armed neutrality and Netherlands joined in the fighting of Britain at sea. On December 20, 1780 Great Britain declared war on the Netherlands.

[6] Coakley & Conn, op. cit. pp. 98-100.

[7] On April 12, 1776 the Provincial Congress of North Carolina instructed its delegates to the Continental Congress to vote for independence. On June 7 Richard Henry Lee, a delegate from Virginia proposed a resolution by Congress declaring independence of the 13 United Colonies from Great Britain. On June 11 Congress appointed a committee of five delegates to draft a declaration of independence, they were; John Adams, Benjamin Franklin, Thomas Jefferson, Roger Sherman and Robert R. Livingston. On July 2 Congress approved the resolution introduced by Richard Henry Lee on June 7.

Then followed the Declaration of Independence as we now know it:

"When in the course of human events, it becomes necefsary for one people to disfolve the Political bands which have connected them with another, and to afsume among the Powers of the earth...."

DECLARATION OF INDEPENDENCE

After Richard Henry Lee, of Virginia, proposed a resolution on June 7, 1776 to declare independence from Great Britain, Congress, on June 11, appointed a committee of five to draft a declaration of independence. They were: John Adams, Benjamin Franklin, Thomas Jefferson, Roger Sherman and Robert R. Livingston.

This page of rough draft in the handwriting of Jefferson has corrections and changes by Adams and Franklin. It contains phraseology initiated in North Carolina and colonial grievances stated in Virginia. The committee submitted their final draft on June 28, 1776 after about two weeks of labor, mostly Jefferson's. Congress altered the final draft considerably and on July 1 when Delaware voted affirmatively after Caesar Rodney's harrowing night ride from Dover, they declared the resolution originated by Lee to be in effect.

On July 4, a vote was taken to adopt the Declaration of Independence; it was signed by John Hancock, President, and Charles Thomson, Secretary. It was read to the public from the State House on July 8 and published in the Pennsylvania Gazette on July 10. On the 15th it was ordered engrossed on parchment for signatures and most signers affixed their names on August 2nd. On January 18, 1777, Congress, in the euphoria subsequent to Washington's crossing the Delaware and his victories at Trenton and Princeton, authorized facsimile copies of the original document containing all 56 signatures. It was entitled, "In Congress, July 4, 1776. The Unanimous Declaration of the thirteen united States of America."

A Declaration by the Representatives of the UNITED STATES OF AMERICA, in General Congress assembled.

When in the course of human events it becomes necessary for one people to dissolve the political bands which have connected them with another, and to assume among the powers of the earth the separate and equal station to which the laws of nature & of nature's god entitle them, a decent respect to the opinions of mankind requires that they should declare the causes which impel them to the separation.

We hold these truths to be self-evident: that all men are created equal, that they are endowed by their creator with equal rights, that among these are life, liberty, & the pursuit of happiness; that to secure these rights, governments are instituted among men, deriving their just powers from the consent of the governed; that whenever any form of government becomes destructive of these ends, it is the right of the people to alter or to abolish it, & to institute new government, laying it's foundation on such principles & organising it's powers in such form, as to them shall seem most likely to effect their safety & happiness. prudence indeed will dictate that governments long established should not be changed for light & transient causes: and accordingly all experience hath shewn that mankind are more disposed to suffer while evils are sufferable, than to right themselves by abolishing the forms to which they are accustomed. but when a long train of abuses & usurpations [begun at a distinguished period, &] pursuing invariably the same object, evinces a design to reduce them under absolute Despotism, it is their right, it is their duty, to throw off such government, & to provide new guards for their future security. such has been the patient sufferance of these colonies; & such is now the necessity which constrains them to [expunge] their former systems of government. the history of the present king of Great Britain is a history of unremitting injuries and usurpations, [among which appears no solitary fact to contradict the uniform tenor of the rest, all of which have] in direct object the establishment of an absolute tyranny over these states. to prove this, let facts be submitted to a candid world, [for the truth of which we pledge a faith yet unsullied by falsehood.]

LIBRARY OF CONGRESS

The war continued in July with Governor Lord Dunmore's destructive, though indecisive, raids in the Chesapeake Bay area. On August 27, 22,000 British and Hessian troops defeated 10,000 Americans on Long Island. Washington's masterful military withdrawal with his out-numbered troops after the engagement on Brooklyn Heights, and subsequent maneuvering in September and October during evacuation from Manhattan Island, won him the highest respect from military tacticians then and now.

On September 16, 1776, Congress asked the states to raise 88 battalions for the Continental Army — to be enlisted for the duration of the war. That was important, because most of the earlier enlistments were to expire on December 31, and had it not been for our victory at Trenton on December 26 it would have been most difficult, if not impossible, to hold the ragged remains of our army together.

On September 26 Congress appointed Benjamin Franklin, Silas Deane and Thomas Jefferson as commissioners to the court of France. Jefferson declined; he remained at his home in Virginia and took no further active part in the entire Revolutionary War. He served for a brief, but unhappy term as governor of Virginia late in the war.

On October 11 - 13 General Benedict Arnold blocked a superior British force at Valcour Island on Lake Champlain. He was defeated but he thwarted any further enemy action from Canada for that year of 1776. There were various successful British actions that month at Throg's Neck, Pelham and Mamaroneck and Washington withdrew to White Plains where there was a heavy engagement in which Howe again failed to trap him. He retreated northward and crossed the Hudson westward with part of his army.

In November the remaining American forces fought at what is now Fort Washington, New York, and Fort Lee, New Jersey; presently at either end of the George Washington Bridge. Our losses were disastrous at both and the remnants of our army had to flee across New Jersey with Major General Lord Earl Charles Cornwallis in close pursuit.[8]

---

[8] N.B. Researchers seeking further details of the military and political action during the retreat from New York across New Jersey; Washington Crossing the Delaware; the battles of Trenton, Princeton, Brandywine, Germantown, Whitemarsh, and the engagements on the Delaware are respectfully referred to the works in the bibliography by authors John Cunningham, Douglas Southall Freeman, Edward S. Gifford, Jr., Ann Hawkes Hutton, Samuel Stelle Smith, William S. Stryker and Edwin Wolf II.

Samuel Stelle Smith has done an outstanding service with his minute details and elaborate source references. Ann Hawkes Hutton has combined historical accuracy with her delightful story telling ability to make the facts interesting.

The large number of footnotes required for referencing in this part of the treatise became unwieldy and have mostly been omitted.

In COUNCIL of SAFETY,

Philadelphia, November 14*th* 1776,
12 *o'Clock, Thurfday.*

SIR,

WE have certain Intelligence that the Enemy has actually failed from New York Five Hundred Ships for this City, and that great Numbers had got out of the Hook on 12 o'Clock Yefterday and were fteering towards our Capes: As you value the Safety of your Country, and all that is dear and valuable to Men, we moft earneftly folicit your immediate Affiftance, and that you will march all your Battalion to this City without the leaft Delay.

As nothing but the moft hafty Marching of the Militia will enable us to make a Stand, it is hoped that your Battalion will manifeft their ufual Spirit, and come forth on this trying Occafion with the Alacrity that will do them Honour. If you can collect any Shovels, Spades, Grubbing Hoes and Pitching Axes, beg you will bring them forward and the People fhall be paid for them a full Price.

By Order of Council,

THOMAS WHARTON, Jun. Prefident

COURTESY LIBRARY COMPANY OF PHILADELPHIA

COUNCIL OF SAFETY BROADSIDE

After the British had captured New York, we believed, correctly, that their next objective would be the capital. Philadelphians feared the attack would be by sea, as indicated by this broadside. General Howe sent Cornwallis by land instead and he reached as far as Trenton, where his well trained Hessian troops were repulsed on December 26, 1776 by Washington. Their successful attack on the capital came during the late summer and autumn of the following year — that time by land and by sea.

On December 5th Washington completed moving his baggage and stores from north of Trenton across the Delaware, and on the 7th, having learned that Howe's forces were advancing from Brunswick, now New Brunswick, toward Princeton, began moving his men across to the Pennsylvania side. Heavy Durham boats, named for Durham Furnace, an iron making works 40 miles farther up river, and all other suitable craft had been gathered in advance. Howe divided his army at Princeton and himself led troops into Trenton on December 8 just as George Washington's rear guard evacuated the east bank farther up river. On the next day Howe and Major General James Grant, who accompanied him as field commander, made plans to take Philadelphia, the capital of the United States. Also on the 9th, beginning at one o'clock in the morning Cornwallis moved his division of 4,000 men from Maidenhead, now Lawrenceville, six miles southwest of Princeton, to Lambertville, New Jersey, with the intention of crossing the Delaware at Coryell's Ferry, now New Hope, Pennsylvania.

The defense there was only 400 men, Germans from Maryland and Pennsylvania under Colonel Nicholas Haussegger. However, thanks to Washington's previous orders to clear all boats from the Jersey shore, they found none and gave up the crossing. They returned next day, the 10th, to Pennington, New Jersey. Cornwallis' failure to make a crossing, and the lack of boats, changed Howe's mind about pushing on to Philadelphia and he then issued orders to establish winter quarters. That took four days.

On December 14th General Howe personally departed Trenton, traveling via Princeton and arriving at Brunswick on the 15th. There he was joined by Cornwallis and the two arrived in New York at 2:00 A.M. on the 17th. The latter was brevetted to lieutenant general and had a grant of leave to return to London for the winter. That left General Grant in command of all British forces in New Jersey. He made his headquarters in Brunswick.

When Howe had reached Trenton and sent detachments south to Bordentown, Washington warned Congress of his fears for the capital. Whenever the river froze solid Howe could march superior forces across, or he could go south on the Jersey side to Cooper's Ferry, now Camden, opposite Philadelphia, and cross there. Congress acted promptly. Their minutes record under date of Wednesday, December 12, 1776:

"Refolved, That this Congrefs be for the prefent adjourned to the town of Baltimore . . . to meet on the 20th instant . . . ."

There was also a resolution giving General Washington dictatorial powers, and upon meeting at Baltimore on Friday, December

20 they resolved:

"....That Robert Morris, George Clymer and George Walton, Esquire; be a committee of Congrefs, with power to execute fuch bufineff as may be proper and neceffary to be done at Philadelphia...."

Betsy Ross, who was now a widow of less than a year and trying to make a living with her flag making and upholstery business, had not much choice but to carry on and bear with the emergency. She left no record of how much she feared, but with the burnings and ravishing that had visited other places earlier[9] there is little doubt that she trembled and that it was her sterling fortitude that carried her through. Perhaps it was fortunate that she was busy making flags, for most other commercial activity was at a standstill. It is said that she had orders to make all the flags she could for the government.

Washington's worries were many; Canada had been lost, New York had fallen, and now our heartland and capital were about to be crushed. On December 18, 1776 he wrote a confidential letter to his brother, John Augustine, saying "....If every nerve is not strained to recruit the New Army with all possible expedition, I think the game is pretty near up...." But the deep determination of his spirit and his innate refusal to accept defeat prompted him to close the same letter with "....under a full persuasion of the justice of our cause, I cannot entertain an idea that it will finally sink, though it may remain for some time under a cloud."

Major General Charles Lee was slowly making his way down from northern New Jersey, despite urgent requests to come with haste. There was a surprise raiding party of the British near Basking Ridge on the 13th and Lee himself was captured, his troops escaped however. Major General John Sullivan brought them to Washington on the 20th, but they were not the "5,000 troops in good spirits" Lee had said he had; there were only 2,000 and they were poorly clad and poorly equipped. Major General Horatio Gates arrived on the same day but his regiments, New Englanders, had no more than 600 rank and file. Formal returns at this time reported only 7,659 effectives in the entire army on the west bank of the Delaware. "The Cloathing of the troops is a matter of infinite importance," the Commander-in-Chief informed Congress, "Their distresses are extremely great, many of 'em being entirely naked[10] and most so thinly clad as to be unfit for service."

9 See Appendix F
10 "Naked" was not synonymous with "nude" in those days. In this sense it meant ill, or scantily clothed; possibly only in blankets or sacks.

49

The situation in late December was that 14,000 British, including their Hessian contingents, were stretched from Brunswick through Princeton and Trenton to Bordentown, Burlington and Mount Holly. Major General James Grant was in overall command. Colonel Carl Emil Ulrich von Donop had charge of the brigades between Princeton and Mount Holly. His headquarters was at Bordentown. Colonel Johann Gottlieb Rall, reporting to von Donop, had a bridgade of 1586 men at Trenton.

On the American side troops were extended from Coryell's Ferry (now New Hope on the Pennsylvania side and Lambertville on the New Jersey side) along the river southward as far as Washington dared thin his force, namely, to just below Bristol, a distance of about 33 miles. The principal divisions were: Washington's army in the northern sector around McKonkey's Ferry, now Washington Crossing, Pennsylvania; Brigadier General James Ewing's sector in the Trenton Ferry, now Morrisville, Pennsylvania area opposite Trenton, where he had a brigade of Pennsylvania militia; and Colonel John Cadwalader's 1800 militiamen responsible for the river front from what is now Penn's Manor, opposite Bordentown, southward through Tullytown, Bristol, and to Dunk's (Duncan Williamson's) Ferry just below the mouth of Neshaminy Creek.

The stretched out positioning of the British forces invited American hit and run raiding parties to annoy their outposts from December 15 onward, and also invited Washington to take the desperate chance that a victory, sorely needed, might be obtained at Trenton. On the 22nd he wrote Robert Morris, ". . . .unless the militia repair to the city of Philadelphia for defense of it, I see no earthly prospect of saving it after the last of this instant. . . I am satisfied the enemy wait for two events only to begin their operation upon Philadelphia . . . thick ice on the Delaware, and the dissolution of the poor remains of our debilitated Army."

In Philadelphia General Israel Putnam, who had been sent by Washington to recruit troops, received none except for a company of 50 Dover militia, newly arrived from Delaware.

It began to snow and get extremely cold on the 19th. Blocks of ice from up river had begun to pack and in a few days the Delaware could be completely frozen over in places north of tidewater at the falls of Trenton. Colonel Rall, in Trenton, asked General Grant for an additional detachment of troops to protect the town but the British General wrote back from his headquarters in Brunswick saying the Americans had neither shoes nor stockings and were ". . . .almost naked, dying and cold, without blankets and very ill supplied with provisions." He refused Rall's request but added that Rall should be prepared for an attack at any time[11] ". . . .though I do not believe they will attempt it."

One can imagine the plight of the soldiers who lacked sufficient tents, blankets, clothing and provisions. There was no heat except for the little warmth afforded by campfires for those lucky enough to be huddled closely. Today, at the reenactment of the crossing held annually on Christmas Day, the men who participate and man the Durham boats never fail to wonder how it was possible for soldiers to endure such privation and achieve that important military objective.

A conference was held about December 22 and 23 at the headquarters of Brigadier General Lord Stirling (William Alexander) at the Thompson-Neely house on the Delaware about midway between Coryell's Ferry and McKonkey's Ferry. William Alexander's ancestral title of Lord had been denied him by Parliament but his patriot friends and associates always accorded him the distinction. This was the fateful meeting that set the course of our nation onward to victories that sustained the revolution and made possible eventual triumph at Yorktown.[12]

Washington knew he would have to surprise the Hessians at Trenton with a night crossing and nine mile march, then a dawn attack. There was some comfort in knowing he would have illumination without tell-tale torches because there would be a full moon on the 24th[13] and it was at the zenith of its high winter orbit. With the ground covered by snow there would be soft light even if the sky were overcast.

The importance of secrecy required many of the orders just prior to the crossing to be passed by word of mouth; cryptography was not in the army of 1776, hence history lacks many details. For that reason the meetings at the Thompson-Neely house probably included the principal officers of the northern division of Washington's army along the Delaware. They were young men; Washington himself was 44; his two major generals were Nathanael Greene, 34, and John Sullivan, 36. Of the brigadier generals there would have been Lord Stirling, aged 50; Hugh Mercer, 56; Adam Stephen, 46; Arthur St. Clair, 40; Philemon Dickinson, 37; and Roche deFermoy. Major General Horatio Gates was not there; he had departed for Philadelphia, claiming illness. Captain Alexander Hamilton, aged

---

[11] Grant's admonition to be prepared for an attack (after rejecting the request for help) is a British military command custom known as — "clearing one's yardarm!" Grant's record would be clear, no matter what happened to Rall.

[12] Hutton, Ann Hawkes, *House of Decision,* Philadelphia: 1956.

[13] From calculation by the Franklin Institute, Philadelphia, 1982.

WASHINGTON CROSSING STATE PARK COMMISSION, WASHINGTON CROSSING, PA.

HOUSE OF DECISION
The Thompson-Neely House, headquarters of Brigadier General Lord Stirling (William Alexander) where American officers met with General Washington and the decision was made to cross the Delaware on Christmas night 1776 and attack the Hessians at Trenton. This lovely home is now a museum at Washington Crossing Historic Park, Washington Crossing, Pa.; it is furnished in contemporary style and is open daily to visitors.

19, would have attended, as well as Lieutenant James Monroe, quartered with Stirling. Monroe was 18 and destined to become the fifth president of the United States. Colonels Henry Knox, only 26; John Glover, 44, and John Stark, 48, were in the area and doubtless in attendance when called.

On the 23rd the weather warmed somewhat but was still below freezing, however the ice in the river began to loosen up and gently swirl with the currents. It made a crisp, relentless, crunching sound, still familiar to residents along the banks. On the 24th, from his headquarters at the Keith house,[14] about three miles west of the Delaware, Washington set his well laid plans in motion. At Nathanael Greene's headquarters at the Samuel Merrick house nearby there was a final meeting on that same day. In attendance were Washington, Greene, Stirling, Sullivan, deFermoy, St. Clair, Stephen, Mercer, Sargent, Stark and Knox.[15] Their men were ordered to prepare three days cooked rations and to have all equipment in the best order. Under those grim conditions they

WASHINGTON CROSSING FOUNDATION, ANN HAWKES HUTTON COLLECTION

WASHINGTON CROSSING THE DELAWARE

The crossing was on December 25, 1776. The flag is a Betsy Ross version of our stars and stripes. Betsy is firmly believed to have made the first one in June of 1776 although the Continental Congress did not officially adopt the stars and stripes until June 14, 1777. Leutze made this magnificent painting in 1850-51, twenty years before the Betsy Ross story was first revealed.

[14] The Keith house was destroyed by fire in 1981.
[15] Callahan, North, *Henry Knox,* New York: Rinehart & Co. 1958.

would probably have done the preparing themselves as there would have been few camp followers here. Wives of the soldiers comprised most of the bands of camp followers that accompanied an army in those days. They did the cooking, sewing and laundry required.

The above named officers and their brigades, except Dickinson's then posted at Yardley, Pennsylvania, closer to Trenton, formed up in daily parade on the Wrightstown road a mile west of the river at four o'clock on the afternoon of the 25th. It was a Wednesday, Christmas, the sunset was at 4:41.

Tom Paine's new pamphlet, "The American Crisis, Number 1" had been published on the 19th in the Pennsylvania Journal and a part was read to the men: "These are the times that try men's

THE AMERICAN CRISIS

Thomas Paine's Essay, printed Dec. 19, 1776, was read at least in part, to Washington's army assembled before crossing the Delaware to the Battle of Trenton. The ringing words - "These are the times that try men's souls...." helped stiffen the resolution of the men, whose watchword of the day was "Victory or death."

LIBRARY OF CONGRESS

souls — the summer soldier and the sunshine patriot will, in this crisis, shrink from the service of his country, but he that stands it now deserves the love and thanks of man and woman."

The diary of one of Washington's officers records as of December 25: "6:00 P.M. The regiments have had their evening parade but instead of returning to their quarters are marching toward the ferry. It is fearfully cold and raw and a snow storm is setting in. The wind is northeast and beats in the faces of the men. It will be a terrible night for the men who have no shoes. Some of them have tied old rags around their feet, others are barefoot. . . ."

At about this time and when the men were being embarked at McKonkey's Ferry the Commander-in-Chief received word that things were not going well with the crossing attempts down river. Washington nevertheless was determined to get his men across at this ferry. Colonel Glover and his Marblehead mariners knew their job well, as did Colonel Knox in boarding the heavy artillery. Only a year ago, Knox, as Washington's artillery chief, had transported 55 guns captured at Ticonderoga through the wintry Berkshire Mountains all the way to Cambridge, Massachusetts.

FROM "GEORGE WASHINGTON CROSSED HERE," ANN HAWKES HUTTON

OLD FERRY INN, McKonkey's Ferry
Washington Crossing, Pennsylvania
This fine old building, now a museum in Washington Crossing Historic Park, Penna., is at the site of the crossing before the crucial Battle of Trenton.

General Cadwalader's[16] difficulty in trying to cross just below Bristol was that ice floes had been packed by the wind onto the Jersey shore, and while some of the men had managed to climb over them from the boats, the artillery could not be landed. The word back to Cadwalader from the Commander-in-Chief was, "Notwithstanding the discouraging accounts I have received from Colonel Reed... I am determined... to cross the river and make the attack on Trenton in the morning. If you can do nothing real at least create as great a diversion as possible." Cadwalader got 600 men on the Jersey side but since he could not give them artillery support he recalled all of them. He was in command of a force of 1500 Pennsylvania and Delaware militia plus a brigade of 822 Rhode Island and Massachusetts troops under Colonel Daniel Hitchcock.

Evidences of the severity of the night and the river ice which thwarted Brigadier General John Cadwalader from crossing just below Bristol are told vividly in the excerpts below from the journals of Adjutant General Joseph Reed and Colonel Thomas Rodney:

> After sunset, the boats moved down from Bristol, and the troops began their march, the light infantry and militia in front and the Continental troops in the rear. On arrival at the ferry, some of the light infantry pushed over in the first boats and landed on the opposite shore. The weather was very cold. An effort had been made to keep the troops from kindling fires before they embarked, but it was found impossible. Col. Reed and one or two field officers of the militia crossed over in advance, but to their great surprise and mortification found the ice had drifted in such quantities on the Jersey shore that it was impossible to land the artillery. It was with difficulty that they were enabled to get on shore with their horses. Advice being sent over to the Pennsylvania side, the troops, which by this time were mostly in the boats, were ordered to disembark, and the ice beginning to drive with such force as to threaten the boats with absolute destruction, and a heavy storm of hail and snow setting in, the expedition was reluctantly abandoned, and the troops, with the exception of a few light infantry, were marched back to Bristol. The Adjutant General and

---

[16] On the 24th Washington promoted Colonel Cadwalader to Acting Brigadier General.

Colonel Cowperthwaite, who alone had crossed with their horses, proceeded about daybreak to Burlington, where the former had many friends, and where they remained for several hours, their object being to ascertain the exact position of the enemy.

    Life and correspondence of Joseph Reed, Adjutant General
    Library of Congress

About dark, I received Orders to march immediately to Shaminy [Neshaminy] Ferry and wait Orders. We prepared and moved up, and met Colonel Matlack at the ferry, he being the advanced party of the Brigade from Bristol. We soon received orders to march to Dunkin's Ferry on the Delaware, and after we arrived there the whole Brigade came up and also Col. Hitchcock's Brigade of New England Regulars. The light Infantry Battoln was embarked in boats to Cover the landing of the Brigade. When it Reached the Jersey Shore, we were obliged to land on the ice 150 yds. from the Shore, the River also very full of floating ice and the wind blowing very hard, we had great difficulty. We advanced about 200 yards from the Shore and formed in four columns of Double file and after we had waited there about 3 hours we were informed that the Artillery could not be got over and that the troops that were over were ordered back. We had to stay about three hours more to cover the Retreat, by which time the wind blew very hard and there was much rain and sleet, etc.

    Journal of Col. Thomas Rodney, Delaware Militia
    Library of Congress

    General Ewing's brigade of 800 Pennsylvania militia was to have crossed at Trenton Ferry and seize the bridge across Assunpink Creek at southern edge of the town. Holding there would prevent reinforcements from Colonel von Donop at Bordentown. He did not succeed in getting a single boat across the icy river on Christmas night.
    Of the pitiful remains of an army that had known nothing but defeats since the Declaration of Independence the supporting forces had failed and Washington could only raise 2400 men able enough to make the crossing at McKonkey's Ferry. He knew as an experienced leader, however, that to turn back now would bring overwhelming enemy forces to bear later on. With the army in

wretched condition, supplies not forthcoming, and enlistments expiring at the end of the year our fight for liberty might forthwith collapse. He determined to press onward; it was "Victory or Death," the watchword of the day.

The snow and sleet which plagued the men abated somewhat during the crossing but Colonel Knox, despite heroic efforts of the men, could not get his artillery of 18 field pieces over until three in the morning and it was four before the lines of march were formed. That was four hours behind schedule and a surprise attack in darkness or even at dawn would not be possible. The sunrise would be at 7:23 and there would be daylight at seven. Still, Washington did not hesitate.

To move 2400 men, their equipment, horses and cannon into crude boats and rafts, and to cross the ice choked Delaware at night, was a military feat that fills modern military men with wonder and admiration. A pause to contemplate the stupendous effort and the magnificent spirit of those men gives a reverence for the patriotism that inspired them.

The army moved southward with rain and sleet again stinging the men's faces. According to plans they soon split into a first division under Major General John Sullivan and a second division under Major General Nathanael Greene. Sullivan took the river road and had three brigades under Colonel Paul Sargent, Colonel John Glover, and Brigadier General Arthur St. Clair. Greene, with his second division approached Trenton via Scotch, then Pennington Roads and had four brigades under Brigadier Generals Adam Stephen, Hugh Mercer, Lord Stirling and Mathieu Alexis Roche de Fermoy. During the march, Greene sent a message to Washington, "Muskets wet and can't be fired." The reply to the courier was brief. "Tell your general to use the bayonet. The town must be taken." The two divisions converged at Trenton at the end of a nearly nine mile march and firing began about eight o'clock, well after daylight.

Colonel Johann Gottlieb Rall, aged 50, was in command of the Hessian forces and as his pickets fell back into town he was hastily aroused. Christmas in the eighteenth century was marked only by religious observance in Christian countries, except in Germany, where it was a day of celebration as well. There are plenty of stories that the Hessians had enjoyed Christmas revelry and were allowed to sleep late in the morning of the 26th, although no official report was noted in their records. At any rate, many soldiers were not dressed and none but guards were ready for battle. Rall tried to rally his regiments and to assemble his artillery but only succeeded in getting horses to six pieces and they could not be brought to bear effectively. The American artillery did much better. The battle was fought in snow and sleet with Americans firing from behind houses and barns with what muskets would fire. The surprised Hessians also had trouble with their muskets, and as they could not be mustered into formation strength, confusion reigned. At one point a brigade under Lord Stirling marched to within 40

THE ATTACK ON TRENTON, MAP I

FROM JOHNSON'S FERRY TO TRENTON *This map shows the road complex north of Trenton in 1776 and the route taken by the American army in its march on Trenton. Gen. Washington was in over-all command. Maj. Gen. Greene commanded the left or 2nd division of the army, and Maj. Gen. Sullivan the right or 1st division. Brigades headed by their commanders are numbered according to their position in the line of march down Bear Tavern Road as follows: 1. Brig. Gen. Stephen; 2. Brig. Gen. Mercer; 3. Brig. Gen. Stirling; 4. Brig. Gen. Roche de Fermoy; 5. Col. Sargent; 6. Col. Glover; 7. Brig. Gen. St. Clair. This map of the area has been constructed from the study of the following maps and records: "A Complete plan of part of the Province of Pennsylvania East and West Jersey . . . compiled from original surveys . . . by I [J] Hills vol. with the Brigade of His Majesty's Foot Guards, New York, August 1778; A Survey of the Roads of the United States of America, by Christopher Colles, 1798; A Map of The State of New Jersey with part of the adjoining states . . . by Thomas Gordon 1828; Map of Mercer County New Jersey from original surveys by J. W. Otley and J. Keily, Surveyors, 1849;" plus Hunterdon County, New Jersey, Road Records, etc.*

COURTESY SAMUEL STELLE SMITH, *THE BATTLE OF TRENTON*

yards of the men of von Knyphausen's regiment. Hessian escape by the Princeton road was blocked by de Fermoy's brigade and Lord Stirling's. Some escaped by fording or swimming the icy water of the Assunpink and some crossed the bridge before it was taken by Colonel Glover's brigade. General Ewing, who was to have secured that point, managed to get a few boats over the Delaware by ten o'clock but by that time the battle was over. Three Hessian officers and 50 men made it to Princeton and another 600 reached Bordentown. As the captured men were rounded up and threw down their arms, the Americans, in an act of magnanimity seldom seen in warfare, discharged their own firearms over the heads of the defeated.

According to Hessian reports 22 were killed, 83 wounded, and 891 captured. Washington reported 918 captured, which figure

ATTACK ON TRENTON, MAP II
American Brigades: 1. Brig. Gen. Stephen; 2. Brig. Gen. Mercer; 3. Brig. Gen. Stirling; 5. Col. Sargent; 6. Col. Glover; 7. Brig. Gen. St. Clair. *Hessian Regiments:* A. Rall; B. von Lossberg; C. von Knyphausen. *Hessian Detachments:* D. Rall's two gun cannon crew; E. Jaegers from The Hermitage.

COURTESY SAMUEL STELLE SMITH, *THE BATTLE OF TRENTON*

may have included some of those listed by the Hessians as wounded. He also listed six brass three pounders, three ammunition wagons, 12 drums, four colors, and as many firearms as prisoners. Under casualties he listed two officers and one or two privates wounded. By late morning the men began streaming northward to return to Pennsylvania. Washington visited Colonel Rall, who had been mortally wounded, and in the evening he re-crossed with his rear guard to Pennsylvania.

He did not allow himself to relax after this single victory however. After being on the expedition all night the 25th, in battle the 26th, re-crossing and having a few hours sleep, he made his report to the Continental Congress in Baltimore. It was a usual, modest Washington letter; it gave the facts, praised the men, and avoided superlatives. That was on the 27th, the day after the battle, and he also found time then to promote Colonel Knox to Brigadier General.

The prisoners were soon well cared for and were paraded in Philadelphia. Tension in the capital relaxed and gave way to jubilation. It must have been a great relief to our Betsy. Otherwise, who would have ordered upholstery with the city about to be captured, houses to be commandeered, furnishings to be sequestered? Who would have ordered flags with the government in Baltimore?

Most of the Hessians were released to the rich farmlands surrounding Lancaster and Reading, where they replaced hands who had left to join Pennsylvania regiments. They became perhaps the luckiest prisoners of the war for they were among the Pennsylvania Dutch immigrants with whom they could speak; they lived well, ate well, married, and many descendants are still there. Supplies and recruits were again forthcoming as the victory news electrified Philadelphia and spread throughout the colonies.

Washington, in a speech to the men at Newtown, was able to obtain large numbers of re-enlistments among those whose terms were expiring at the end of the year and he was able to go on to another victory at Princeton on January 3, 1777; just eight days after Trenton. There he defeated General Cornwallis, who had been recalled by Howe just before Cornwallis' ship was to sail from New York.

After those victories, Lord Stirling wrote, "The effect is amazing; the enemy has deserted Bordentown, Black Horse, Burlington, Mount Holly and are fled to South Amboy." Later, the British historian, the Right Honorable Sir George Otto Trevelyan, wrote in *The American Revolution*, "It may be doubted whether so small a number of men ever employed so short a time with greater and more lasting results upon the history of the world." Years later, when Cornwallis again surrendered to Washington at Yorktown and the hostilities of the war were ended, a dinner was given in Washington's honor and Cornwallis said in a toast, "When the brilliant successes of your excellency become matters of history, fame will gather your brightest laurels from the banks of the Delaware...."

Still later, Washington, in writing on February 6, 1783 to General Nathanael Greene, said in regard to the hardships of the soldiers at the time of crossing the Delaware, and ensuing privations, "....it will not be believed [in history] that such a force as Great Britain has employed...could be baffled...by numbers infinitely less, composed of men half starved, always in rags, without pay, and experiencing, at times, every species of distress which human nature is capable of undergoing."

That Washington's great military achievement of crossing the Delaware under almost impossible conditions and that his subsequent victories at Trenton and Princeton enabled the almost defeated Revolution to continue is hardly doubted, and that it was a principal turning point of the entire war is widely believed. It's importance has been ably attested to by Presidents Lincoln and Eisenhower, who have signified in their writings the critical portent of the events of those few days in our struggle. Winston Churchill and historian Sir Otto Trevelyan have indicated the same. Recently, the diary of a Hessian officer was translated in Germany. He had been with a Hessian detachment at Mount Holly, New Jersey and in writing about Washington crossing the Delaware and the Battle of Trenton said, "....this great misfortune, which caused the utter loss of the thirteen splendid provinces of England's crown...."

Lord George Germain, Secretary of State for the Colonies, in a speech in the House of Commons two years after the battle said, "All our hopes were blasted by that unhappy affair at Trenton."

CHAPTER V

The War Around Betsy

BETSY REMAINS IN PHILADELPHIA
THE PINCERS - CANADA AND PENNSYLVANIA
BRANDYWINE
FALL OF GERMANTOWN
FALL OF PHILADELPHIA
BETSY IN THE CAPTIVE CITY
FORT MIFFLIN AND FORT MERCER

 The fears Betsy must have endured living alone in her tiny brick house on Arch Street would have been most trying during November and December of 1776. Indeed the city had been badly hurt by the withdrawal of many citizens, the removal of Congress to Baltimore, and the general war tension. But, some of that was remedied now that the victories at Trenton and Princeton had been announced, and a sudden feeling of euphoria and friendliness swept the populace. Betsy, who had watched with apprehension as young men of the militia and the Philadelphia Associators had gone northward, accompanied at first by some of their wives, no longer need shudder at the deep rumble of heavy wagons in the streets, nor the sounds of drums and bugles from the fields and square, for they came from gleeful boys playing and from commerce resuming.

 How much the resumption of nearly normal business affected her was not recorded, but she must have had the benefit of some of it. She would have had to pay more for a cord of hard wood, however. Oak and hickory, which had risen to 29 shillings a cord, went even higher; drovers bringing in pigs and cattle, and herders

COURTESY PHILADELPHIA FREE LIBRARY
CITY TAVERN

Second and Walnut Streets, Philadelphia. A prominent gathering place founded by merchants in the vicinity. Committees of Congress often met there. It is still standing and still in business.

Delegates to the First Continental Congress gathered here September 5, 1774 before their formal assembly at nearby Carpenters Hall.

COURTESY PHILADELPHIA FREE LIBRARY
LONDON COFFEE HOUSE
Front and High (Market) Streets, Philadelphia

A meeting place for travelers, seafarers and influential citizens. Trading was done here and news passed among those in the know. It was originally built circa 1702 and in 1754 became a coffee house operated by William Bradford.

selling sheep, would want more. Fortunately, Philadelphia was surrounded in a perimeter of many miles by highly productive farms, but textiles, coming from abroad, were not plentiful. News was avidly sought and the Pennsylvania Gazette and the Daily Advertiser were eagerly read. The quickest source of information came from inns and taverns, such as the London Coffee House at Second and High (now Market) Streets, and the City Tavern at Second and Walnut Streets. Betsy was probably getting some help from Joseph Ashburn, a former suitor and a friend of her late husband. He was in command of a brig which made trips to the West Indies and may have brought fabrics and sugar to her. Just when their acquaintance resumed is not clear but it could have been at least as early as late 1776.

The year 1777, which had begun with American will and determination revived at Trenton and Princeton, now turned to skillful defense against two major British advances; one from Canada and the other from New York. From Canada Major General John Burgoyne attempted to split the American states by invading through the Vermont and Lake Champlain areas. His immediate objective was Albany, on the Hudson. New York City had been in British hands since September of 1776, and with the North River (Hudson) and the Lake George and Lake Champlain waterway northward secure, American commerce between the north and the central states would be effectively blocked. The Royal Navy off our coast would choke off commerce from the sea and in Long Island Sound. Accordingly, Burgoyne departed from St. Johns, Quebec with a force reported as 7,700 to 10,000 men and in a rapid advance southward via the Richelieu River and Lake Champlain took our lightly defended Fort Ticonderoga on July 6, 1777.

From lower New York Bay inside Sandy Hook a great armada sortied on July 23rd. There were approximately 260 ships under command of Vice Admiral Lord Richard Howe, and 16,498 troops commanded by his brother, General Sir William Howe. Their mission was to take the capital city, Philadelphia, an operation wherein they had been unsuccessful the previous winter.

Upon entering the capes of Delaware Bay on July 30, however, advice from loyalists warned that their objective, 100 miles up the river, was protected by two powerful forts just below the city; Fort Mifflin on the Pennsylvania side and Fort Mercer opposite on the New Jersey side at Red Bank. In addition, they would encounter two lines of cheveaux de frise implanted across the river near the forts. These were stout, iron tipped pikes, secured at an angle downstream in enormous wooden coffers some 63 feet long and forty feet wide, which were sunk to the channel bottom with rocks so that the pikes presumably would pierce the bottoms of vessels attempting to pass. The upper line ran from just below Fort Mifflin on Mud Island on the Pennsylvania side to Fort Mercer at Red Bank, New Jersey; the lower line was about two and a half miles down river and extended from Billings Island on the Pennsylvania side to the fort at Billingsport, New Jersey, just south of Mantua Creek. The Philadelphia Airport now encompasses the site on the west bank of the Delaware. A tiny American navy was stationed just up river from the two lines of cheveaux.

The Howe brothers then decided to move their expedition to Chesapeake Bay and begin the assault overland from the nearest point to Philadelphia. Sir William also decided to seize control of the rich farm land en route in order to supply his army and at the same time deny to the Americans the products from the agricultural center at Reading, Pennsylvania.

COURTESY SAMUEL STELLE
SMITH, *FIGHT FOR THE DELAWARE*

"WARHEAD" OF A CHEVEAUX DE FRISE

This was the wrought iron tip of a long, stout pike about 12 inches thick. It was intended to pierce the bottom of any ship attempting to pass over it. The amount of manpower required to build hundreds of these, and sink them in huge rock filled coffers across the Delaware, staggers the imagination. Two lines of them kept the entire Royal Navy away from Philadelphia for weeks. This one was recovered from the river and is now at the Gloucester County Historical Society, Woodbury, New Jersey.

Accordingly, they sailed southward on August 1, and after rounding Cape Charles proceeded north, landing the troops at the Head of Elk (River), now Elkton, Maryland, on August 25. By the route of march they would have about 57 miles to go to reach Philadelphia.

August was a month of maneuvering for Washington. The movements of the British after July 23 were unknown to him but the size of the expedition suggested something more than their going north to assist General John "Gentleman Johnny" Burgoyne in his southward movement through northern New York from Canada, so he strongly suspected that the enemy intended to take our capital city. Therefore, his Continental Army was assembled at the southeastern edge of Germantown, six miles northwest of Philadelphia. Germantown is now a part of Philadelphia. The encampment reached from the east bank of the Schuylkill River in what is now the East Falls section to a point nearly two miles upland to the northeast.[1] There were two rivers to contend with; The Schuylkill, a barrier to the west; and the Delaware, a barrier to the east. The Delaware was a broad tidewater artery navigable all the way up to the falls at Trenton, and farther north by small boats. The army was stationed between the two rivers and within easy striking distance of Philadelphia. General "Mad Anthony" Wayne was sent to Chester to organize Pennsylvania militia, Major General Nathanael Greene was in command of the army at Germantown, but Generals John Sullivan and Alexander MacDougall had their forces way up on the west bank of the Hudson as far north as southeastern Orange County in the vicinity of Stony Point. All told, Washington had about 11,000 men at his disposal.

Washington himself supervised the strengthening of Philadelphia defenses and the forts on the Delaware, but in the midst of that feverish activity word came from a river pilot, Henry Fisher, that the British vessels moored between the capes had weighed anchors on July 31, and were disappearing at sea.

This posed another dilemma to Washington. Could their destination be Charleston, or would they come north again? He wrote to his brother, John Augustine, on the fifth of August:

"Information received from Congress that the enemy were at the Capes of Delaware brought us in great haste to this place [Germantown] for the defense of the city; but less than 24 hours after our arrival we got accounts of the disappearance of the fleet on the 31st; since which nothing having been heard from them we

---

[1]Thompson, Ray, *Washington at Germantown*. Fort Washington, Pa.: The Bicentennial Press, 1971, p. 5.

remain here in a state of irksome suspense."

Generals Sullivan and MacDougall had been ordered south from the Hudson but were now halted. By August 8th, camp was broken at Germantown and the army moved to Whitemarsh, then to Warminster and Hartsville, destined north to Coryell's Ferry. They had not completed that move when word was received that the British fleet had been sighted off the coast of Maryland 30 miles below the Delaware capes — they were bound southward. The encampment was now along Little Neshaminy Creek, about 20 miles north of Philadelphia and remained there until word came on the 22nd that the fleet had been seen "high up in the northeast part of Chesapeake Bay." The army was ordered to Philadelphia immediately and the forces on the Hudson were to march south to join the main body as soon as possible.

Washington made his headquarters on the 23rd of August at "Stenton," the Germantown home of Dr. George Logan, son of James Logan, Secretary to William Penn. James built the mansion in 1728. It is still standing and the address is 18th and Courtland Streets, Philadelphia. The Colonial Dames of America maintain this outstandingly beautiful example of Georgian architecture. It is of red brick and has a dormered roof. Today it is an attraction for tourists and visiting architects.

There Washington wrote detailed orders for a march through the capital to enhearten the populace that their city would be defended. He also specified that there would be no stopping in Philadelphia and guards were spaced at intervals to see that none fell out of ranks; they marched on to Chester. The route of march specified entering the city via Front Street southward to Chestnut Street, thence westward, passing the State House and onward toward the Schuylkill River.

Betsy must have been mightily impressed on that Sunday, August 24, 1777, for the route of march took them a block and a half from her home and shop. There were fifes and drums in each brigade and the orders were for the "quick step," while going through town, and music accordingly. She probably saw some of her glorious flags on parade because there was a report of them in battle only a few days later. They were marching twelve abreast and the tramp of thousands in quick step, horses hooves, wagons rolling on cobble-stone paving, and the drums and fifes sent thrills and chills to the bone marrow of all who watched. This time it was deadly serious for the enemy was landing and his destination was Philadeiphia.

Excerpts from Washington's orders give us an intimate view of the times:[2]

Head Quarters, at Stanton, (sic) near German Town, August 23, 1777.

No officer or soldier is to leave the encampment this evening, without leave in writing from the Major General or Brigadier under whom he acts; and they are desired not to give such leave unless there be very apparent cause for it.

The Army is to move precisely at four in the morning, if it should not rain. The division commanded by General Wayne is to take its proper place in the line (to wit, between Lord Stirling's and General Stephen's division) and it is strongly and earnestly enjoined, upon the commanding officers of corps to make all their men who are able to bear arms (except for the necessary guards) march in the ranks; for it is so great a reflection upon all order and discipline to see a number of strollers (for they cannot be called guards) with the wagons, that is really shocking.

The Army is to march in one column thro' the City of Philadelphia, going in at and marching down Front Street to Chestnut Street, and up Chestnut Street to the Common. A small halt is to be made about a mile on this side of the City, till the rear closes up, and the line is in proper order.

The divisions march as follows: Greene's, Stephen's, Lincoln's Lord Stirling's. The Horse to be divided upon the two wings. Bland's and Baylor's regiments upon the right, Sheldon's and Moylan's upon the left.

The whole line is to march by subdivisions, at half distance, the ranks and files at the most convenient distance for marching. Which is to be exactly observed in passing thro' the City, and great attention given by the officers to see that the men carry their arms well, and are made to appear as decent as circumstances will admit.

It is expected that every officer, without exception, will keep his post in passing thro' the City, and under no pretense whatsoever leave it; and if any soldier shall dare to quit his ranks, he shall receive thirty-nine lashes at the first halting place afterwards. The officers will be particularly attentive to prevent this, not only in their own divisions, but in others also, if they should see an attempt of this kind. They are also to prevent the people from pressing the troops.

[2]Thompson, Ray, *Washington at Germantown*, op. cit. p. 11

Not a woman belonging to the Army is to be seen with the troops on their march thro' the City. The Wagon Master General and all his assistants ... are to attend the wagons and prevent any men who are alloted to attend the wagons from slipping into the City.

The soldiers will go early to rest this evening, as the General expects that the whole line will be on their march at the hour appointed. That this may be the case, each Brigadier is to appoint patrols to take up all stragglers from the camp and all others of the Army who do not obey this order.

The drums and fifes of each brigade are to be collected in the center of it; and a tune for the quick step played — but with such moderation, that the men may step to it with ease, and without *dancing* along, or totally disregarding the music, as too often has been the case.

The men are to be excused from carrying their Camp Kettles tomorrow. A proper guard from the Horse is to be posted on the road leading to the City, to take up strollers from the camp.

After writing his orders, Washington wrote to Congress imploring them to push on with the "....several works for the defense of the City... and that no pains should be omitted to complete them." He said he thought it wise to march the troops through the city without stopping. "I am induced to do this," he said, "from the opinion of several of my officers and many friends in Philadelphia, that it may have some influence on the minds of the disaffected there and those who are dupes to their artifices and opinions...."

The army did create a favorable impression despite their rag-tag appearance and lack of uniforms. All was in deadly seriousness, and fears of burning, destruction and looting were in the minds of the citizenry. It took more than two hours for the army to pass. One eyewitness wrote, "I was standing in front of the State House when the parade arrived. There was a small advance guard and then the commander-in-chief, dressed in his finest buff and blue and mounted on his best horse. With him rode Henry Knox, and Tench Tilghman [Washington's faithful aide], the young Marquis de Lafayette and other aides. The Philadelphia Light Horse [now First Troop, Philadelphia City Cavalry] followed, then the Virginia dragoons of George Baylor and Theodore Bland. The clack of hoofs, the rustle of horsehair plumes gave way to the drumming tramp of the infantry and the steady rumble of artillery wheels."

Howe had rehabilitated his tired army after 32 days at sea

during the hottest time of the year and now be began his move northeastward toward the capital. As he did so, Washington moved southwestward to meet him. On September 3rd, Brigadier General William Maxwell, of New Jersey, was posted with an advance brigade of 800 men at Cooch's Bridge over the upper reaches of the Christiana River in Delaware. Hessian General Knyphausen came upon them and forced the Americans to retreat. Cooch's Bridge was one of the early engagements of the war where our new American flag is said to have flown. About 30 to 40 men were killed or wounded on each side. By the 9th, Howe's army was at Kennett Square, six miles west of the Chadd's Ford crossing of Brandywine Creek.

On September 11 the main forces met on the Brandywine from Chadd's Ford, Pennsylvania, to a point north about two miles. General Sullivan had been assigned to guard the crossing upstream on our right flank but General Cornwallis drove him back. Washington sent Greene to Sullivan's aid but it was too late, the crossing had been made. With our main position at the Ford weakened by Greene's attempt to save Sullivan, General Knypausen was able to cross the stream and attack our left flank under Generals Wayne and Maxwell. The action was heavy; of the patriot force of 11,000, we lost more than 1,200, including 400 taken prisoner; the British had 12,500 engaged and lost nearly 600.

Colonel Louise du Portail, a French engineer with the Continental Army wrote to a friend after Brandywine: "If the English had followed up their advantage that day, Washington's army would have spoken no more; since that time, also, Howe has, in all his operations, exhibited such slowness and timidity as to strike me with astonishment."[3]

Retreating eastward, a force of 1,500 continentals under Brigadier General Anthony Wayne was surprised by a British bayonet attack at Malvern, just west of Paoli, Pennsylvania, on September 20 (the Paoli Massacre). He was badly routed in that night attack, losing 150 men.

On September 18, 1777, Congress, at Washington's urging, left Philadelphia. They met briefly at Lancaster, Pennsylvania, on the 27th and then convened at York, Pennsylvania, on September 30. They remained there until June, 1778 and re-convened at Philadelphia 2 July 1778.

Along the route of Howe's army, and especially in Chester County, destruction and thievery were wanton, houses were

---

[3]Thompson, Ray, *Washington at Germantown*, op. cit. p. 15.

destroyed, furnishings taken, cattle slaughtered or seized, young boys were taken from their homes to serve as orderlies, and Whigs and Tories suffered alike.

How much of this Betsy was aware of we do not know, but being alone and defenseless she must have feared. Because of her interest in the American cause, she may have read Benjamin Franklin's satirical essay, written some time ago, and prior to his departure for Paris. He entitled it, "Rules by Which a Great Empire May Be Reduced to a Small One:"[4]

> Convert the brave, honest officers of your navy into pimping tide-waiters and colony officers of the customs. Let those who in time of war fought gallantly in defence of their country, in peace be taught to prey upon it. Let them learn to be corrupted by great and real smugglers; but (to show their diligence) scour with armed boats every bay, harbour, river, creek, cove or nook throughout the coast of your colonies; stop and detain every coaster, every wood boat, every fisherman; tumble their cargoes and even their ballast inside out and upside down; and, if a penn'orth of pins is found unentered, let the whole be seized and confiscated. Thus shall the trade of your colonists suffer more from their friends in time of peace than it did from their enemies in war. Then let these boats' crews land upon every farm in their way, rob the orchards, steal the pigs and the poultry, and insult the inhabitants. If the injured and exasperated farmers, unable to procure other justice, should attack the aggressors, drub them, and burn their boats, you are to call this high treason and rebellion, order fleets and armies into their country, and threaten to carry all the offenders three thousand miles to be hanged, drawn and quartered. Oh, this will work admirably!

Washington, aware of the British desperate need for supplies, and observing a northward movement of Howe's army, also moved northward, placing his army so as to protect our stores at Reading.

---

[4]Stout, Neil R., *The Royal Navy in America, 1760-1775*. Annapolis: Naval Institute Press, 1973, p. v.

On September 22, he encamped near Pottstown and next morning the British came to Gordon's Ford, now Phoenixville. Howe no longer needed to fear a patriot army from points west of Philadelphia along what is now Philadelphia's Main Line, so he gave up any thoughts of moving in the direction of Reading, crossed to the east side of the Schuylkill, and the way was open to his main objective, the capital.

As matters stood late on September 23 Washington was more than 15 miles to the northwest near Pottstown, his army had marched 140 miles in the past 11 days, many of his men had no shoes, blankets had been discarded in the hot weather retreat and a forced march in pursuit of Howe was not possible. Congress, before leaving Philadelphia on the 18th, had given Washington virtually dictatorial powers to take whatever he needed, but Alexander Hamilton, who was hastily dispatched to collect blankets, clothing, shoes and supplies, reported that Whigs departing the city had taken their supplies along and those remaining had already given all they could spare; Tories had hidden what they could. Colonel Clement Biddle, who had attempted to round up supplies north of the city, paying with cash and promises, was mostly unsuccessful also.

By September 24, the British were in the Norristown area and they arrived in Germantown next day. Their march was described as a mighty machine in perfect order, moving without drums or music or the flying of colors. Occasionally men dropped out of line to ask for milk or cider.

On September 26, Howe sent Lieutenant General Lord Charles Cornwallis with four battalions into defenseless Philadelphia, and then wrote to Lord George Germain, the British Secretary of State for North American Colonies, that the capital had fallen to him. Philadelphia was then secure for the British, but their army was woefully low on supplies after the long sea voyage from New York and the wearing trek overland from Maryland. Supplies could not come up the Delaware. The city was in a state of shock and confusion; eight to ten thousand of the citizens had fled, taking with them food, horses, livestock and such furnishings as they could move. Markets were rapidly drained by the remaining populace as well as the invaders, and they were not readily restocked. Houses which had been abandoned, and spare rooms everywhere, were taken over by the British for needed quartering of officers and men. In addition to the four battalions in Philadelphia, Howe placed 3000 men in New Jersey, which left 9000 in Germantown.

Our Betsy was not among those who fled. She remained at her tiny house and shop. Within a few short years this young girl had lived a long life. First, a deep love and daring elopement; then a spiritual change upon alienation of her family, disownment and a new faith for worship. Soon following were the setting up of a business and a home; the death of her husband; carrying the upholstery work on alone; and the good fortune of an in-law relative bringing distinguished gentlemen to her shop who wanted a new flag made. And now this capture of America's capital and largest city; the ominous sounds of marching feet, of horns, drums and caissons rolling over cobble-stone paving. Cornwallis' men were knocking on every door inquiring the number of rooms and number of occupants. There were shortages of everything except the ribaldry and relaxation of an army which has achieved its objective. Later, Susan Satterthwaite Newport, a grand niece of Betsy, told in her story that the British officers quartered at Betsy's called her "The Little Rebel."

The fortitude of our pretty, young lady was immense, but nevertheless, Betsy must have suffered not only fear, but at times intense and cruel grief.

PLAN OF ATTACK FOR THE BATTLE OF GERMANTOWN

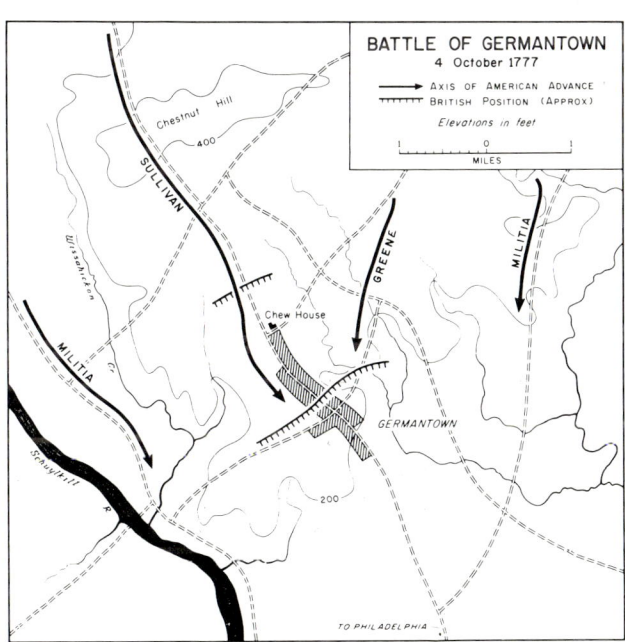

CENTER OF MILITARY HISTORY, U.S. ARMY

While General Howe was giving his men what comforts were obtainable at Germantown Cornwallis was in Philadelphia preparing for the general movement of the army into the city and for the destruction of the fort defenses which prevented Admiral Howe's fleet from coming up the Delaware. Washington, at Potts Grove, was taking measures to prevent supplies from coming into town where the British could get hold of them, and then moved his army eastward and southeastward to engage Howe at Germantown. From September 27 to 29 he camped near Schwenksville on Perkiomen Creek, but soon moved to a strong position at Center Point (Worcester P.O.) and at the Peter Wentz farm there he wrote detailed orders for the attack, which was to take place before dawn on Saturday, October 4, 1777.

He formed two main divisions of the army; a right wing, or column, under Major General John Sullivan; and a left wing under Major General Nathanael Greene. The roster of general officers and colonels read like those at Washington Crossing, Trenton and Princeton. Militia units were present from neighboring counties, Maryland, New Jersey and elsewhere.

On October 3 the army sortied at 6:00 P.M. The right wing advanced via the Germantown Road, entering on the present Germantown Avenue; the left wing marched down Skippack Pike and entered Germantown via Limekiln Pike. Militia columns covered the outside flanks of each column as far right as the Schuylkill River and as far left as Old York Road. There was a reserve corps of two battalions of militia under Major General Lord Stirling which also took the Skippack Pike. The battle plan was excellent and heartily agreed to by the commanding officers, but as in all large scale movements, it depended on communication and timing.

It so happened that an autumn fog blanketed the scene before dawn and all morning, which disrupted communications and led to uncertainty and confusion. Initial contact with the enemy was by Sullivan's right column at Beggarstown, now Mount Airy, at Allens Lane. The British pickets were quickly subdued but the firing of shots alerted their posts further down Germantown Avenue. At the Chew Mansion[5] a regiment of British made a defense and used the stoutly built house as a fort. About 120 of them barricaded themselves inside to escape the bayonets of Anthony Wayne's

---

[5] The Chew Mansion, "Cliveden," was built in 1763 by Benjamin Chew, Chief Justice of the Province of Pennsylvania. It withstood cannon fire, musket balls and an attempt to burn it down. Six generations of the Chew family occupied before it was given by them to the National Trust in 1972. It occupies an entire block at 6400 Germantown Avenue and is now open to the public.

men smarting for revenge after the Paoli Massacre. In the fog the Americans believed they had encountered the main enemy force and halted to lay siege to the place; it could have been by-passed. By now it was daylight but the fog persisted. Howe himself had come up when he heard the initial firing and rode back to rally his main forces in the center of Germantown.

The left column, under Greene, was somewhat late advancing down the Limekiln Pike. Firing was heard from the direction of the Chew Mansion, and in the dense fog, and unbeknownst to Greene, Adam Stephen ordered his brigade to break off and turn toward the firing. That unauthorized diversion weakened the left column. Greene, with three remaining brigades, met the British at daybreak where the Pike joins Church Lane, fought his way to the center of Germantown, and still in the fog, engaged them around the Market Square vicinity and penetrated nearly as far as the Stenton Mansion, a mile eastward. Had Sullivan and Greene been able to meet near Market Square on schedule the route of the British could have been complete but lack of communication and fog prevented that. Sullivan did proceed after the initial confusion at the Chew Mansion to the center of Germantown, however, the militia units which had approached that village on the extreme right and extreme left never did make it in time for the battle. Some of the troops who had run out of ammunition reversed direction to replenish, and advancing units unable to see beyond them thought

GERMANTOWN HISTORICAL SOCIETY
DESHLER-MORRIS HOUSE

One of the beautiful homes that escaped burning by the British after the Battle of Germantown.

For a short time General Sir William Howe made his headquarters here. In 1793, when most of our government moved to Germantown to escape the yellow fever epidemic in Philadelphia, it was occupied by George Washington. It is thus the oldest "White House" in the nation.

it was a general retreat and likewise reversed. Some units mistakenly fired upon each other. Soon the retreat was general and commanding officers, unable to communicate or be seen for any distance, could not stem the movement. The battle was over by ten o'clock in the morning and the army retreated all the way to Schwenksville. Patriot losses were 673 killed and wounded and over 400 captured out of an army of 11,000; British losses were 537 killed and wounded and 14 captured out of 9,000 engaged.

British soldiers were incensed that the local citizenry had not helped them in their efforts to ward off the rebels who sought to destroy his majesty's government in their land and later, upon departing Germantown they burned a number of houses in the village and on the route to Philadelphia.

Howe moved the balance of his army from Germantown into the city on October 19th. Industry and commercial movements stopped and with the city paralyzed there was no way to replenish fodder, equipment and victuals for a tired army. Unless the Delaware could be cleared for British ships, the army was in an uncomfortable position. Moreover, Lieutenant General John Burgoyne's campaign in New York state had taken a bad turn; he was defeated and surrendered at Saratoga on October 17th, losing his entire army of about 7,700 men when surrounded by a superior force (variously reported at 13,000-17,000) under Major General Horatio Gates. That was doubtless bad news to Howe. Washington, with a force of about 8,000 Continentals and 3,000 militia stood just outside the city, and the river forts blocked sea communications. General Sir William implored his brother to relieve the situation and that the admiral set out to do.

The forts were to be reduced by naval and shore gunfire, and the cheveaux were to be raised by purchase between two vessels at low tide and then removed as the tide flooded. Cornwallis' four battalions, the initial British force in Philadelphia, brought up cannon on the waterfront to contend with the small American naval ships, floating batteries and row galleys ranging from there to the Jersey side north of the upper line of cheveaux.

At Billingsport, New Jersey, at the terminus of the lower line of cheveaux, was a third, lightly armed fort which became the first target of the British. Washington had realized the fort was untenable and ordered the personnel of 112 under Colonel Bradford, and supplies, moved to Fort Mifflin. But before the order could be carried out, the British attacked by land. Patriot militia of about 300, with two field pieces, went out to meet their 1500 and some brisk skirmishes ensued, but by October 2nd the British occupied the fort. They evacuated on the 5th for fear of superior American forces by land, however, the installation was by then useless as a fort. The British also removed a few cheveaux. Light American naval forces then came down river through a secret opening protected by a heavy chain and sank two ships to seal a breach where the cheveaux had been taken out. Nevertheless, the British succeeded in making a passage on October 14th of about 100 feet width through which it was possible, though risky, to maneuver a large ship.

Meanwhile, beginning October 6th or 7th, despite American harassment, batteries were constructed by the British on Carpenter's Island directly behind Fort Mifflin, where it was lightly defended. Province Island, adjacent to the north, and only separated by a narrow tidal run, received royal batteries soon after. On October 10th the Carpenter's batteries began bombarding Fort Mifflin from the rear across the narrow inner channel between Carpenter's Island and Mud Island, on which Fort Mifflin is situated. Mud Island is sometimes called Fort Island. The channel was about 400 feet in width, much of it in tidal flats, and too shallow for deep draft shipping. Today all the passages have been filled in and Mud Island, Little Mud Island, Carpenter's Island, Province Island, Boon's Island and Hog Island are all a part of the mainland adjacent to the Philadelphia Airport and extending northeast to the Schuylkill River mouth.

Sir William Howe complained bitterly about his lack of supplies and mobility; 400 of his horses had died on the sea voyage in August. A trickle of provisions had resumed soon after his occupation of the city but Washington soon stopped that. The Fort Mifflin garrison of about 200 men continued to hold out despite constant shelling. A reinforcement of 128 men from Fort Mercer on October 19th bolstered that garrison.

General Howe also needed to silence Fort Mercer on the Jersey side in order to gain access to Philadelphia for his brother's large fleet, then in the Delaware near Chester. He sent Colonel Carl Emil Ulrich von Donop and a brigade of 1228 Hessians and they crossed on October 21st from Philadelphia to Cooper's Ferry in 14 flatboats which had been brought up from the fleet off Chester. Colonel Christopher Greene, in command at Fort Mercer, had a garrison of 614 men, mostly Rhode Islanders and Virginians. The Hessians camped overnight at Haddonfield and attacked Fort Mercer the afternoon of the 22nd. The small force of American naval vessels off the fort were to be taken care of by British warships coming through the passage in the cheveaux.

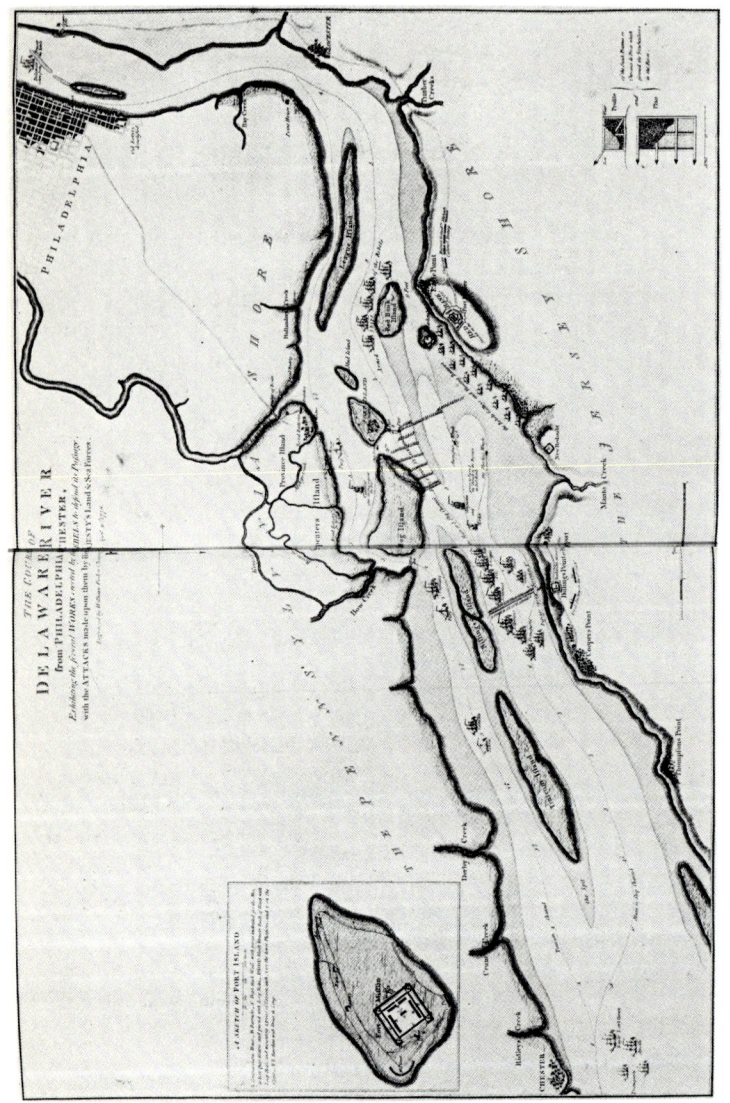

BRITISH ATTACK ON DELAWARE DEFENSES   COURTESY MARTIN P. SNYDER, ESQ.

Engraving made in London 1778 shows British ships of Admiral Howe's attacking force, the American Navy, the cheveaux de frise; Fort Mifflin (shown here on Fort Island), and Fort Mercer at Red Bank. Land batteries of both sides are also indicated.

A contrary wind, however, prevented arrival of the warships which were to bombard Fort Mercer and engage the American vessels. The Hessians made a brave attack on Fort Mercer and reached a 15 foot ditch outside the breastwork of the fort. When they could advance no further, and their leader, von Donop, fell mortally wounded, they retreated in disorder, gathering such wounded as they could. There were 514 Hessian casualties out of 1207 men, and 14 Americans were killed, 23 wounded. On October 23 the remnants of the assaulting force arrived at Coopers Ferry for return to Philadelphia. Observers on the distant side of the river reported that the rebel flag was still flying on Fort Mercer on the morning of the 23rd but unfortunately none described it for our historic record.

Earlier, the grand assault plan of the Howe brothers had been well conceived and if all went well the Delaware would be opened for British shipping quickly, but that is not quite the way it worked out. An advance squadron of warships was to negotiate the breach in the lower cheveaux and fire on Fort Mifflin from the river side. A lightened galley, the *Vigilant,* 16 guns, was to work her way through the shallow inner channel between Mud Island, and Carpenter's and Province Islands, then assist the batteries on the two last named islands in shelling Fort Mifflin from the rear. This firing would hopefully draw over the American Continental and Pennsylvania Navy ships off Red Bank and Fort Mercer and expose them to the heavier British ships. Meanwhile von Donop, with his superior Hessian force would storm and capture Fort Mercer from the landward. von Donop's effort came to grief as we learned.

Earlier, a delay caused by adverse winds, was the first difficulty. Nevertheless, by the afternoon of October 21st, the 4th rate ship *Isis,* 50 guns, and the large frigate *Augusta,* 64 guns, got underway. Other vessels followed soon after. The *Isis* promptly went aground, and so did a galley, the *Cornwallis,* 8 guns. On the 22nd, the *Vigilant* also grounded. The remaining ships, all delayed, were the *Roebuck,* 44 guns, and *Pearl* 32 guns, both 5th rate ships. The *Liverpool,* a 6th rate ship which carried 28 cannon, and the sloop *Merlin,* with 18 guns, completed the squadron and had a total of 260 cannon to assault the Americans. The *Merlin,* in a collision situation with the *Roebuck,* went aground.

Courageous American row galleys dropped down river on the Jersey flats and gave battle to the superior British ships, which may have invited a maneuvering development that caused the *Augusta* to go aground off the mouth of Woodbury Creek, opposite the present Philadelphia Airport, late in the afternoon of the 22nd. The

COURTESY NEW YORK PUBLIC LIBRARY, PHELPS STOKES COLLECTION

THE FIGHT FOR THE DELAWARE

The text of this aquatint states that it was "Drawn on the spot and engraved by Lieut. W. Elliot. . . . Representation of the Action off Mud Fort on the River Delaware; the Enemy's fleet consisting of Frigates, Fire-Ships, Galleys &c attacking His Majesty's Ships, *Augusta, Roebuck, Pearl, Liverpool* and *Merlin* 15 Nov. 1777, in which the *Augusta* took fire by accident and the *Merlin* was burnt to prevent her falling into the hands of the Enemy." The picture was printed in London in 1787.

The noted historian, Samuel Stelle Smith, whose book, *Fight for the Delaware* also contains this illustration, points out that the action was on October 22/23 of 1777, not November 15.

The ship in the right foreground with the Royal Navy Ensign flying is the *Roebuck*. At the left foreground with the same flag prominent is the *Pearl*. Other vessels in the full drawing are the *Augusta, Merlin* and *Liverpool*. The *Augusta* went aground, as did the *Merlin*; the former took fire and blew up - the British said by accident but as she was under fire from both Mifflin and Mercer her destruction can be assumed by reason of our action. The *Merlin* was purposely blown up to prevent her falling into our hands.

There are two stars and stripes flags on Fort Mifflin, one with red and white stripes and the other with red, white and blue stripes.

Augusta was a large ship; 153 feet in length and 44 feet, 7½ inches of beam. She drew 18 feet, 10 inches, and she had a complement of 500. There was a concentration of ships about the *Augusta* and so the Americans sent fire rafts against them on the ebb tide, but British small boats succeeded in towing them out of the way. The next day, October the 23rd, the flood tide failed to move the big ship but she fought her guns against American Commodore John Hazelwood's 12 galleys and two floating batteries. By late morning the same day, the *Augusta* was observed to be on fire and it became necessary for her crew to abandon ship; 61 to 160 men, as reported, then perished in the water. She had been, in her stationary position, a helpless target from Fort Mercer and Fort Mifflin. Flames issued from every gun port, and by 2:00 in the afternoon the fire reached her powder magazine and she blew up with a sheet of flame and a roar that rocked all of Philadelphia. People said the city shook like an earthquake.[6.]

On the same date, the *Merlin,* which had defied all efforts to move her, was given up for lost. She was just off the guns of Fort Mercer. The *Roebuck* came alongside and removed her crew and then she was set afire and blown up about a half hour after the *Augusta's* demise.

Despite these setbacks, the British pursued their intentions with vigor. They reoccupied the fort area at Billingsport on October 26th with 300 men to prevent the Americans from doing the same and interfering with passage of their ships and efforts to remove nearby cheveaux. Then a landing on Mud Island and assault by 300 grenadiers was planned, but it never materialized. Two new regiments of English troops were bivouacked on Carpenter's Island in addition to the 470 men already posted. On November 10th the bombardment of Fort Mifflin began in great volume and it was directed mostly against the weak, landward side. Few American guns could be brought to bear on the British land batteries and so the unprotected installations within the fort were soon destroyed. The men at Fort Mercer could see the gradual demolition going on but could not help, except at night when they sent replacements

---

[6]Mrs. Edith Hoelle, curator of the Gloucester County Historical Society, provided this researcher with data from "The Constitution," a Washington newspaper in which an article in the November 17, 1869 issue tells the story of the refloating of the Augusta.

An enterprising group raised her in 1867, apparently to become an attraction at the coming Centennial in Philadelphia. They got her hulk as far as Gloucester Point, a distance of five miles, when contrary weather forced a grounding and she now lies on the New Jersey side about 1/2 mile below the Walt Whitman Bridge where Jersey Avenue, Market Street and King Street come together. She lies off the masonry bulkhead of Camden County Park, as near as 50 feet, and a stone's throw from the site of Hugg's Tavern, where Betsy Griscom and John Ross were married. She is sometimes visible under the surface at extreme low water when strong northeast winds and equinoxial spring tides occur together.

COURTESY NEW YORK PUBLIC LIBRARY, PRINT COLLECTION, ASTOR, LENOX AND TILDEN FOUNDATIONS
THE BLOWING UP OF THE BRITISH FRIGATE *AUGUSTA*, 1777

During the fight for the Delaware the *Augusta* went aground on October 22, 1777 in mid-stream just below Fort Mifflin and Fort Mercer. She could not be moved as the tide had begun to ebb. There was a steady north wind which kept the next flood tide lower than usual, and, either from gunfire or an accident on board, she became ablaze just before noon on the 23rd. Most of her crew were rescued but she blew up about 2:00 P.M. and loss of life was reported between 61 and 160 men.

This spectacular painting was made by an unknown artist, said to be an English naval officer who for a time visited James Peale. The artist did well with the difficult feat of painting an explosion, yet preserving the architectural integrity of that beautiful ship. Actually her entire topsides were blown to smithereens and the blast rocked Philadelphia.

for killed and wounded defenders. By November 12th, Brigadier General James Varnum, who had crossed the river the night before to inspect damages, reported to Washington that the defenses of Fort Mifflin were almost completely destroyed.[7] On the night of 14/15 November the large galley *Vigilant,* with her 16 guns, finally got up the inner channel to within 200 yards of the back of the fort. This was her fourth attempt, but they had lightened her a bit and with a spring tide she made it across the bar. She was accompanied by the *Fury.* Fort Mifflin could not bring guns to bear on them where they lay, and at dawn on the 15th, the island batteries and

[7] At Fort Mifflin, Lt. Col. Samuel Smith had been in command since Oct. 4th. He was wounded on Nov. 11 and relieved on that date by Lt. Col. Giles Russell. By Nov. 12 there were only 306 rank and file at the fort.

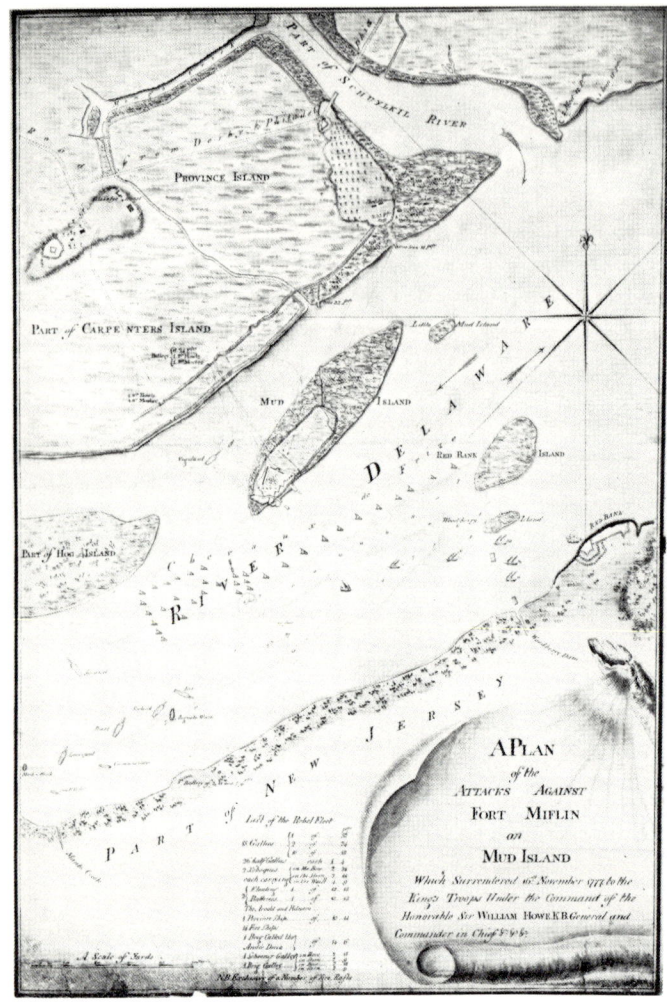

ADMIRAL LORD RICHARD HOWE COLLECTION. LIBRARY OF CONGRESS

PLAN OF ATTACKS AGAINST FORT MIFFLIN

This remarkable map, by Ensign Thomas Wheeler of the British 40th Regiment, is an accurate representation of the military situation about November 15, 1777 just before the fall of Fort Mifflin. Most of the land area shown is now comprised in the Philadelphia Airport.

The British works on Carpenters and Province Islands, and the tremendous fire from heavy guns of the fleet pounded Mifflin mercilessly until that noble fort was finally silenced and her men reduced to handful of survivors. An observer wrote, ".... such a cannonade I believe, was never seen in America. About 350 guns were firing at the height of the final assault.

British ships did not come away unscathed, in fact it was said that every ship engaged was holed, some badly, and loss of life was heavy.

vessels let loose with all they had. Out in the river heavy British ships pounded Mifflin, protected their ships in the inner channel and pounded General Varnum's newly constructed batteries on the east side of the mouth of Mantua Creek on the Jersey shore (which were seriously damaging British ships).

Notwithstanding the superior enemy ships Commodore Hazlewood ordered his galleys to attack the *Vigilant,* however, the latter warped still closer to the rear of Mifflin, within one hundred yards, and continued her murderous fire. The British ships out in the river nevertheless did not come out unscathed, some were badly holed through both sides of their hulls by fire from Mantua Creek and from Mifflin.

By late afternoon of the 15th the British squadron retired to the vicinity of Billingsport and after dark General Varnum sent over from Fort Mercer at Red Bank, New Jersey some small boats with orders to Fort Mifflin to hold or evacuate at the commander's discretion. He had already been in communication with Washington regarding that decision. Major Simeon Thayer, then in charge of Fort Mifflin had informed Varnum that only two cannon remained usable and there was no ammunition to fit them. He sent over to Fort Mercer all the remaining garrison except himself and 40 men at two o'clock on the morning of the 16th, the remainder followed in three bateaux. Mifflin was in flames but the flag was left flying. At daybreak, British soldiers landed and took down the colors, reporting that they had never seen a flag so tattered and ripped by cannonballs. They found dead bodies everywhere and blood around every gun, most of which had been spiked and dismounted. Again, it is unfortunate for history that the flag was not described[8], and since the brave defense of our river forts ranks among the great military sacrifices of history, it is a pity that a poet did not tell in ringing couplets that valiant but losing struggle. Fort Mercer had to be abandoned November 21, 1777.

After the fall of Philadelphia was complete and the British controlled the river, the supply situation was reversed. The enemy could import what they wanted, and for horses, fodder and victuals could live off the rich countryside; the Americans who remained might get what was not barred to them. Under those conditions, the Betsy Ross shop had difficulties obtaining fabrics and other supplies which had to be imported. However, they were obtainable one way or another and one method was from cargoes brought in through a little known inlet on the Jersey seacoast. In that way the

[8] In the portrait of the destruction of the British frigate *Augusta* the flags on Fort Mifflin appear to be stars and stripes.

small town of Tuckerton (Clamtown) suddenly became a busy seaport.

Northward on the coast above the broad entrance to Delaware Bay are a number of inlets between the barrier reef islands off the Jersey shoreline, and just above what is now Atlantic City are the treacherous Brigantine Shoals which mark the south side of a broad and deep inlet called Little Egg Inlet. That inlet permitted access for ocean draft vessels to Great Bay and adjacent Little Egg Harbor. The area was the southern terminus of a line drawn a hundred years earlier by King Charles II to divide his province of West Jersey from East Jersey, a line by now forgotten. Ships drawing as much as 15 feet[9] could find protected anchorage inside the inlet and those of smaller draft could go all the way to the fisherman's wharfside at Tuckerton.

The entrance was tricky but once the shoals were cleared, there was smooth water and in the event of a grounding the next high tide would usually float the vessel off, or it could be kedged from the mud or sand; there was not a rock in the whole area. The larger ships could unload to barges alongside or to a dry sedge. After landing, the merchandise was hauled by dray to Cooper's Ferry and Philadelphia, fifty miles northwest. Ocean cargo vessels had not used the inlet before the war however because of the transshipping encumbrance.

This safe harbor became a rendezvous for privateers also, and the British seldom caught on to the clandestine traffic. After the British vacated Philadelphia in 1778 Royal Navy patrol vessels continued to block commerce from Delaware Bay, so this nearby Great Bay area remained as a refuge for American ships to replenish and to load and unload cargoes.

However, on October 6, 1778, British men-of-war made an entrance and raided the little village of Chestnut Neck on the deep Mullica River where it empties into Great Bay. They destroyed a small fort and then burned every house in the vicinity; 12 homes, a tavern and a store. Some say as many as 400 took part in the raid. The little settlement of Chestnut Neck was never rebuilt but a monument marks the approximate vicinity at what is now Port Republic.

One can imagine the day to day anxiety and uncertainty of a girl in her mid twenties trying to maintain herself and her flag shop amid all the uncertainties of her surroundings. Our Betsy did not flinch.

[9] Depths have been checked with early hydrographic charts in the possession of William J. Holt, U.S.N. (ret.) of Oxford, Maryland. It appears that as recently as 62 years after the event there was ample water and that two boarding houses and Hatfield's store were in business on islands just inside the inlet.

CHAPTER VI

The Flag Resolution of the Continental Congress

NO DETAILS
NO SPECIFICATIONS
SLOW TO ADOPT
FLAGMAKERS FANCIES

Earlier in 1777, and just over a year after Betsy's first flag, the Journal of Congress recorded a minute that became important in American history. A resolution was passed which stated that the flag of the United States shall be of stars and stripes. The date is now celebrated annually as Flag Day.

It is a pity that no mention was made of who proposed the measure, or any discussion there may have been on it. Valuable clues for further research might have been given us. The minutes were entrusted to Charles Thomson, an able and devoted secretary, whose handwriting in the minute book became our sole authority for much of our accepted history of the times. Sam Adams did not always agree with the entries but nevertheless, they were accepted and doubtless were not untrue.

The logic is convincing that the Betsy Ross design of stars and stripes, having been initiated by Washington and found acceptable for use at sea as well as on land, became our recognized national flag about the time of the Declaration of Independence and only needed to be made official, as was done by the resolution. As mentioned earlier, the Grand Union was soon found objectionable as a national flag. Let us then pursue the actual facts we have at hand and see if each of us can arrive at his own logical conclusion on the basis of the evidence.

The Flag Resolution of the Continental Congress was only a single sentence entry along with other routine entries of that particular Saturday, and it merely set forth in concise manner the components that had been selected for our new national banner - 13 white stars, 13 alternate red and white stripes and a blue union. It did not say whether there were to be seven red and six white stripes, or seven white and six red, and it did not say which way they were to run. The arrangement of the stars and their number of points were not mentioned. The original rough draft of the minutes of Congress read:

"Refolved. That the Flag of the united states ~~confift~~ be ~~diftinguifed by of~~ 13 stripes alternate red and white, that the Union be 13 stars white in a blue field representing a new conftellation."

Those elements, simply named, officially distinguished our flag from all others that had confused the issue - particularly at sea. However, we had been slow in 1776 to discard old ensigns then in use, and our lethargy continued even after the Flag Resolution. The Grand Union, flown by Commodore Esek Hopkins, of Rhode Island, was possibly continued on his naval vessels for a time after the Declaration of Independence; another at sea was of plain red and white stripes, no field, no stars; the nickname by the British was, "the Rebellious Stripes." Much later, the flag flown during the victorious engagement of September 23, 1779 on the *Bon Homme Richard* and on the *Serapis* had red, white and blue stripes.[1]

A resolution of that nature today would hardly be evolved in debate on the floor of our Congress, but would come after committee recommendation, public demand or executive request. In 1776 there was no constitution for the Continental Congress to legislate with, not even articles of confederation, and also very little of that important element — money. The members were not elected representatives of the people, they were delegates appointed by the states, and their collective power was derived from committee action, persuasion, mutual grievances and mutual trust. From today's viewpoint one can reason any way he wishes as to how many months advance thinking, if any, were involved in 1777 before that resolution was passed.

[1] Morris, Robert, *THE TRUTH ABOUT THE AMERICAN FLAG*, op. cit., p. 50

NATIONAL ARCHIVES

FLAG RESOLUTION OF CONGRESS

Original minute under date of June 14, 1777 of the rough journal of the Continental Congress in the handwriting of Charles Thomson, Secretary. This resolution officially established the stars and stripes as our national flag. The date is now celebrated annually as Flag Day.

The Flag Resolution is seen near the top, second entry. The crossed out words are: confist, diftinguifhed, of and by. The words "united" and "states" are not capitalized. The word "be" is inserted above "states."

Interestingly, this same page of the journal tells of the appointment of Captain John Paul Jones as commander of the ship *Ranger*.

It appears that little notice was taken of it officially or publicly for some time. The first press notice was apparently in the "Pennsylvania Evening Post" of August 30, 1777; on September 2nd it was in Dunlap's "Pennsylvania Packet, or General Advertiser;" the "Boston Gazette" carried the story on September 15th and the "Massachusetts Spy" did so on September 18th.[2] Of course there may have been earlier publications that have now escaped us, and most likely our Betsy, working for the government, knew of it. She must have derived a great deal of satisfaction that her flag was officially adopted as the flag of the United States. Our patriotic young widow was achieving an enviable record of accomplishments in her young life.

Benjamin Franklin and John Adams, our commissioners in Paris, did not correctly know what the American Flag was in 1778.[3] The king of the two Sicilies, upon opening his ports to American vessels, asked his ambassador to the Court of France to obtain a description of our flag. Our commissioners replied:

> Passy, Oct. 9, 1778
> It is with pleasure that we acquaint Your Excellency that the flag of the United States of America consists of 13 stripes alternately red, white and blue; a small square in the upper angle, next the staff, is a blue field, with 13 white stars, denoting a new constellation.
> Some of the States have vessels of war distinct from those of the United States. For example, the vessels of war of the State of Massachusetts Bay have sometimes a pine tree; and those of South Carolina a rattlesnake, in the middle of the 13 stripes; but the Flag of the United States, ordained by Congress, is the 13 stripes and 13 stars above described.

An interesting similarity in the use of the term from the minute book, "representing a new constellation," was revealed in the early part of this century. A letter dated London, September 12, 1908, from Smith Burnham to Lloyd Balderston, Ph.D., of West Chester, Pennsylvania, husband of a Betsy Ross descendant, related that Burnham was researching at the British Museum Library on the

---
[2] Morris, Robert, *The Truth About The American Flag*, op. cit., p. 40.
[3] Ibid. pg. 60.

subject of captured American flags and he quoted from a diary of a British lieutenant, William Digby, Mss 32413, writing under the date of July 24, 1777:

" '....at that action [Fort Ann, July 8, 1777] the 9th took their colours, which were intended as a present to their Colonel Lord Leganeer [Ligonier] they were very handsome, a Flag of the United States, 13 stripes, alternate red and white, in a blue field representing a new constellation....' " Burnham continued, "In my mind, however, it does not establish the fact that Digby had heard of the resolution of Congress of June 14th [1777 - the Flag Resolution]. It is not impossible that he may have heard of it, but the whole diary seems to be the work of a keen observer who writes very clearly what he sees."

Since there is no known publication of the Flag Resolution until August 30, 1777, one wonders how the term "representing a new constellation" got to an enemy officer writing under the date of July 24. Under battle conditions it is hardly likely that the flag would have been made and supplied between June 14 and July 8, so this could very probably be one more instance of the stars and stripes flying with a military outfit before Congress got around to making it official. Until further information comes to hand, it should be regarded as another enigma.

With the absence of directions in the flag resolution, flagmakers were free to make their own designs, and although there is ample evidence of the 13 five-pointed stars in a circle both before and after the resolution, there is also evidence of rectangular arrangements, horizontal rows, a circle of 12 with one in the middle, and one of a square of 12 with one in the middle. Later, as more states came into the union and more stars were added, there were all sorts of patterns; an outline forming one large star, an heraldic lozenge (diamond shape), a parallelogram, a bell, and others. In 1818 a congressional representative noted in a speech on the floor of Congress that the national standard then flying over the Capitol contained only nine stripes, while that at the Navy Yard had 18! During the Civil War our ensign took many forms, as can be seen from paintings and photographs.

In the long history of our armed forces, there are numerous official regulations concerning identifying flags for the army and its various units all the way from the early years down to the present. Mostly the regulations concerned unit flags, their design, devices and how and when they were to be displayed. Seldom were national colors mentioned because they were standard and the

July.   1777.

cover him with leaves. At that Action the 9th took their Colours, which were intended as a present to their Colonel Lord Leganeer, they were very handsome, a Flag of the United States, 13 Stripes, alternate red & white, in a blue field representing a new Constellation.

In the Evening our Indians brought in two Scalps, one of them an Officers, which they danced about in their usual manner. Indeed the cruelties committed by them were too shocking to relate, particularly the melancholy catastrophe of the unfortunate Miss McCrea, which affected the General & the whole Army, with the sincerest regret & concern, for her untimely fate. This young Lady was about 10, had a pleasing person, her family were Loyal to the King, & she engaged to be married to a Provincial Officer in our Army, before the war broke out. Our Indians (I may well now call them Savages) were detached on Scouting Parties both in our Front, & on our Flanks, & came to the house where she resided——

BRITISH LIEUTENANT DIGBY'S DIARY AT FORT ANN, NEW YORK

A page from the diary of British Lieutenant William Digby which describes a captured American flag. Digby apparently had in mind white stars on a blue field when he wrote "....blue field representing a new Constellation...." but we should not jump to conclusions as it remains an unresolved enigma to this day. Colonel John R. Elting, who probably knows more about the history of Revolutionary War military action in New York State than any historian alive today, wrote to this researcher in 1978 saying, "....This whole business [the flag description and the battle] is full of holes. The 9th [British regiment of foot] could hardly have 'took their colours,' since the Americans engaged were a gaggle of mixed New York/New England militia who would be most unlikely to have a flag with them and, besides, the 9th got pretty well whipped. All in all, it's a puzzle. As of now, I'm prepared to consider the similarity of the language in the diary and in the Flag Resolution of Congress as a coincidence but I certainly am going to keep an eye open for more information on those 'Colours'...."

It is interesting that this same page of the diary describes the well known massacre of Jane McCrea (sic), an incident that was widely printed and inflamed hatred against the British.

rules covering them did not change nor need repeating.

Incredibly, some flag historians have built a story that the U.S. Army did not carry American national flags during the entire Revolutionary War — because the historians did not find them mentioned in reports or in regulations. They could have carried that shallow reasoning on through our other wars had they wanted to because the presence of flags was always taken for granted and battle reports did not mention them. Indeed, we would not have any record of our flag on Mount Suribachi, Iwo Jima if it were not for the famous photo by Joseph Rosenthal on February 23, 1945.

During our struggle for independence there were actually many evidences of them with our army however, and a few that come to mind are the stars and stripes which British Lieutenant Digby just described; also the stars and stripes with Washington at Princeton which Charles Willson Peale painted (see frontis color plate). Peale, who was at the battle, finished it in 1779 and Washington would have most likely disapproved an incorrect flag so prominently displayed. Colonel Trumbull showed the stars and stripes even earlier, in 1776, in his *General Washington at the Battle of Trenton,* picture, which he completed in Philadelphia in 1778. In 1777, General Schuyler said he had one with his army; one is believed to have been with Washington's army at Cooch's Bridge the same year. General Gates must certainly have had one when he accepted the surrender of General Burgoyne at Saratoga on October 17, 1777; Colonel Trumbull painted one in his depiction of the scene. What about the Bennington Flag and the Cowpens Flag? Are we to believe there were no such things? They have never been proven false. And finally, when Cornwallis surrendered at Yorktown our American flag was not mentioned in reports but are we to suppose Washington did not have the stars and stripes there to match the white banners with the fleurs de Lis of France when the British marched toward us on the surrender grounds.

Milo M. Quaife,[4] one of the best known modern flag historians of that war said, "The year 1834 marked several outstanding developments in the history of the American Flag. It witnessed the first significant changes in the colors carried by the United States Army since the reorganization of 1796; saw the first official attempt to prescribe the details of the flag; and for the first time the Stars and Stripes was admitted to the Army."

[4] Quaife, Milo M., Weig, Melvin J. and Appleman, Roy E. *The History of the United States Flag.* New York: Harper & Row, 1961, p. 87.

The first time the Stars and Stripes was admitted to the Army! How presumptuous! The clause containing the word "official" may be the excuse for that outlandish statement but the way writers following him have interpreted it is to say the army did not fly the American flag before 1834. Quaife allows in other parts of his book that American flags are reported to have been in several battles but he does little or nothing to dispel the picture that the army did not use them until 1834.

There are letters from important military leaders direct to Congress and the Board of War requesting colors, among other things, though no particular description of design was given and they were apparently unfulfilled. But supplies generally came through quartermasters in those days just as they do today. They also came through the states, and most importantly in the matter of flags, through patriotic persons and organizations. Incidentally, this author still has a navy blue woolen scarf and watch cap (stocking cap) that arrived aboard the U.S.S. Nevada from a generous ladies auxiliary of the North Carolina Red Cross during grim North Atlantic days of World War II. I don't think I could have got them through Congress!

We will have to pursue Betsy's activities and study other contemporary flags in order to learn her true story and the interesting development of our national standard.

CHAPTER VII

Widow Betsy's Suitors

JOSEPH ASHBURN
JOHN CLAYPOOLE
CLAYPOOLE'S DIARY
MILL PRISON

    Joseph Ashburn's renewal of his acquaintance with Betsy came as a natural sequel to his having been a former suitor. He was the young sea captain of the brig *Swallow* and had been placed in command by his aunt, a Mrs. Ashburn, who was a principal owner, back in 1772 when he was only 21 years of age.[1] Now, in 1777, the vessel was sailing between Philadelphia and the West Indies under letters of marque.[2] Another former suitor was John Claypoole who was in training with the Pennsylvania militia. The two men had been old friends with each other as well as with Betsy, but by this time saw little of one another because Joe was at sea and John was away with his military company. By a curious turn of fate, however, the two men were destined to come together across the seas in a strange triangle of tragedy and romance.
    Still estranged from her Quaker meeting, alone in her upholstery business and at Christ Church, Betsy needed love and understanding. Joseph Ashburn was an old friend from whom she could obtain help and companionship, and as for Joseph he was probably still in love with the girl he had lost to Ross. The old friendship became a love affair during time in port in Philadelphia and on June 15, 1777,

---

[1] Parry, Edwin S., op. cit. p. 125
[2] A letter issued by a state to an individual authorizing reprisals at sea upon the vessels of another nation - acts without which would be considered piracy.

when she was 25 and he 26 they were married at Gloria Dei, Old Swede's Church, in Wicaco, an Indian name for a settlement now a part of South Philadelphia. Gloria Dei is still in service and is the oldest church structure in Pennsylvania. The building was started in 1698 and dedicated in 1700, an outgrowth of the original church of the Swedish settlers who had a colony on the Delaware called Christina, established in 1638 at what is now Wilmington, Delaware, and on up to Tinicum, just below Philadelphia.[3]

Betsy's flag making and upholstery business apparently flourished, and although there are few actual records remaining we do find in Pennsylvania Archives the following minute of the Board of War:[4]

> State Navy Board, May 29, 1777. Present William Bradford, Jofeth Marfh, Jofeth Blewer, Paul Cox. An order on William Webb to Elizabeth Rofs, for fourteen pounds, twelve fhillings, two pence for making fhips colours & put into William Richards' ftores. . . .
> £14•12•2

It is unfortunate that there was no description of those flags. Since they were for ships, and since Pennsylvania did not have a state flag at that time, it has been presumed that they were Betsy Ross American Flags, stars and stripes. However, we cannot rest upon such an assumption.

The William Richards mentioned was a Philadelphia ship chandler. Back in August of 1776 he had requests for national flags and wrote to the Pennsylvania Committee of Safety stating that he could not supply the galleys in the Delaware River with flags until a design was settled upon. That letter has been held by some reviewers to show that he did not know Betsy Ross and did not know her flag. The letter did not say he was unacquainted with her but Philadelphia was a thriving city of more than 30,000 and he may not have.[5] Further, he did not say he was unacquainted with her design; his concern was in determining one that had official

---

[3] In 1638 the Swedes laid claim to lands called New Sweden, which encompassed all of the tidewater area on both sides of the Delaware River from the capes to the falls at what is now Trenton. Governor Johann Printz chose Tinicum Island, near present Essington, Pennsylvania, as his capital in 1643. Government ended when the Swedish Colony was taken over the Dutch in 1655.

[4] Pennsylvania Archives, Second Series. A(2)1, Minutes of Board of War, 1777.

[5] There have been various estimates of population in the mid-1770's from 31,000 to 36,000. According to the 1775 constables' returns there were 31,410 registered inhabitants in Philadelphia, including the Northern Liberties and Southwark Districts.

Marriages For the Year 1777 ———— 61

Knight Gilbert and Mary Grames May the 23
James Ward and Eleanor Loreley May the 23
John Burk and Eleanor Leery May the 23
John Weaver and Jean Davis May the 28
Richard Page and Mary Winters May the 29
Benjamin Chue and Mary Payton May the 29 by Licence
Crenius Jones and Mary Brooks May the 30 ————
James McDole and Eleanor Angel June the 6 ————
Edward Rowan & Elizabeth Cox June the 8 by Licence
Martin Murphey and Hannah Smith June the 8 ————
Henry Abbot & Elizabeth Marshall June the 9 ————
John Hitton and Elizabeth Page June the 9
Edward Flinn & Sarah Johnson June the 11
William Dudley & Mary Bryant June the 11 by Licence ————
James Gold & Elizabeth Clemons June the 13
Joseph Ashburn and Elizabeth Ross ←
June the 15 by Licence ————
William Clark and Pristilla Peerce June the 16 ————

ARCHIVES OF GLORIA DEI CHURCH

BETSY AND JOSEPH ASHBURN MARRIED
At Gloria Dei Church (Old Swedes') the Book of Marriage Records, p. 61 records the marriage of Joseph Ashburn and Elizabeth Ross on June 15, 1777, second entry from bottom.

approval, there was none having such official sanction at that time.

Joseph continued sailing his brig to the West Indies and Betsy remained at her shop. Since she had no children by John Ross we can imagine her happiness when her first child, a girl, was born on September 15, 1779.[6] They named her Zilla. Betsy's marriage and the joys with her baby must have been a gratifying relief from some of the trials of previous years.

The voyages of the *Swallow* had been profitable but she was only a small brig and could not mount effective armament for a vessel of marque and also would be easy prey for larger British vessels on patrol off the American coast and in the West Indies. Sometime in late 1780, Ashburn was offered a new and larger ship to be built by the firm of McClenachan and Moore on the Delaware, but as she would not be ready until 1781 he was meantime given a first mate's commission on the brigantine *Patty*, which was commanded by one of his sailing friends, Captain Francis Knox. The *Patty* carried six brass nine-pounders.

Ashburn's experiences as first mate of the *Patty* and as master of the *Swallow* were hazardous indeed, but the rewards were good if voyages were successful. West Indies ports were the exchange points for cargoes which could not be carried directly between Europe and America. Manufactured goods; fabrics, tools, glass, chemicals and the specialized works of master European craftsmen would be sent to the West Indies ports of France, England, Spain, Netherlands and others. Ship captains would then either purchase or take them on consignment for disposal at American ports. Contraband and items traded with the enemy were thus got through as well as legitimate stores, and a lively trade went on. It was up to the master's ingenuity to cargo his vessel and get it through to his destination.

All manner of ships were used, and they were almost all armed in one way or another. During the last half of the eighteenth century there was almost continual warfare at sea, even at times when there was peace on land. Under such conditions privateers commissioned by governments, and pirates flourished. Even navies were not above taking a prize. In those days when a merchantman happened upon a naval squadron it was common courtesy for him to signal, "Request permission to pass." Sometimes an admiral, perhaps needing the stores anticipated to be aboard the merchantman, would signal back, "Join me." The luckless captain had better well comply.

[6]Parry, Edwin S., op. cit. p. 188.

A small brig like the *Swallow* could not mount very effective armament but she would be fast and could elude some of the privateers, pirates and Royal Navy patrol vessels. The captain of a pursuing ship would weigh his chances: did he have superior gun power; could he overtake before darkness or weather set in; would he risk damage to his own vessel; would he be able to dispose of his prize at a port safe to him; and most important, would the prize be worth the risk? The *Swallow* would not be worth much.

Ashburn had been lucky and had used good judgment, however he was ambitious and wanted to go after a bigger trade. He had an opportunity for a larger ship, and to gain experience by becoming first mate of the *Patty*, which was engaged in more extensive commerce, was attractive to him.

Ships from ports of north Europe; the North Sea, Irish Sea, Scandinavian and English Channel ports would sortie in squadrons for protection, often being convoyed by men of war. They would sail southward well off the coast of France and the saying goes that the masters of ships in the lead would bellow out, "I'm sailing south 'till I see flying fish, then I'll head west." The prevailing westerlies and inclement weather of the Western Ocean (North Atlantic) were to be avoided. Sometimes ships from Spanish and Mediterranean ports would fall in en route if they met a friendly group. At a point in mid-ocean convoys would split according to their several destinations and the risk taking proclivity of the various skippers. It was there that predators were most likely to seize the laggards. Eastbound skippers did not have all those course options so they would take more northerly and more direct routes across.

Meanwhile, John Claypoole, whom we left in early 1777 in training with the Pennsylvania militia, was by September of that year with General Washington's army at the Battle of Brandywine. He was commissioned a second lieutenant in Colonel Jehu Eyre's regiment on the 13th,[7] two days after that disastrous battle. To have received such a commission in the field must have been a recognition of some extraordinary service, but the details of it have not survived. He was badly wounded at the Battle of Germantown on October 4th, and when partly recovered was mustered out and returned subsequently to Philadelphia.

He renewed his friendship with Joseph and Betsy Ashburn and before long developed a hankering for the sea. Fortunately, he

[7] Parry, Edwin S., op. cit. p. 150.

kept a memorandum book.[8] It tells that he left Philadelphia in the *Luzerne,* a vessel sailing under a letter of marque and carrying 18 six-pound cannon, he shipped aboard in October, 1780. She was detained in the Delaware by contrary winds until November 7 and after a difficult passage finally made Port L'Orient, France, on January 1, 1781. Claypoole suffered a serious illness in port but was nursed back to health by a kind family, whose three daughters taught him French during his convalescence. The *Luzerne* discharged her cargo of tobacco and re-loaded another cargo but did not set sail for the return voyage until the 26th of March, when seven or eight other ships became available to accompany her. By that time he had recovered and re-joined his ship. His memorandum book then relates:

"On the 4th of April . . . fortune that fickle jade Threw a Privateer in our way who soon made a Prize of us and with us shap^d her course for Ireland she was call^d, the *Enterprize* commanded by a Thomas Eden and mounted 32 guns. . . ."

Some of the other ships in company had apparently angled off earlier on course for the West Indies. Upon reaching Ireland, anchorage was made in the River Shannon and the prisoners, 37 of them, were taken to Limerick.[9] The Irish people were quite civil but the prison accommodations were miserable. For a time they had to sleep on wet ground, resulting in sickness. By the 6th of July, the prisoners were tried for high treason in England at Plymouth Dock, as John wrote at Mill Prison, Plymouth, England, on 2 September 1781.

Back in Philadelphia, Betsy now had the joy of a second child, Eliza, born February 25, 1781,[10] and she continued in her shop, busier than ever. By this time flagmaking was more important than upholstery. She had not heard from Joseph since he departed in October, 1780, however it was to be a long voyage and with a stop in the West Indies, so she did not worry until well into 1781. But by the time we left Claypoole at Mill Prison in September, Betsy

[8]Jenkins, Charles Francis, *John Claypoole's Memorandum Book,* Philadelphia: Pennsylvania Magazine of History and Biography, Historical Society of Pennsylvania, Vol. 16, pp. 178 - 190.

[9]Claypoole's memorandum book provides an interesting description of life in Ireland at the time: ". . . . I must here take notice to you the manner in which the Poor people live, which I cannot help calling beastly. For upon the same ground and frequently without any partition are lodged the Husband & Wife and the multitudinous brood of children all huddled together upon straw or rushes with the cow and the calf, the pig & the horse if they are rich enough to have one. Their Houses are of several sorts, but the most common is the sod wall as they call it. . . The only solace these miserable mortals have is in matrimony accordingly they all marry young Most Girls are one way or another mothers at Sixteen and every house has Shoals of children. . . nothing can be more elegant than the manner in which the rich live another thing which surprised me. . . is the thousands of Ruined houses and castles and villages. . . occasioned as I am told by the war of Ireland in Oliver Cromwells days."

[10]Parry, Edwin S., op. cit. p. 199.

had indeed become apprehensive; it had been nearly a year since Joseph Ashburn had sailed away and her inquiries of shipmasters at the docks below Front Street, near her shop, yielded no information. Zilla was two years old now and Eliza was seven months.

When Claypoole made entries in his memorandum book he often made them in the form of letters, as though he were writing to a friend. On may 20, 1782 he wrote in that form but addressed it to no one as he could not post letters from the prison: "....As I believe you were acquainted with Mr. Joseph Ashburn, I beg leave to inform you that he was brought to this prison in a short time after me, he died in the night of the 3^d of March after an illness of about ten days which he bore with amazing fortitude, retaining his sences till the last moment of his life."

Joseph would never see his second child, little Eliza, and for Betsy her anxiety would only be amplified by the crushing loss of her first child, Zilla. In those days infant mortality was high and Zilla became one of the unfortunate victims.

Prison conditions were rugged everywhere then and Mill Prison was no exception. There was no heat, quarters were crowded and ill furnished, if equipped with anything at all; rations of food and water were the minimum required to sustain life. In 1782 there were said to be as many as 700 Americans there. Captain William Donaldson, husband of Betsy's sister Sarah was a prisoner also, being the third patriot close to Betsy to be in that one gaol.

Susan McCord Turner, granddaughter of Captain Donaldson, writing in 1909 said:

"Although rebels, they had the sympathy of many London people. One humble admirer and friend was a baker who furnished bread to the prisoners. Whenever news favorable to the colonies was received, this good man informed the prisoners through scraps of paper concealed in one of their loaves."

Throughout the war there were many instances in England of sympathy and affection for the rebels and the rebel cause in America. Such feelings extended all the way up to the halls of Parliament. Nevertheless, officialdom moved slowly after the end of hostilities in 1781 and it was many months before the inmates of Mill Prison began to be returned to the United States. Claypoole was embarked on 22 June 1782 on a cartel ship (prisoner exchange ship) with 215 others bound for Philadelphia via St. Michaels in the West Indies. They made Cape Henlopen, at the mouth of

Delaware Bay after a voyage of 50 days and were shortly afterward at their destination. He wrote in his journal:

"On the 11th of August [1782] in the morning was chased by the ship Genl Washington who came up with us and spoke with us. Same day made the land and came to anchor within Henlopen."

It was John Claypoole who upon reaching Philadelphia a few days later, confirmed to Betsy the rumors she had previously heard that her husband had passed away. Five months had elapsed since his demise and Betsy, at age 30, was now twice a widow. Her anxious queries when ships arrived in port had been unrewarded and were now ended. So far as we know she had not regained the love of her family. Apparently she asked for no help and received none. She carried on her flagmaking and upholstery business and had the respect and admiration of a few friends and neighbors. When they were distressed, she gave comfort, and being a natural healer, brought relief during times of illness.

Claypoole may have seen her frequently as he knew her well from years past, though his diary does not mention courtship and he did not stay in port long before taking to the sea again. A letter written by him and copied into his memorandum book reads:

Philadelphia, the 16th of Aug. '82

". . . .I have the pleasure to find all my friends in good health at home which I assure you is no small satisfaction after so long a separation.

"I am now about to go on the ship *Hyder Ally* bound on a cruise, and as soon as I return you shall hear from me again."

Miscellaneous information in the journal reveals that the daily ration at the prison was 3/4 pound of beef and a pound of coarse bread per day. That was augmented by an allowance of six pence per week which apparently came for a time through popular subscription in England and through the efforts of Benjamin Franklin, who increased it to a shilling a week in the winter months.

John soon gave up the sea after peace came and pursued a romance with Betsy. It was not easy for a woman to be in business alone and doubtless he could help, so a partnership was found in the shop as well as in love. Security came into Betsy's life at a time of need.

They married on May 8, 1783, probably at Christ Church, as they both were parishioners there in 1783, however, the marriage book at the church does not record it. Betsy was now 31 and had her third husband; John was not quite 31, having been born August

15, 1752 at Mount Holly, New Jersey.[11]

There were five children born to them:[12] Clarissa Sidney was the first, born April 3, 1785, she married Jacob Wilson; Susannah, who married Abel Satterthwaite; Rachael, who married Richard Fletcher; Jane, who married Caleb H. Canby; and Harriet, who died in infancy. Thus Betsy bore seven children in all, and they were all girls.

---

[11] Pennsylvania Magazine of History and Biography, op. cit. Vol. 16, pp. 178 - 190. (Additionally contains genealogical information, family life, addresses, prison experiences, etc.)

[12] Betsy Ross Historical Papers, Bucks County Historical Library, Doylestown, Pa. Morris, Robert, microfilm, op. cit.B-2-A-a.

CHAPTER VIII

The Free Quakers

THE DISCIPLINE
A NEW MEETING HOUSE
LYDIA DARRAGH
CLAYPOOLE DECEASED
BETSY DECEASED

The Society of Free Quakers was an organization formed during the war of Quakers who did not adhere to the discipline forbidding the bearing of arms or supporting warlike activities. They would hold meetings for worship at the homes of various of their number, much the same as any Quaker "preparative meeting." Samuel and Sarah Wetherill were early members, as was Clement Biddle. Colonel Biddle we heard of previously with Washington's army prior to crossing the Delaware, later he was the Commissary General at Valley Forge.[1]

The Free Quakers of course permitted military service, they also allowed marriages with those of other faiths. Those factors appealed to Betsy and it was only natural that she should go back to the religion of her childhood so long as it did not prohibit those precepts against which she was so bitterly opposed and which had brought her so much hurt. Their new Discipline contained this maxim:

> We acknowledge the kindnefs of Providence in awakening us to a view of the deplorable fituation in which we have been. Difowned

---

[1] Biddle, in this capacity, was stationed at Moore Hall, about two miles northwest of Valley Forge, near the present Phoenixville. General Nathanael Greene, when appointed Quartermaster General, also occupied Moore Hall. Per letter dated Dec. 1, 1981 to author from John F. Reed, Director, Valley Forge Historical Society.

and rejected by thofe among whom we have been educated, and fcattered abroad as if we had been aliens in a ftrange land, the profpect of our fituation has indeed humbled us. But he whofe mercy endureth forever, has preferved us and induced us to confide that he will care for us. And being made fenfible of the indifpenfible neceffity of uniting together, we have caft our care upon the great preferver of men, and depending upon him for fupport, conceive it to be a duty which we owe ourfelves, our children and families to eftablifh and fupport among us public meetings for religious worfhip. . . .

Membership grew and soon exceeded the capacity of homes. When there were enough to support their own place of worship they built a substantial, red brick meeting house at Fifth and Arch Streets and dedicated it in 1783. It is still there and high on the

ROBERT H. WILSON, "PHILADELPHIA QUAKERS, 1681-1981"

FREE QUAKER MEETING HOUSE
Still standing at Fifth and Arch Streets, Philadelphia.

Arch Street wall, under the gable, is a marble dedication stone which plainly reads:

> By General Subfcription
> For the
> FREE QUAKERS
> Erected in the YEAR
> of OUR LORD 1783
> of the EMPIRE 8

Although members of this Meeting were high in the affairs of our new nation, it is clear that they did not know in 1783 what form of government we would have, a fact not clearly written in history but well indicated by this stone.[2]

There is a membership roster dated February 17, 1785 on which this researcher counted nearly 400 names; the members signed and added the names of their children.[3] Not all names went on at one time, as revealed by dates placed opposite some of the signatures. John and Elizabeth Claypoole appear in an early position, doubtless before 1785, although the exact date has not been found. As noted, they were listed as parishioners at Christ Church in 1783. Lydia Darragh's name appears; as well as her husband's, William; and daughter, Susanna.

There is a quaint story of the patriotism of Lydia. She and her husband and two of her five children were living in their home, Loxley Hall, at 177 South Second Street, in 1777 when the city fell and they were told to move out to make room for officers. Through some pull they were permitted to remain but one room was reserved as a conference room for the use of British officers. On December 2, 1777, she overheard a plan to attack Washington's army, which had camped at various points north of the city after the Battle of Germantown and was at that moment at Whitemarsh, close enough to be a worry to General Howe. She was vitally interested because her son, Charles, was an ensign in the army and she decided to warn Washington.

Under pretext of visiting Pearson's Mill at Frankford to obtain a sack of flour, she obtained a pass and walked from her home on

---

[2] On November 15, 1777 the Continental Congress approved the Articles of Confederation, the first constitution of the United States, but those articles did not become effective until March 1, 1781 after the required number of states had ratified it on January 30, 1781. Even then our form of government was precarious and as late as 1783 was unstable, for on June 17 of that year the United States Congress fled Philadelphia to Princeton before mutinous, unpaid American troops.

[3] American Philosophical Society, Betsy Ross Papers. 289.6 So 22p
Morris, Robert, microfilm, op. cit. AP-1-A.

MEMBERSHIP BOOK OF THE RELIGIOUS SOCIETY OF FREE QUAKERS
The preface and some of the signatures are shown here. Among them are Elizabeth Claypoole, John Claypoole, Margaret Boggs (Betsy's niece), Lydia Darragh, C.S. Wilson (Clarissa, daughter of Betsy), many Wetherills, of whom Samuel, Proctor and Reeves are signed, Matlacks, Hansells, Logans, Sarah M. Wilson, Janeways, Lewises, Mannings and other prominent Philadelphia patriots.

breathed by the Breath of God into the Hearts of all Men, to leave every Man to think and judge for himself according to the Abilities received, and to answer for his Faith and Opinions to him who seeth the Secrets of all Hearts, the sole Judge and sovereign Lord of Conscience."

Being now through divine Favour, in some measure established as a religious Society, we trust by an Adherence to those Catholic Principles, we shall be favoured with the Blessing of the Almighty, and therefore relying upon him for Protection, We do hereunto subscribe our own Names, and the Names of our Children, as Brethren and Sisters in Community, the seventeenth day of the Second Month (called February) in the Year of our Lord One Thousand seven hundred and eighty five. 1785

Isaac Howell   Lydia Darragh
                       Sarah Wetherill &c.
Peter Thomson
Thomas Renshaw   Elinor Karcher
Samuel Crispin   Ann Lenton
Nathaniel Browne   Ann Darah
Moses Bartram 18 feb 1785 Susanna Darragh
Sam.l Wetherill Jr.   Isabella Renshaw
Jehu Eldredge   Sarah Paschall
John Piles   Elizabeth Parry
Edward Tiffets   Esther Parry
Benjamin Say   Susan Smallwood
Joseph Stiles

Joseph Warner	Charity Warner
William Darragh	Mary Lawn
Bowl'd Parry	Elizabeth Thomson
Samuel Eldredge	Lidia Crispin
[?] Matlack	Elizabeth Neave
Jonathan Scholfield	Elizabeth Neave Jur
Rebecah Scholfield	Hannah Carmalt
Jacob Lahn	Elizabeth Claypoole ←
William Thomson	Margaret Rauferin
Samuel Crispin Junr	Sarah Wetherill Daughter of
William Milnor	Samuel Wetherill & Sarah his Wife
Eli Lewis	Mary Cripps
Will'm Matlack	Martha Wetherby
Samuel Wetherill Min	Thomas Lang — Margare
Mord Wetherill	Wife of Thomas Lang and
John Wetherill	Margaret & Agnes his
Ruth James	daughters
William Smallwood	James Lang
→ John Claypoole	Mary Elton
Jacob [?]	Susannah Elton
George Kemble	John Elton
Thomas Elton	Thomas Elton
	Elizabeth Elton
	Anthony Elton

Samuel Crawford
Elizabeth Crawford
Mary Crawford
Charles Crawford
Elizabeth Crawford
Ann Warner
William Warner
Mary Warner
Elizabeth Warner
Sarah Warner
Sarah Stewart
Elizabeth Murphy
Sarah Cribs
Joseph Burden
Elizabeth Trippe
Silas Crispin
Catherine Trippe
Maria Trippe
Margaret Boggs

Saml. C. Wetherill
Adam Trippe Senr.
Adam Trippe Junr.
John Price Wetherill
Charles Wetherill
William Wetherill
Thomas Wetherill
George Wetherill   } Children of Saml. Wetherill Junr.
Fairman Marshall
Saml. Wetherill
John P. Wetherill
Elisha Wetherill   } Children of John P. Wetherill
Charles Wetherill
Henry M. Wetherill
Thomas Wetherill
Margaretta M. Wetherill
Maher Wetherill April 20 1842
Samuel Wetherill
John Macomb Wetherill   } Children of Charles Wetherill
Saml. W. Lippincott
William Lippincott
Joshua Lippincott
Selina Lippincott
Mary Lippincott   } Children of Joshua & Sarah Lippincott
Timothy Mattack
Chas. Kimble

AMERICAN PHILOSOPHICAL SOCIETY

Second Street up Frankford Road to the mill on Frankford Creek; leaving her empty sack there, she went westward along Nicetown Lane near what is now Erie Avenue to find the Continental Army outpost believed to be near Rising Sun Lane. She came upon a mounted officer whom she recognized as Lieutenant Colonel Thomas Craig, who knew Lydia well. She gave him the information and returned to Pearson's Mill; from that point she carried her 25 pound sack of flour six miles to her home. This doughty patriot, clad in a heavy shawl, had trudged on snowy roads for 16 miles.

With Lydia's information, Washington prepared a defensive position and when the attack came on schedule on the fifth of December, Lord Cornwallis, in the van, was repulsed. By the eighth, the entire British army began retiring back to Philadelphia, driving cattle with them and leaving a swath of destruction and burned houses all the way from Chestnut Hill. The Battle of Whitemarsh ended with about 350 enemy killed and wounded; there were under 100 American battle casualties but the toll of illness due to almost 100 hours of standing under arms in winter elements was very considerable.

As the years rolled on, and the war became a struggle of the past, members having old ties with former meetings began to leave the Free Quakers. However, new members were received also, as

ROBERT H. WILSON, "PHILADELPHIA QUAKERS, 1681-1981"
LOXLEY HALL
Home of Lydia Darragh, where she overheard British officers plan to attack Washington's Army at Whitemarsh and warned him in time. One of the unsung heroines of the war, she became a Free Quaker later.

indicated by a business meeting held at the home of John P. Wetherill on July 6, 1832. The minutes show six members present, including Betsy, and applications for membership were received from ten persons, among them: Clarissa S. Wilson, daughter of John and Elizabeth Claypole (sic). The same precepts and qualifications used among the Quakers were observed, as noted in the minutes: "On Motion of George D. Wetherill it was agreed that a Committee be appointed to examine in the customary Manner those applying for Membership - George D. Wetherill & Dr. Wm. Wetherill were appointed members of this Committee. . . ."

Numerous descendants of Betsy were active in the Society. At the Philosphical Society Library there are a number of boxes of memorabilia containing miscellaneous notes and receipts. For instance, there is a receipt for $8.00, undated, signed by Susan McCord, a grand niece of Betsy, for her mother, Sarah McCord, ". . . .for cleaning and opening the Meeting House to June 12th." Although it is believed that Betsy's parents and most of her sisters and brothers had always remained cool to Betsy, her own children and some of her nieces and nephews were loyal and affectionate toward her.

At another meeting in 1832 the Treasurer, William Wetherill, reported a balance of funds of $335.92. G.D. Wetherill reported that the clerk had authorized reshingling of the meeting house and necessary repairs to the building. Apparently meetings for worship were being sparsely attended, however, and by 1834 there were only two regular attenders, Elizabeth Claypoole and John Price Wetherill, grandson of one of the first leaders. It is related that at the close of one of the meetings in 1834 John Wetherill said:

"Widow Claypoole, there are but two of us remaining. It is not right that thee and I should continue to meet here. . . ."

Whereupon they locked the door with its heavy, old fashioned key and the Free Quakers, as a religious society, passed out of existence.[4] The corpus is still very much alive nevertheless. Descendants and others who have joined it for philanthropic reasons meet and dispense income from properties to worthy poor.

Currently, Mr. Reeves Wetherill, a prominent Philadelphian, is the Clerk of the Society of Free Quakers. He generously provided important historical details which have been in the records of the Society and which have come down through Wetherill and Reeves family ancestors. They inform us that Samuel Wetherill, a well known Quaker of the Revolutionary War, called at the Betsy Ross

[4]Parry, Edwin S., op. cit. p. 234.

shop and she told him that General Washington had just been there and asked her to make a new American Flag. She said he wanted stars and stripes and she told Wetherill of the proposed design. When Wetherill asked how she would make all those stars she folded a piece of paper and cut a five-pointed star with one snip of a scissors. He asked Betsy for it and wrote the design on the star. Subsequently, he put it away in an envelope in his office safe.

Reeves then said, "The safe, unopened, remained in my family for many years. One day, about 1925, my father invited me to go to town on a Sunday because he had hired a safe blower to open the original Samuel Wetherill safe...it was blown open and in it we found the star with the notations." Reeves mentioned that long ago he loaned the star to the Atwater Kent Museum and while there it was examined scientifically for verification and it "....checked out perfectly by chemical analysis as to its age. It is hard to read the writing."

The fact that Samuel Wetherill, a well known and active patriot, was so impressed by what had transpired at Betsy's shop that he kept that paper star and made notes of his visit on it is a powerful verification that Betsy was indeed the maker of our first stars and stripes American Flag. Reeves Wetherill, having complete faith in the integrity of his father and ancestors, said, "The paper star which was found in Samuel's safe provides the key link which proves that Betsy did indeed make our first American Flag." None can deny his logic, and none can disprove his contention.

The ownership of the meeting house has been transferred to the State of Pennsylvania and Reeves, as Clerk of the Society, asked the commonwealth to allow the Junior League of Philadelphia to use it as a headquarters, which was accomplished. The League also set up a small museum there. The paper star was eventually given by Reeves to the Society of Free Quakers and it is now in the museum in the meeting house. Presently, ladies of the Junior League dressed in Quaker costume take visitors through the museum and give a slide film presentation of the history of the Society narrated by Mr. Wetherill.

Although no meetings for worship were held after 1834, Samuel Wetherill, being a wealthy man and having custody of the treasury kept the property up and the remaining members of the Society would meet for the purpose of dispensing charity in the form of coal and food orders. Presently, an annual meeting is held to give income funds to worthy charitable organizations.

John Claypoole, as noted, had suffered wounds at the Battle of Germantown and his experience at Mill Prison had also taken its toll of his otherwise good health. Pensions and disability benefits were not granted to Revolutionary War soldiers until the first meager pension was enacted in 1818. Soldiers were allowed government jobs as a sort of relief though, and John did take a civil service position at the United States Custom House in Philadelphia for a short time, otherwise he and Betsy worked together in the upholstery shop. In about 1815, he had a stroke which crippled him, and so, in addition to her flag making and upholstery work, she had to attend to him. He died on August 3, 1817 at age 64.

She had able assistants in her widowed daughter, Clarissa S. Wilson; a granddaughter, Sophia B. Hildebrandt; and a niece, Margaret Donaldson Boggs, who carried the business on. For a time Betsy lived with another daughter, Susan Satterthwaite, in Abington, a few miles north of Philadelphia, but she returned to center city and then lived with a third daughter, Jane Canby. A city directory of the 1830's still listed Betsy as, "Elizabeth Claypoole, Upholsterer."

Her eyes failed in her last years but she continued sewing items like quilts and coverlets as long as she could. A few artifacts have been handed down; one, a silver snuff box, and Betsy's descendants who knew her tell that she did use snuff occasionally. They also remember that her hair was a beautiful reddish titian, or auburn color and that her eyes were clear and of bright blue to her final years.

Betsy was apparently a natural nurse, as mentioned in earlier text. In her neighborhood people would come to her for minor illnesses, such as rheumatism, gout or slight fevers. She would give them herbs and other home medicines of the day. She was an outspoken "Anti-Rushite," a term for those who opposed the medical theories of Benjamin Rush.[5]. Betsy was never one to go along with a prominent person because it was not fashionable to question his competence. Courageous in every facet of her life was this surprisingly modern woman of the 18th century.

It is only fair that we keep in mind that during her lifetime, Betsy was not famous. The story of her making our first flag was cherished by her family, a few friends, and by herself, but it had not then received nationwide attention. Yet she was truly a great lady in her own right as can be realized by following the facts of her life

---

[5] Benjamin Rush was a prominent physician of that time; he was a "man into everything," a devout patriot, a signer of the Declaration of Independence, and during the war was surgeon-general of the military hospitals - a duty he performed with energy and maximum employment of what meager facilities were available.

His medical views, however, were not in agreement with other learned doctors of the day. He practiced bleeding, and it was he who insisted, over the strong objections of three other doctors, in bleeding George Washington, who then died - on December 14, 1799. Some doctors, "Anti-Rushite," said his stubborn obstinacy cost hundreds of lives.

available to us.

She was also witness to dynamic changes in our country. By the time of her girlhood we had had a hundred years of prosperous growth, then we became a budding free nation taking our place on the globe with an army, a navy and a maritime entity. Betsy lived on to see us survive two foreign threats; one from France in the 1790's which was settled without war, and the other from Great Britain which resulted in the War of 1812. The latter a totally unnecessary war which we found ourselves in largely because of absurdly naive unpreparedness under President Thomas Jefferson and more of the same plus timid and irresolute foreign policy under President James Madison. At the time it was called "Mr. Madison's War." During the course of it we made our second attempt to annex Canada but that ended in failure too.

Betsy lived on to see the beginning of our vast expansion to the west. On January 30, 1836 she passed away quietly and peacefully at the age of 84 at the home of her daughter, Jane Claypoole Canby, at 63 Cherry Street, Philadelphia. She was buried beside her husband, John Claypoole, in the graveyard of the Society of Free Quakers on Fifth Street below Locust. In 1857, when that ground was required for city development the remains of both were moved to Mount Moriah Cemetery at 63rd Street and Kingsessing Avenue. In recent years her remains, and those of John Claypoole, were re-interred in the park beside her home on Arch Street. Popular philanthropy and a vast amount of legal work on the part of the American Flag House and Betsy Ross Memorial Association were required. In addition, the school children of an Upper Darby, Pennsylvania public school were prime movers in this patriotic project; without their enthusiasm and help it might never have been accomplished.

The American Flag is permitted to fly 24 hours a day at Betsy's grave. Let us hope it will always wave there and be forever a patriotic shrine for our people.

William J. Canby, Betsy's grandson who first revealed the Betsy Ross Story to the public in his address before the Historical Society of Pennsylvania in 1870, was reticent in giving facts about her life from his own recollections because he was only 11 years of age when she died. However, he later made an appendix which he entitled, "My Own Recollections of Grandmother Elizabeth Claypoole." Since he did not add to or change historical facts, but only related personal matters of interest, parts of his remembrances are given here. Of course, they apply to her final years.

"I was in the country at Uncle Abel Satterthwaite's house

[Betsy's son-in-law], where Betsy was then living [at Abington]. She was an active, bustling woman, yet full of sweet womanly dignity and grace. As her eyes began to fail she would have us children read the bible to her... she sat in her arm chair by the fire grate in the back parlor in serene dignity..."

Canby sat with a bible and spelling book and when he stumbled over words she would correct him, always pronouncing "ed" endings distinctly, as "gain-ed." She was not talkative but told the story of her making the first flag as had been told to her daughters years before.

"....When the children would cry she would call the weeper and bestow comfort and caresses, wiping the bedewed face with her ample handkerchief, soft and sweetly scented, and bringing back sunshine to the little heart. We often called her handkerchief 'Grandmother's flag,'...[she said] 'Yes boys, I made the first star spangled banner with these old hands. My fingers were not so crooked as they are now. I sewed it well, and they were all delighted with it. It was a beautiful flag.'"

"Did they go to battle with it Grandmother?" one of us asked.

"Yes, my dear, it was wartime then, and a great many battles were fought after that."

"What battle did they take that flag to, Grandmother?"

"I do not know. It was made for Congress, and they hung it to the mast of one of the ships at the wharf, and then took it into their meeting and adopted it; that is, they said it should be the flag of this nation."

"And what did they do with the flag after that, Grandmother?"

"That I cannot tell, my dear. I made a great many flags after that one. I made pretty much all the flags then, and I never knew what became of them; but I could tell one of my flags well enough when it came back to me to be mended, if it was years after, but they did not often come back."

"Did they get shot to pieces?"

"Yes, some were burnt up or sunk in the ships which carried them."

Canby said a conversation turned to Washington and reference was made to a large engraving with a well known caption. One of the children asked, "Was he first in war and first in peace?"

"Yes, and where else was he first?" she asked.

My memory supplied the answer, "First in the hearts of his countrymen."

"Yes, my dear," said she stroking my head, "he was truly first in the hearts of his countrymen...we all loved him...."

Canby said that in her final days, "....although bent with age [there was] scarcely a wrinkle in her smooth white face...about which there always seemed to shine a soft, mild radiance....She always wore a silver hook at her waist with two silver chains, to which were attached her scissors and a pin ball, the latter encircled with a silver band. These were insignia of her former occupation... These and her silver snuff box, which occasionally came out of a very deep pocket to be most daintily used and quickly returned, were the invariable accompaniments of her quiet person.

"She once sent me to replenish her box, and I purchased a large bladder of Scotch snuff...I remember her amused smile...I fell heir to the unopened bladder at her death. I learned afterward that she used Rappee and never the Scotch article.

"She was seized with an apoplectic stroke, and on the third night we were all led in to see her die...and so gently, like her whole life, that we could not see that she was still not sleeping."

CHAPTER IX

Critics and Doubters

WILLIAM J. CANBY'S ADDRESS
THEODORE J. GOTTLIEB'S CRITICISMS
THE AFFIDAVITS

The Betsy Ross Story is the most beautiful flag story ever told. This tale of a young Revolutionary War girl, widowed by her husband's war effort, and being called upon by great men of the times to make the flag for our emerging nation, has been told to generations of school children and grown-ups. No other country has anything similar to its quaint simplicity and patriotism. However, it was not a tradition that would ordinarily be made a matter of record in the early days of our young country. In England the design of a flag would be a matter for the King's heralds and the exact description would be recorded in the College of Arms, but here nothing was written down until the flag resolution of Congress a year later. By then a description was necessary in order to put an end to the multiplicity of flags, especially for proper identification of our vessels at sea. Even so it was years before one single design of ensign represented us and indeed 136 years, 1776 to 1912, before the layout of that ensign was standardized and specifications written.

Although the flag tradition was well known within Betsy's family and friends nothing was written down until 21 years after her death. It was in 1857, at the time that her widowed daughter, Clarissa S. Wilson, was finally giving up the operation of the flag making and upholstery shop when William J. Canby, a grandson in his 32nd year, persuaded his aunt, Mrs. Clarissa S. Wilson, that it should be reduced to writing. They made notes and others of Betsy's children added valuable bits of information.

The notes were carefully put away for future reference and no attempt to publish them was made, largely because there was no public interest in the subject. After the Civil War, however, when our nation was once more united, feelings of grief over the severe devastation of life and property gave way to intense patriotism.[1] In 1870 the Executive Council of the Historical Society of Pennsylvania asked Canby to relate the details of the flag story at a meeting of the Society in Philadelphia, which he did on March 14, 1870. Canby was then in his 45th year and his address began with:-

"Mr. President and gentlemen of the Historical Society of Pennsylvania:

"A number of persons, who, like yourselves, are impressed with the importance of preserving every item of history relating to the origin of our beautiful national standard, being aware of the existence, in an unpublished form of certain information relating to the making of our flag, in the possession of a few individuals, now far advanced in years, deemed it desirable that a paper should be prepared and presented to your honorable body, with a view to having said information put on record as a part of our local and national history. These facts being laid before the Executive Council of this Society, they have done me the honor to appoint me to perform this duty. . . ."

Canby noted that research was made among national archives journals of Congress and other works without disclosing any references to the subject, ". . . .It was hoped that some official testimony could be obtained to establish the truth. . .but none was found." He said that (as of 1870) no history of the origin of our flag existed, and most importantly, he noted that, ". . . .tradition, passed down from generation to generation, is an uncertain recourse to a researcher seeking facts. . .it is only the truth that the real student of history is trying to reach." He stated that three daughters of Betsy confirm the statement that Betsy made the first flag and that they heard the tale oft told by her and by others who were cognizant of the facts during their childhood. He added that a niece, Mrs. Margaret Boggs, who worked in Betsy's shop, well remembered hearing the story from her aunt. Canby did not rely on his own recollections of his grandmother because he was young (aged 11)

---

[1] Most of our present patriotic, hereditary societies were founded in the period from 1870 to the end of the nineteenth century.

when she passed away. Notwithstanding, this weight of reliable, first hand information, the lack of positive documentation made it possible for this precious tale to be disputed, and indeed it was, in every small detail.

The most extensive diatribe against our story came from one Theodore D. Gottlieb, Esquire. Gottlieb was a lawyer of Newark, New Jersey and was identified with a well known and respected patriotic organization, although the organization did not join him in his anti-Betsy Ross thesis. Writing in the 1930's[2] he proceeded against the story with a fervor unmatched since, but often copied in part by other writers and historians unwilling to inquire themselves behind his contentions.

Perhaps the most widely quoted Gottlieb argument is his statement that the flag story refers to the visit of Washington, Morris and Ross to the Ross upholstery shop as a "committee" of Congress, although there is no record in the Journals of Congress of the existence of such a committee. This one deserves study, as well as the statements of some writers that Washington was not in Philadelphia at the time the interview was alleged to have taken place — at the end of May and early June of 1776.

Six published proceedings of the Journals of Congress were perused: John Dunlap's, Evans', Claypoole's, the Way and Gideon work of 1823, Folwell's Press of 1823, and Robert Aitken's of which he began publication in 1777. The secret journals were also scanned in an original publication found among the rare books at the Huntington Library entitled, "U.S. Continental Congress, Secret Journals." Finally National Archives, at Washington, produced photo copies of pertinent sections of the original rough draft of the minutes of the Continental Congress in the handwriting of Charles Thomson, Secretary.

A study of the journals gives one great respect for the work of Thomson as secretary. He devoted himself assiduously to the task of keeping accurate records and he held delegates together at times when they had not been paid and when there were scarcely enough in attendance to make a quorum. John Adams severely criticised him for omissions and sometimes a biased slant in various entries, but nevertheless, we were fortunate to have had so dedicated a secretary. In 1775 and 1776 that body had very limited ability to legislate, tax or command. Its power was largely

---

[2] The 1930's was a period when "debunking" became a popular means for a writer to attract attention. Rupert Hughes was notorious in that field and some of his writings were especially scathing.

His principal debunking was directed to George Washington, apparently because picking on Washington would bring the author the most publicity.

the power of persuasion and it was held together mostly by mutual grievances suffered alike by the colonies. As noted earlier, even the Articles of Confederation, under which our government operated, were not agreed to by the delegates until November 15, 1777, and did not become effective until they were completely ratified on January 30, 1781. Our principal interest in reading the journals was to learn about the committee system and it appears that a great deal of the work of Congress was so delegated. While most were quite formal and official, others were casual. There were any number of them, sometimes six or more being appointed in the course of a single day. Some were designated "secret." Reports of committees were noted but in many cases they either did not report or their reports were not recorded. There were reports of committees of which there was no traceable record of their having been previously appointed. At least one historian has said that committees charged with the duty of obtaining flags were appointed in December of 1775 and in January of 1776. This researcher could not find any in January but did find the following:

Thursday, December 21, 1775.
"Resolved, That it be recommended to the committee of safety of Pennsylvania, to provide arms, for the three companies which are ordered to march; . . .and likewise to furnish the said battalion with drums, colours and fifes."[3]

So we did not find documentation for a specific flag committee. Whether there was ever an actual flag committee; whether the gentlemen calling upon Betsy Ross said they represented a committee, using the term as a figure of speech to introduce their group and purpose; or whether the family so used the term, we will never know. The word "committee" stuck with the tradition and its employment should not rule out the story.

The minutes of late May and early June definitely establish that

---

[3] At this juncture it may be of interest to quote two other minutes which, although they do not directly relate to our flag story, do help to put us in tune with those times:

"Thursday, December 21, 1775. Resolved, that the said battalion [Pennsylvania] be paid one month's pay as soon as may be, that afterwards they receive a half month's pay only, until so much is retained, as will amount to the money advanced for their fire arms, clothing, &c after which they shall receive their full pay monthly."

"Wednesday, December 27, 1775. The committee appointed to confer with Captain [Edward] Motte, brought in their report, which being read was agreed to as follows: That they find some of said guard have upwards of 240 miles to march: that they will be content with eight dollars each, and bear their own expenses to their respective homes. . . ." The last minute refers to Captain Motte's guard which had conducted prisoners from Kingston, N.Y. to Lancaster, PA. They were either being given home leave or their enlistments were expiring.

Washington was in Philadelphia at that time,[4] refuting those who said he was not. Some historians have placed the dates between May 18 and June 5, but it is certain he was there by May 23. He is known to have been in New York City on June 9 and there are ample records that he left Philadelphia about the 5th, possibly the 6th. The journey directly between the two cities took two days, in inclement weather three.

Christopher Marshall, an influential Quaker and a member of the prestigious Philadelphia Committee of Correspondence, kept an accurate diary which has provided history with many facts. Under date of May 24, 1776 he wrote: "Yesterday, about two o'clock P.M., came into town from New York, General Washington, as did his lady, the day before. Past ten, went to meet the Committee at Philosophical Hall...."

We can thus be convinced that the General was in Philadelphia when our Betsy Ross Story says he was, and further, that there were great numbers of committees at that time. Perusal of the journals reveals a number of facets of history which have become slightly distorted with the writing and re-writing of them over the years, thus it is well to go back to original records. In doing so, it is interesting to note the casual mention expressed at that time of items which we now hold of the greatest importance.

It is possible that some writers may have been mislead by a

---

[4] From the work, *Journals of Congress, Proceedings 1776*, printed by Robert Aitken, Philadelphia 1777 by resolution of Congress September 26, 1776, we have:

"Saturday, May 18, 1776. A letter of the 17th from General Washington, and three from the commissioners of Canada...were laid before Congress and read. Resolved. That the committee to whom the former letter from the commissioners was referred be augmented to the number of eight and these letters be referred to them. The additional members chosen, Mr. R. Morris, Mr. Duane, Mr. R.E.Lee, Mr. Rutledge and Mr. Livingston." On that day alone five committees were referred to, appointed, or reports heard from them.

"Tuesday, May 21, 1776. [Received] Three letters from General Washington of the 18th, 19th and 20th, inclosing sundry letters and papers of intelligence from England, and a copy of the treaties made by his Britannic majesty with the Duke of Brunswick for 4084 of his troops; with the landgrave of Hesse Cassel for 12,000 of his troops; and with the count of Hanan for 663 of his troops... Resolved that a farther consideration be postponed till the arrival of General Washington...."

Under May 22 there is further mention of letters received from General Washington, and under Thursday, May 23:

"Resolved, that a committee of five appointed to confer with General Washington, Major General Gates, and Brigadier General Mifflin, upon the most speedy and effectual means for supporting the American Cause in Canada. Ordered. That General Washington attend in Congress tomorrow."

The next two days contain brief mention of his being in Congress and at least one routine item which was crossed out in the original journal does not appear in any printed work. It was probably changed or cancelled. The principal business was the raising of troops and the disposition of stores; disposal of prisoners, ammunition and military supplies which had been captured; and disposal of ammunition and stores taken by the armed schooner *Franklin* and other armed vessels in the pay of the United Colonies.

There is no further mention of Washington in the minutes for the next four days until the 29th when his report containing a detailed listing of the military forces in the various provinces was read. This entire minute was omitted in Dunlap's published work.

On June 3rd letters which had been received by Washington were laid before Congress and read. There is no mention of when he departed Philadelphia, but on the 10th two letters from him dated the 7th and 8th were read to Congress.

publication entitled, *Secret Journals of the Acts and Proceedings of Congress from the First Meeting Thereof to the Dissolution of the Confederation by the Adoption of the Constitution of the United States.* Boston, Thomas B. Wait, Printer and Publisher, 1820. It contained no mention of Washington between May 23 and June 5, 1776, nor any reference to his visit to Philadelphia. It was not intended to be a complete record of minutes of those years.

The matter of the inexact date when Betsy was said to have produced the first flag became a big point with critic Gottlieb. He said, ". . . .Admiral Preble[5] proved in his correspondence with Canby that the latter's memory was not as exact or consistent as the paper which he read before the Historical Society, and which, as aforesaid was received without much comment or belief. . . . "

This is an example, out of many, of Gottlieb's propensity to twist information to suit his own preconceived opinions. The actual correspondence to which Gottlieb refers was found by this researcher in the Rare Manuscripts Department of the Huntington Library. It was most amicable, and Admiral Preble, noting that Canby had not mentioned in his address a specific date when Washington, Morris and Ross called upon Betsy to ask her to make the flag, then asked Canby if he could state one. Preble was at that time writing his monumental work on flags referred to in the previous footnote; it was and still remains a most comprehensive and accurate work on the subject. Canby then replied that he could not place it more exactly than early June when Washington was in Philadelphia, about a month before the Declaration of Independence (as Canby had stated in his address at the Historical Society). There was nothing to warrant Gottlieb's way of putting it in a way to make Canby look imprecise or inept, and the only quotation he could have got from Preble was on Preble's p. 194 where he says, ". . . .[quoting Canby] I fix the date to be during Washington's visit to Congress from New York in June 1776, where he came to confer upon affairs of the army, the flag being — no doubt one of these affairs. . . ." The family never recorded an exact date nor did any of Betsy's daughters remember their mother mentioning one.

Gottlieb's statement that the address of Canby was received, ". . . .without much comment or belief. . . ." is completely wrong. It was received with approbation, the story was published many times and it spread rapidly throughout the country.

Gottlieb said, ". . . .It [the Betsy Ross Story] rests on nothing

---

[5]Preble, George Henry, U.S.N., *The Story of the United States Flag,* op. cit.

more substantial than the supposed conversation a young boy had with his grandmother years after the alleged event, and the date, which is very material, was inferred by him rather than told him by any one, and the record of this supposed conversation was not written out until many years after and even then did not receive full credit by members of the family."

That statement is completely misleading and was apparently made by Gottlieb for people he expected would not inquire further. No member of the family has been found by this researcher who has discredited the story, and three daughters and a niece have told of Betsy relating it first hand. Canby, a grandson, remembered her telling it too but as mentioned earlier, he did not make a point of it because of his youth, being only 11 years old when she died.

There had been no reason for supporting affidavits to be made hitherto but with the story's popularity and nationwide spread Canby asked three members who had first hand knowledge to make legally affirmed statements. They were: Rachel Fletcher, daughter of Betsy by John Claypoole, whose affirmed affidavit was executed on July 31, 1871; Sophia B. Hildebrandt, a granddaughter (daughter of Clarissa S. Wilson who was a daughter of Elizabeth Claypoole), who made an affirmed deposition on May 27, 1870; and Margaret Donaldson Boggs, a niece (daughter of Sarah Donaldson who was a sister of Elizabeth Claypoole), whose affidavit was affirmed on June 3, 1870. All three, being Quakers, did not take oaths; the duly affirmed statements of Quakers having equal legal status.

Mrs. Fletcher's affidavit began:[6]

"I remember having heard my mother, Elizabeth Claypoole, say frequently that she, with her own hands made the first star spangled banner that was ever made. I remember to have heard her also say that it was made on the order of a Committee, of whom Colonel Ross was one, and that Robert Morris was also one of the Committee. That General Washington, acting in conference with the Committee, called with them at her house. This house was on the north side of Arch Street a few doors below Third Street, above Bread Street, a two story house, with attic and a dormer window, now standing, the only one of the row left, the old number being 89 [now 239]. . .That it was in the month of June 1776, or shortly before the Declaration of Independence that the committee called on her. That the member of the committee called Ross was

---

[6]Morris, Robert, microfilm, op. cit. Item B-1-F, a,b,c. Also Appendix C.

an uncle of her deceased husband. That she was previously well acquainted with Washington. . .That they then showed her a drawing roughly executed. . . ."

The affidavit went on to state that Betsy made several suggestions during the conference; that the flag be rectangular instead of square as in the drawing; that the stars be in some form of pattern such as lines or a circle rather than scattered promiscuously; that the stars be five-pointed instead of the usual heraldic six-pointed stars because the former could be cut with a single snip of the scissors from properly folded fabric. Mrs. Fletcher's statement continued:

". . . .General Washington, seating himself at a table with a pencil and paper, altered the drawing and then made a new one according to the suggestions of my mother. . .That the committee then requested her to call on one of their number, a shipping merchant on the wharf [Robert Morris], and then adjourned. . .the gentleman drew out of a chest an old ship's color which he loaned her to show how the sewing was done. . .The drawing of the flag was then done in water colors by William Barrett, an artist who lived on Cherry Street above Third Street. . . ."

Also contained in the affidavit were statements that she worked diligently and soon produced the flag. It was run up on the rigging of a vessel belonging to one of the committee, Robert Morris, to the cheers of bystanders. It was taken to the State House, where it was approved and the next day Colonel Ross informed her that it was adopted and he gave orders for as many flags as she could make. Mrs. Fletcher went on ". . . .and from that time forward, for over fifty years she continued to make flags for the United States Government."

Margaret Boggs' affidavit[7] gave facts in agreement with Mrs. Fletcher's and she went into detail about the five-pointed stars. She said that for many years she was a member of her Aunt Betsy's family and aided her in the flag business.

Sophia B. Hildebrandt's affidavit[8] was also in agreement and said that her mother, Clarissa S. Wilson, daughter of Betsy, succeeded Betsy in the business and she, Sophia, assisted her mother. They carried on the flag business until the late 1850's, as mentioned earlier, and it was then that cousin William (J. Canby) felt that the tradition should be reduced to writing. He wrote down his aunt Clarissa's recollections and put his notes away until being called

[7] Morris, Robert, microfilm, op. cit. Item B-1-E, a & b. Also Appendix C.
[8] Ibid. Item B-1-D, a & b. Also Appendix C.

upon, as stated earlier, to relate the story to the Historical Society of Pennsylvania.

So much for Gottlieb's statement that the story ".... rests on nothing more substantial than the supposed conversation a young boy had with his grandmother many years after the alleged event...."

Gottlieb quotes John Spargo[9] as saying in his, *The Stars and Stripes in 1777*, published in 1928 at Bennington, Vermont, that "....no competent authority accepts this [Betsy Ross] story as told ...[it is] morally certain that she did make a flag at Washington's request, perhaps from a pencil sketch by him, but it was not and could not have been the stars and stripes. The flag she made at Washington's request was undoubtedly the Grand Union Flag, the first ensign of the American Navy. The flag which was raised when Washington took command of the Army, January 2, (sic) 1776, and hence commonly called the Cambridge Flag."

That so called quotation is so full of holes it defies detailed refutation. This author could not find the quotation in Spargo's work, nor anything to warrant what Gottlieb attributes to him, however, that is not to say the quotation does not exist somewhere. Spargo wrote the history of the famous Bennington Flag (the American Flag with the numerals "76"), and told of other Revolutionary War flags in his *The Stars and Stripes in 1777*.

As for the Grand Union, or Cambridge Flag, the facts are, as partly related earlier, that Washington, in Philadelphia, was appointed by Congress as Commander-in-Chief of the Continental Army on June 15, 1775, the day after the army was established. He accepted on the 16th and on the 17th departed for Cambridge, Massachusetts. There he took command of the recruits coming in from the various colonies for the siege on Boston, then held by the British. He began their training on July 3, 1775.

No flag was provided for the new army by Congress, but at that time, or soon afterward, the Grand Union Flag appeared — the one with 13 red and white stripes, and the British Union Jack in the upper left. As detailed earlier, this is the flag Washington ordered flown on Prospect Hill overlooking Boston in view of the British on January 1, 1776. It also flew at that time over ships of our new navy in the Delaware River. One cannot find the authority by which Gottlieb quoted Spargo as making such a positive and unequivocal statement as, "....The flag she made at Washington's request was

---

[9] John Spargo was the President of the Bennington Battle Monument and Historical Association. He was also President of the Vermont Historical Society. He was a distinguished humanitarian and patron of the arts as well as an historian of note.

undoubtedly the Grand Union Flag...."

Thus it appears that critic Gottlieb has apparently misquoted and used to support his own theories the works of two prominent historians, and they are not all. He has categorically stated that historians do not believe the story; "....that they hold it to be certain that the Betsy Ross Story is one of the most unwarranted renowns in history, and that the stars and stripes were never carried during the Revolution." He quotes Ballard Thruston as saying, "... the stars and stripes were meant for the navy, while Washington and the Board of War agreed on an entirely different design [not described] for the army to carry as national colors... the stars and stripes we find in paintings are purely artistic license and were made long after the events portrayed." Such postulations, however irresponsible and incredible they may appear, nevertheless should be analyzed.

CHAPTER X

Early Stars and Stripes

FIVE IN EXISTENCE
STARS AND STRIPES IN PORTRAITS
CHARLES WILLSON PEALE
COLONEL JOHN TRUMBULL

There are five flags with 13 white stars and 13 alternate red and white stripes from Revolutionary War years which are still in existence. They are:

1. The Schuyler Flag at the Fort Ticonderoga Museum. A true Betsy Ross design with 13 white, five-pointed stars in a circle on a blue field[1] with a banner of seven red and six white alternate stripes. It was made for General Philip Schuyler by Betsy Ross when he was in Philadelphia in 1777 and was intended to fly at his headquarters. This flag is described more fully in Chapter XIII.

2. The Cowpens Flag at the State House, Annapolis, Maryland. It is similar to the Betsy Ross type except that there are 12 stars in

---

[1]"Field" is a term in heraldry meaning the plain portion upon which distinctive charges are placed. In flags it is commonly the upper left portion next to the staff. The British Union Jack is found there in various British ensigns, hence that portion is also called the "union." The heraldic term "canton," meaning a rectangular quarter or smaller, has come to be used to denote the upper left section of a flag also.

the circle and the 13th is in the middle of the circle. It is a relic of the Third Maryland Regiment, members of which fought at the Battle of Cowpens, South Carolina. Just when the flag was made is not known. Its history begins with the Battle of Cowpens but it is believed to have been designed and carried as a national ensign with the regiment much earlier. It conforms in all respects to the stipulations of the Flag Resolution of 1777. This flag is described in more detail in Chapter XIII.

3. The Bennington Flag, with 13 seven-pointed white stars, seven white and six red alternate stripes and the numerals "76" on the blue field with the stars. Except for the numerals this ensign is in keeping with the meager directions of the Flag Resolution. It is a relic of the Battle of Bennington, August 16, 1777 and its known history begins with that battle, but it may well predate the Flag Resolution of June 14, 1777. This was the popular stars and stripes flown nationwide during the Bicentennial. The actual flag has been carefully preserved and is now at the Bennington Historical Museum, Bennington, Vermont. It measures 10 feet by 5½ feet and it is described in greater detail later in this treatise.

4. The General Philip Schuyler Flag of the Independence National Historical Park collection in the Army and Navy Museum in the Pemberton House, south side of Chestnut Street between Third and Fourth Streets, Philadelphia - Item SN 26.063. Robert L. Giannini III, Assistant Curator,[2] provided a detailed description and the story of its restoration and remounting for display, a work of infinite patience and skill. It is a silk flag, 42" x 62" and contains seven white and six red sewed stripes. Painted in oil colors on the blue field, upper left next to the staff, is an eagle, wings spread, facing viewer's right. A white scroll is in its beak with the motto: E Pluribus Unum. There are three arrows in its left claw and in its right an olive branch. Arched between the wing tips are 13 white stars; 12 with five points and one with six points. Around the perimeter

[2] Letter to author dated October 31, 1980, Robert L. Giannini III, and enclosure - treatise on restoration of this particular flag by Colonel Rice, National Park Service, 1968.

INDEPENDENCE NATIONAL HISTORICAL PARK COLLECTION, SN 26,063 PHILADELPHIA, PA

SCHUYLER FLAG

A silk flag, 42" x 62" of seven white and six red stripes, with a fringe of red. The union is blue and contains a painted eagle "to the right," with wings spread and a shield centered. In its beak there is a white scroll with the motto, E Pluribus Unum. Arched between the wing tips are 13 white stars; 12 of five points and the 13th, on the extreme right, has six points. In its talons are the arrows of war to the right, and the olive branch of peace to the left. The devices in the union reflect the influence of the Great Seal of the United States, which was new when this flag was made. In the seal the eagle "to the right" was later changed to face left toward the olive branch rather than the arrows of war. Eagles were common in American national flags late in the war. The one with Washington at Yorktown contained an eagle, as painted by Charles Willson Peale in his *Washington, Lafayette and Tilghman at Yorktown*, now at the State House, Annapolis.

This flag was presented in 1782 or 1783 to Major General John Philip Schuyler by admirers from his former command. Schuyler was one of the first four major generals in the Continental Army, appointed by Congress June 17, 1775. It was passed down through the Schuyler family and finally presented to Independence Hall when the hall was under the management of the City of Philadelphia. It was hung in the Congress Hall section until the hall was taken over by the National Park Service, at which time it was painstakingly restored by experts of the service. It now hangs in the second floor of the Army - Navy Museum, Pemberton House, Chestnut Street between Third and Fourth Streets, Philadelphia.

This flag is not to be confused with the Schuyler Flag (Schuyler-Hamilton) at Fort Ticonderoga, which is also a precious relic of the Revolution.

GRAND UNION FLAG. Our adaptation of the British Red Ensign which was familiar to the colonists as seen on British merchant ships in harbors. It was simply the addition of six white stripes across the banner, making seven red and six white stripes, or 13 in all. The Union Jack in the upper left signified our allegiance to the king and the stripes were symbolic of the colonies.

BETSY ROSS FLAG. The American ensign first made by Betsy Ross; this style of our flag has borne her name evermore. There is ample evidence, by reason of the well founded story and by the work of artists who accurately portrayed what they saw, to believe that she made this flag at the end of May or first days of June, 1776.

COWPENS FLAG. The Flag Resolution of Congress did not specify how the stars were to be placed in the union, so this flag with 12 in a circle and one in the center, as carried by the Maryland Third Regiment, was as valid an American flag as any. When it originated and by whom is not known; but it was carried at the Battle of Cowpens, South Carolina on January 17, 1781 and takes its name from that important and victorious engagement. The actual flag from that battle now hangs in the State House, Annapolis, Maryland.

BENNINGTON FLAG. One of a number of American flag types during the early days of the Revolution. It participated during the repulse of the British at the Battle of Bennington, August 16, 1777 and the actual flag from that battle is now framed at the Bennington Museum, Bennington, Vermont.

of the three outer sides is a fringe of red. The devices in the field somewhat resemble the first Great Seal of the United States, which was adopted in 1782.

Eagles are not uncommon in early American flags. A similar example is portrayed by Charles Willson Peale in his famous painting at the State House, Annapolis, entitled, *Washington, Lafayette and Tilghman at Yorktown,* which shows in the background a French and an American flag. The blue field of the American flag contains an eagle and the stars are in an irregular, circular fashion surrounding the eagle.

This flag is said to have been presented to the General in 1783 prior to the Peace Treaty of September 3, 1783 by members of his former commands. It was passed down through his family and presented to the nation by his great, great, great granddaughters, Miss Elizabeth Schuyler and Mrs. Anna Schuyler Killie. At some time a label was attached which reads, "Regimental Flag." Whether it was originally intended to be a national flag or regimental is not certain. It would not have been out of keeping of the time as a national flag, and the devices from our new Great Seal would be timely. Normally regimental flags had banners matching the facings of the uniforms of the regiment, not red and white stripes.

5. United States Navy Ensign 1780. This flag is now at the Germantown Historical Society, Philadelphia, and is the only one of these five remaining 13 white stars and 13 red and white stripes flags with the stars in rows. They are placed 3-2-3-2-3. It was presented to the Society by a Mrs. Woodruff[3]. This flag is also mentioned in Chapter XIII.

The stars and stripes are prominent in paintings of Charles Willson Peale and Colonel John Trumbull of military scenes during the Revolutionary War. Their biographers relate that they were most meticulous in portraying flags, uniforms and the accoutrements of war. They felt a responsibility to be accurate in things that would not otherwise be carried down through history. Even the variations

[3] Letter to author from Laurence Hallinan, Germantown Historical Society, October 22, 1980.

in design, which were indulged in by flagmakers after the incomplete terms of the Flag Resolution of 1777, were carefully preserved by these contemporary artists. They were in positions to observe and to know. Peale was captain of a company of foot with Washington; Trumbull, son of the colonial and revolutionary governor of Connecticut, Jonathan Trumbull, was adjutant of a Connecticut regiment at Bunker Hill and later became an aide directly to Washington.

A number of pictures of Washington at the Battle of Princeton, January 3, 1777, were made by Peale. He was there with the General. This author has traced 13 with Princeton and other backgrounds and has viewed most. Flags are prominent and Washington is in about the same stance in a number of them. Peale made replicas and sometimes varied the backgrounds from Princeton to Trenton to Yorktown. One now hanging in the faculty room at Nassau Hall, Princeton University, clearly shows a stars and stripes flag. It is entitled *George Washington at the Battle of Princeton,* and contains five-pointed white stars possibly in circular fashion (not all 13 are showing) on a blue union, and red and white stripes. Some of Peale's works show Washington's own flag, a blue banner with 13 six-pointed, not five-pointed, white stars in a circle and no stripes. The points are thin and are proportioned exactly like those on the actual headquarters banner which Washington's collateral descendants gave to the Valley Forge Museum, now on view there. Peale began his portraits of Washington in 1772 and had a number of sittings in 1776 and later years.[4] His son, Titian R. Peale wrote in a letter some years later that "....the trophies [four Hessian flags] at Washington's feet I know he painted from flags captured [at Trenton and Princeton] which were left with him for the purpose. He was always very particular in matters of historical record in his pictures."

Colonel Trumbull, in his *General Washington at the Battle of Trenton,* now at the Yale University Art Gallery, New Haven, shows a stars and stripes flag with the stars in a circle, Betsy Ross fashion. The battle was on December 26, 1776. This portrait, as mentioned earlier, was completed two years later in Philadelphia. Not all his paintings showing flags had the stars in a circle, some were in squares. of which a number had one star in the center of the square. Theodore Sizer, Trumbull's biographer,[5] stated, "Colonel Trumbull was a faithful recorder of men and events at the birth of this nation...

---

[4]Sellers, Charles Coleman, *Portraits and Miniatures by Charles Willson Peale,* Philadelphia: Transactions of the American Philosophical Society Vol. 42, Part 1, 1952, p. 217.

[5]Sizer, Theodore, *The Works of Colonel John Trumbull,* New Haven: Yale University Press, 1967, p. 1.

being a soldier he understood military gear and accoutrements ...and recorded with punctilious accuracy...."

There are four Trumbull portraits in the Rotunda of the Capitol at Washington, all have Revolutionary War figures and all have true facial likenesses. For his *The Surrender of Lord Cornwallis at Yorktown, Virginia, 19 October 1781* he went to Paris, and while there wrote to his brother Jonathan, "I have been in this capital of nonsense and dissipation for near six weeks for the purpose of getting portraits of French officers who were at Yorktown, and have happily been...successful." In his *The Declaration of Independence, 4 July 1776 at Philadelphia,* he faithfully painted the facial likenesses of 48 of the 56 signers. To do so required an enormous amount of research and travel. This portrait, which also hangs in the Rotunda of the Capitol at Washington, is now on our two dollar bills of currency in circulation.

Gottlieb, when confronted with examples of flags in works of art which did not fit in with his own ideas of history, swept them aside saying they were "artistic license." A convenient way to deny opposition with one stroke. The fact is that, before the invention of photography, much of the historic information we have about flags, uniforms, sailing ships, and accoutrements of war has come from the faithful and painstaking efforts of artists. Specifications and designs were seldom written down, and only a few items have survived in corpus. Incidentally, with respect to later years, we would hardly know what Indians looked like in their colorful tribal garb were it not for the artist, Frederic Remington.

CHAPTER XI

Site of The Betsy Ross House

THREE NUMBERING SYSTEMS
DIRECTORIES
TAX LISTS
AFFIDAVITS

    The matter of the address of the house in which Betsy made our first flag has come under the fire of detractors. The inexact data concerning that important street number has been held to be evidence of the incredulity of the whole story.
    Most anyone attempting to trace the addresses at which his grandparents or great-grandparents lived at various times of their lives would have difficulty, especially if they moved as many times as Betsy. There are additional complexities in her case for a number of reasons:
    1. There have been three different address numbering systems used along Arch Street. In 1776, the crucial year for our purposes, there were no numbers at all.
    2. There were no city directories in 1776. The first was published in 1785.
    3. Tax lists of individuals and of property owners could be expected to yield addresses but there were no tax lists for the war years of 1776, 77 and 78. The name "John Ross, Upholsterer," does appear, however, on certain prior tax lists, he being taxed for his occupation.
    4. Neither Betsy, nor any of her three husbands, ever owned any real estate. Hence deed books do not enlighten us except to provide the names of landlords from whom they may have leased

property.

5. The name of the street was changed from Mulberry to Arch at some unrecorded and indefinite time in the mid-eighteenth century but the old name persisted for many years. Recorded deeds as late as 1835[1] used the term, "Mulberry Street, commonly called Arch Street."

These factors do not confuse careful flag researchers, but do some flag historians who wish to create doubt.

Theodore Gottlieb never troubled himself to go into all this research, however. He merely found someone who claimed Betsy lived at another address and through his prejudice and negativeness on the subject has led many to believe she at no time had her shop on the north side of Arch Street between Third and Second Streets. He held that since her daughters and other family members couldn't even come up with her correct address they didn't know what they were talking about and the whole thing should be declared a hoax. He ignored the affidavit of Betsy's daughter, Rachel, which did give a specific address, number 89 Arch Street, now 239.

The hope that public records might be found to definitely place the location has enticed a number of able researchers. Mr. & Mrs. Charles B. Barclay have exhaustively searched among old original records and archives at City Hall, Philadelphia. He is the President of the Genealogical Society of Pennsylvania and she is a collateral descendant of Betsy. She has compiled property descriptions from deeds, wills, tax lists and other documents of the seven houses that have been considered, erroneously or not, as possible addresses of the shop and home. Mr. Barclay has searched deeds, tax lists and other documents and has constructed property maps of the area according to the various numbering systems used through the years. In 1975 Linda A. Fisher, Esq., of the University of Pennsylvania, researched on much the same material as the Barclays, and William A. Kingsley, Director of the American Flag House and Betsy Ross Memorial, published that valuable treatise.[2]

At the outset, the earliest city directories were consulted, but since none was available for 1776 they only served as something to work backward from. Of the first two, published in 1785, one by Frances White did not contain street numbers; the other, by John MacPherson, did contain numbers. Both White and MacPherson listed "Claypole, (sic) John, Upholsterer," the latter providing a

[1] Philadelphia Deed Book A-71, p. 531.
[2] Fisher, Linda A. Esq. and Kingsley, William A., *Authenticity of the Betsy Ross House*, Philadelphia 1975.

number, 335, which translates after a changed numbering system to the present site, if not the exact number. By 1785 Betsy was Mrs. John Claypoole.

Referring to tax lists, John Ross was listed as of March 31, 1775 as a taxpayer in the Walnut Ward.[3] He did not own any real property there but taxes were levied not only on real estate but on occupations; such as carpenter, cordwainer, baker, etc. The entry read, "John Ross, Upholder," (Upholsterer). Personal property, such as horses and cattle, were also taxed and it even extended to the number of servants and slaves. Indeed, each person living in a given taxable area was required to be included in the tax assessment list thereof in those colonial years. Being in the Walnut Ward in 1775 would place Betsy and John near the shop where they worked, which, as mentioned earlier, was William Webster's Upholstery Shop, on Second Street below Chestnut and above Walnut.

Pursuing documentary information we find no help from tax lists during 1776, 1777 and 1778 because, as mentioned, none was made during those war years, and nothing helpful can be disclosed for 1779. However, in 1780 when Betsy was Mrs. Joseph Ashburn, we find Joseph Ashbourne (sic), Mariner, on the Mulberry Ward tax list and in addition to his occupation tax he paid property taxes for the estate of Jesse Jones.

Similarly, Elizabeth Asbourne (sic) is shown in 1781 and Joseph Osbourne (sic) in 1782. The Mulberry Ward encompassed the present Betsy Ross site on Arch Street.[4] There is significance in the payment of those estate taxes because the estate of Jesse Jones owned at that time two adjacent houses on the north side of Mulberry (Arch) Street between Bread and Third Streets The properties are located by deeds[5] and accurately positioned as present numbers 241 and 243.

In order to trace the street numbers through the three systems it is necessary to consider all of them. As previously noted, the very first was MacPherson's in 1785. He began at the Front Street terminus of Arch Street and numbered consecutively along the south side westward to the last location of a building; thence returning consecutively eastward along the north side of Arch

---

[3] Philadelphia County Tax Assessment Ledger of March 31, 1775, p. 31.
[4] City of Philadelphia Effective Supply Tax.
1780 - Joseph Ashbourne, Mariner, for Jesse Jones Estate.
1781 - Elizabeth Asbourn, for Jesse Jones Estate.
1782 - Joseph Osbourn for Jesse Jones Estate.
[5] Philadelphia Deed Book D15, p. 166. Isaac Jones and Evan Jones, executors of Thomas Griffin to Jesse Jones. Indenture made 26 Nov. 1762, acknowledged 18 Dec. 1762, recorded 21 March 1786.

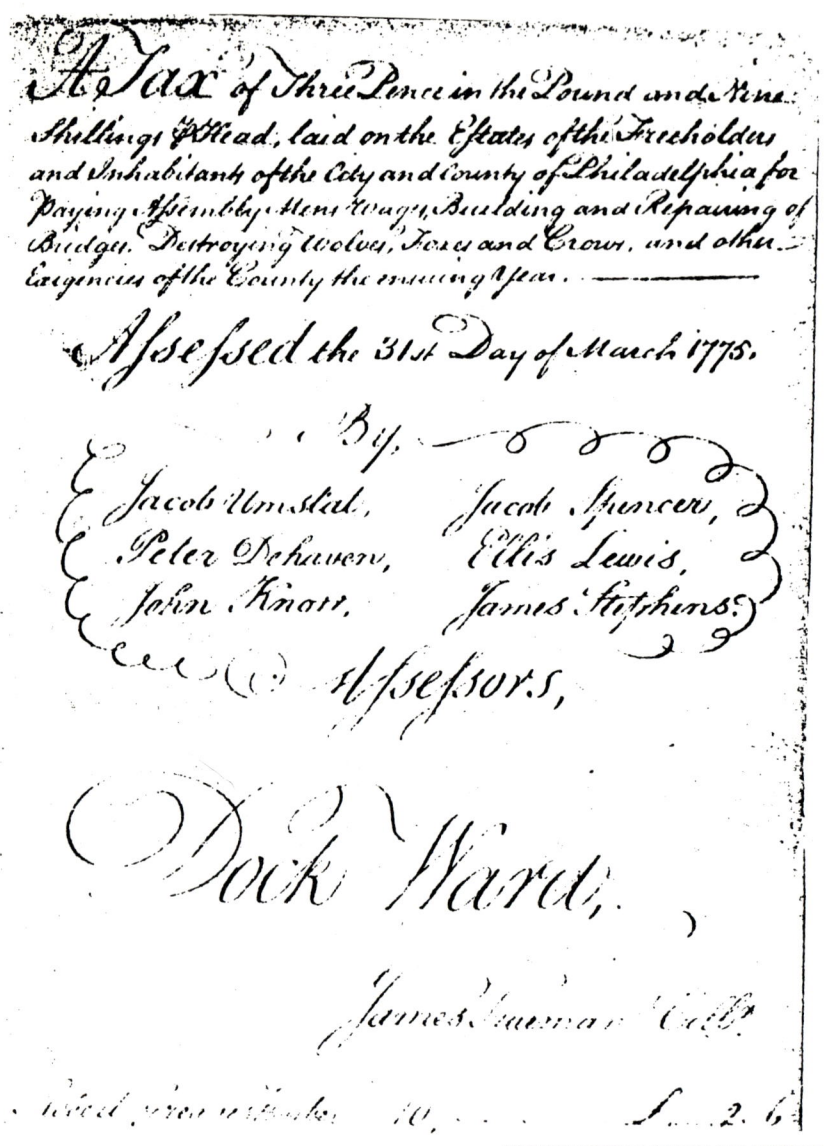

ARCHIVES OF THE CITY OF PHILADELPHIA

"For...Destroying wolves, foxes and crows..." Tax assessment of March 31, 1775 in what is now downtown Philadelphia. Mr. and Mrs. Charles B. Barclay made these two excerpts from the Dock Ward, Walnut Ward section of the Philadelphia County Tax Assessment Ledger.

John Ross was taxed as an upholsterer, as shown at the bottom of the second print.

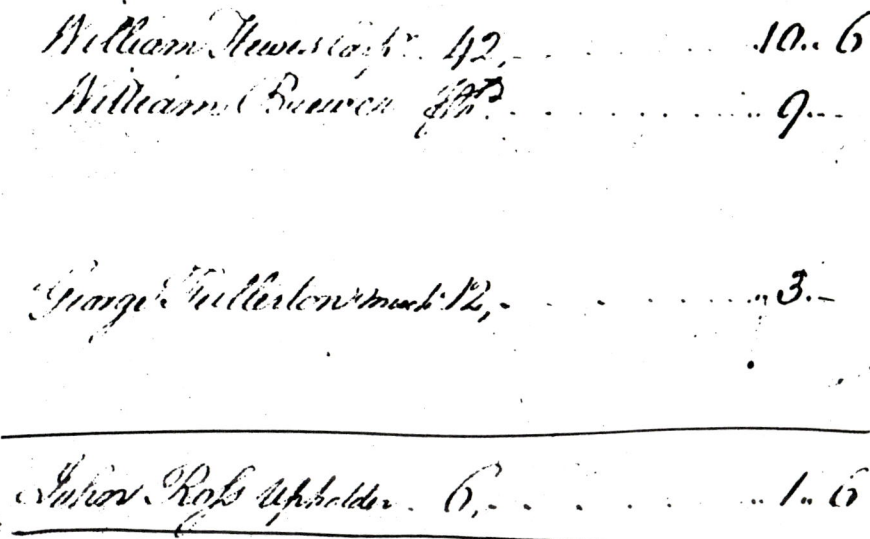

ARCHIVES OF THE CITY OF PHILADELPHIA

John Rofs, Upholder (upholsterer) was assessed as of March 31, 1775. His name is seen at the bottom of this print, which is page 31 of a continuation of the Dock Ward photo.

Street back to the beginning at Front Street. Under his system the Jones Estate twin houses were numbered 334 and 335.

In 1791 Colonel Clement Biddle published a directory which replaced the previous ones. He numbered alternately from side to side, increasing from east to west, as is done today. Under his system, MacPherson's 334 and 335 became 93 and 91, respectively. The Biddle method remained in effect until 1857, when a uniform, city wide plan was instituted and his 93 and 91 became 243 and 241. So it can be seen that Joseph and Betsy Ashburn paid taxes in 1780, 81 and 82 on the Jones Estate houses which at first had no numbers, then were numbered successively, 334 and 335; 93 and 91; and now 243 and 241. We now have reliable information that Betsy and John Ross were on Arch Street in 1775, having moved there after March 31, 1775 as shown by the tax lists. We also believe that Betsy lived at what would be present number 241 in 1780 to 1785.

With all the weight of direct evidence we have it seems that there is little reason why the three affidavits of a daughter, a granddaughter and a niece should not be accepted. All three were associated with Betsy in their daily lives and all three agreed that

COURTESY WM. A. KINGSLEY, DIRECTOR, BETSY ROSS HOUSE

THE BETSY ROSS HOUSE
239 Arch Street, Philadelphia. Today this house, with its adjacent A. Atwater Kent Park and Burial Site, is second only to Independence Hall and the Liberty Bell as a tourist attraction. School children by the many bus loads stop here every week.

she lived on Arch Street below Third at the time she made our first flag.

Margaret Boggs, her niece, gave the place as being on the north side of Arch Street below Third; Sophia Hildebrandt, her granddaughter, gave it as Arch Street below Third. Rachel Fletcher, Betsy's daughter, was even more precise, stating in her affidavit, as partially mentioned earlier:

"This house [where the first flag was made] was on the north side of Arch Street a few doors below Third Street, above Bread Street, — a two story house, with attic and a dormer window, now standing, the only one of the row left, the old number being 89; it was formerly occupied by Daniel Niles, Shoemaker. Mother at first lived in the house next East, and when the war came, she moved into the house of Daniel Niles."

Rachel's statement, "when the war came," probably meant July 4, 1776, but she may have meant 1775 because in 1775 the Continental Congress in Philadelphia was surely on a war footing. A Continental Army had been established and warships of the new Continental Navy were then in the Delaware River. Lexington, Concord, Fort Ticonderoga, Crown Point, Bunker Hill and Quebec all became matters of Revolutionary War history in 1775.

Rachel's reference to Daniel Niles house stimulated further detailed research of deeds and the Barclays obtained abstracts from Philadelphia Deed Book AM71, p. 531 in which there is a property of Daniel which traces to number 247 Arch. The house next east, number 245 is in the book of Philadelphia Sheriff's Deeds B-3, C.P. 3, p. 507 as belonging to William Niles, father of Daniel. However, the dates of ownership are many years after Betsy quit the location in 1785 and are not conclusive as to whether occupied by Daniel in 1776. He could, of course, have occupied 241 or 239.

The property map of the area which the Barclays constructed shows owners and locations under the three numbering systems. They used tax lists, deeds, insurance company surveys, directories and census data gathered from state and city archives and libraries. The tax lists covered years from 1767 to 1811, excepting 1776, 77 and 78. Deeds extended earlier and later. Such material provided information as to names, but not always addresses, so they had to learn who lived next to whom, and so on. As of passing interest — the preamble of a 1773 tax list for the Dock Ward contained:- ". . . .A Tax of Three Pence in the Pound and nine shillings a head. . .for. . .Destroying Wolves, Foxes and Crows, and other exigencies of the County the ensuing year."

Rachel Fletcher's mention of Daniel Niles house, and the one next east, does not allow us to conclude that she was mistaken about her number (old 89) because we do not have proof of where Daniel was situated in 1776. This area was one of row houses, unnumbered, similar one to another, and often in pairs separated by three foot alleyways on the ground level only. A handsome example of such a pair exists today at numbers 219 and 221 Arch Street.

It has been found that number 239 appears to have been owned from 1765 to 1779 by Hannah Lethgo. Records of the Philadelphia Contributionship Insurance Company show that it was insured for Hannah Lythgo (sic) under policy No. 847 and that policy was renewed for her twice for seven year terms each on August 7, 1770 and September 2, 1777. Incidentally, the first house that lady owned on the street was number 219, mentioned above.

All this leads to possibilities for Betsy to have been at locations presently numbered 247, 241 and 239 in 1776. The work of the Barclays and of Miss Fisher is most impressive and is in more detail than can be expressed here, and what is of great importance to all Americans is that these numbers are all comprised in the present Betsy Ross site. There will probably never be more exhaustive work than they have produced and they together with William A. Kingsley, agree without hesitation that there is no evidence to deny that the house where Betsy made our first flag was on the foregoing site.

The house was given to the City of Philadelphia by the American Flag House and Betsy Ross Memorial Association; the remainder of the grounds, including her burial place, was given by the philanthropist, A. Atwater Kent.

CHAPTER XII
More Critics

WHITNEY SMITH
QUAIFE, WEIG AND APPLEMAN
THE HOPKINSON FLAG

Whitney Smith, a flag author, has summarized his version of the arguments against the Betsy Ross Story in his book.[1] He does not present facts against it; he just gives his own ideas, and starting with a negative view he of course winds up with negative conclusions. Such tactics are necessary in jurisprudence where a lawyer must present an opposing view to win his case, but not in matters of history.

For instance, Smith says,[2] "There is no contemporary reference in any known letter, newspaper, government document, or other source to the existence of a 'flag committee,' of the acquaintance of Washington and Mrs. Ross, of the adoption by Congress of any flag before 1777, or of any other detail of the story...."

Since Betsy's pew at Christ Church was adjacent to that of Martha and George Washington, and knowing that the Washingtons were modest and courteous people, it could be assumed that there would be at least a nodding acquaintance there. Colonel George Ross and Robert Morris, the members of the "flag committee," also worshiped at Christ Church and are buried there. Betsy's family never claimed any closer familiarity than sewing work she had done for the Washingtons, and that would be unlikely to be documented

---
[1] Smith, Whitney, *The Flag Book of the United States*. New York: William Morrow & Co., 1970.
[2] Ibid. p. 67.

in any way. All of us have friendships during our lives for which our children and grandchildren would have no documentation. This author's father was a friend of President William McKinley at Canton, Ohio near the close of the nineteenth century but I have no provable record of it.

The matter of the "flag committee," and whether there actually was one, or whether the term was used as a figure of speech, has been dealt with earlier in this work. But Smith asks,[3] "Would Washington be likely to have a flag made which clearly asserted American independence at a time when independence had not been proclaimed by Congress?" To answer it is necessary to repeat some points already made in this treatise. At the time Smith questions, instructions were already being received by the delegates to vote for independence. Washington was well aware of that and indeed he had been Commander-in-Chief of the Continental Army since June 15, 1775. Many of the important battles of the Revolution had already been fought. Historians Douglas Southall Freeman[4] and Ann Hawkes Hutton[5] have amply elucidated the political situation at this time to dispel any doubt that Washington would be free to have an appropriate flag made then. In fact, the General had written numerous times in past months about the importance of flags for identification and for the morale of the troops; one letter being about a week prior to his visit with Morris, and Colonel Ross at Betsy's shop. There is no question that there was a distinct need in mid-1776 for an American ensign, on land and at sea, which was unlike any British counterpart.

Smith also asks,[6] "....Indeed would either the Commander-in-Chief of any army at war or a committee of Congress take off an afternoon to visit the shop of a common upholsterer....?" The Betsy Ross Story does not say that they took an afternoon off, and furthermore it is not up to us two centuries later to question whether they would or would not have made the visit. All we need to know is that they felt the matter was important. That we know from evidence. Incidentally, at the time of Washington's visit he "took time off" on May 29 and again on May 31 to sit for a portrait by Charles Willson Peale.[7]

Another of Smith's points is that there is no contemporary reference (evidence) "....of the adoption by Congress of any flag before 1777...."[8]

[3] Smith, Whitney, op. cit. p. 67.
[4] Freeman, Douglas Southall, *George Washington*. New York: Charles Scribner's Sons, 1951, Vol. IV.
[5] Hutton, Ann Hawkes, *The Year and the Spirit of '76*. Philadelphia: Franklin Publishing Co., 1972, Ch. 2 & 3.
[6] Smith, Whitney, op. cit. p. 67.
[7] Sellers, Charles Coleman, op. cit. p. 220.
[8] Smith, Whitney, supra, p. 67.

Are we to suppose that if Congress did not officially adopt a flag before 1777 that we did not have one? Did our soldiers fight all those battles under an ensign which bore the royal crosses of a monarch who had spilled their blood? Did all our ships at sea continue to carry a flag (the Grand Union) identical with one on the vessels of the British East India Company?

Congress sometimes was a long time taking official action on important subjects — and is today. They did not adopt a national anthem until March 3, 1931 but it is hoped we are not telling our school children there was none. Not all the actions of our young government originating at the State House were brought to the floor of Congress, nor were all the items of discussion handwritten into the minute book.

It might be observed, incidentally, that the now well known Flag Resolution of June 14, 1777 apparently did not get outside the minutes of Congress until months later, as previously stated, and it was not celebrated as "Flag Day" until 1877, when the patriotic fervor generated by the Centennial was still with us. From then on it was observed annually by numerous hereditary and patriotic organizations but it did not achieve executive notice until it was proclaimed by President Woodrow Wilson on June 14, 1916; national feelings were then running high because of the war in Europe and on the sea. Finally, Congress officially recognized what we had been celebrating for at least 72 years and on August 3, 1949 President Truman signed an Act of Congress designating June 14th as Flag Day.

Smith allows that there are paintings by contemporary artists, such as Colonel John Trumbull and Charles Willson Peale, showing the stars and stripes early in 1777. But he says, "Although Trumbull and Peale show thirteen-star flags in paintings of battles which occurred early in 1777, the paintings themselves were made years afterward when patriotism was likely to have overruled historical accuracy by insisting that the Stars and Stripes be shown in preference to the Continental Colors (sic-Grand Union) with its Union Jack." That, of course, is merely a contention, in no way provable, made two centuries later in support of a personal thesis. A study of the works of those artists and their biographers gives us a higher respect for the historical accuracy of their paintings.[9] Many of their works were begun while the war was still on.

---

[9] As has been partly related, Trumbull's *General Washington at the Battle of Trenton December 26, 1776* shows the American Flag with 13 white stars in a circle and red and white stripes - Betsy Ross style. His *The Capture of the Hessians at Trenton, New Jersey, 26 December 1776* also shows the stars and stripes. His *The Death of General Mercer at the*

Smith finally dismisses our Betsy by saying, ". . . .But the popular image of the young girl in her shop showing Washington how to cut five-pointed stars in one snip undoubtedly began in the faulty recollections of an elderly lady and the impressionable mind of her young grandson. No useful purpose is served in perpetuating such false or highly doubtful tales. . . ."

Well, there certainly is a use in perpetuating the Betsy Ross Story. For our children it is the most popular story of the entire Revolutionary War; and Betsy is the most endeared, the most lovable person of those grim times in our glorious history. She instills patriotism and a reverence for our founders which is only approached by Washington himself. The pity is that we have so called historians who denigrate the story without factual foundation. This researcher has not found one of them who can come up with proof against the story; he has found many however, who repeat one another and offer latter day opinions of their own invention. As stated before, the legend did not begin with the elderly recollections of Mrs. Claypoole, and as grandson Canby freely stated, he did not rely on his own early recollections of his grandmother Betsy.

Another recent flag book was authored by Milo M. Quaife, Melvin J. Weig and Roy E. Appleman.[10] Quaife did the writing, Weig served as general editor and Appleman obtained illustrations and supplementary material. Quaife had the same failing we have seen before of historians inserting their own conjectures and theories when convenient. He says,[11]". . . .until that step was taken [the Declaration of Independence] there could certainly be no very logical reason for replacing the Great or Grand Union Flag with a national banner of new design. . . ." Ample reasons for a new ensign in June of 1776 have been brought out heretofore and are facts of history which have long been apparent to students of the Revolutionary War.

<small>Battle of Princeton, New Jersey, 3 January 1777 distinctly shows two stars and stripes flags. All three portraits are at the Yale University Art Gallery.

Peale's *George Washington at the Battle of Princeton* prominently features a stars and stripes flag. It is now in the Faculty Room of Nassau Hall, Princeton University. Peale painted Washington many times, usually with flags, and they are known to be historically accurate. His son, Titian, said he even had captured flags brought to him so that he could be historically accurate. Peale began his paintings of Washington and his flags while we were still at war and as early as 1776 - see fn. supra, Ch X.

We observed earlier in this treatise that there were variations in the stripes and in the positioning of the stars. Artists followed such variations faithfully, as they carefully did with the many variations in military uniforms and accoutrements.

[10] Quaife, et al, op. cit.
[11] Ibid. p. 97.</small>

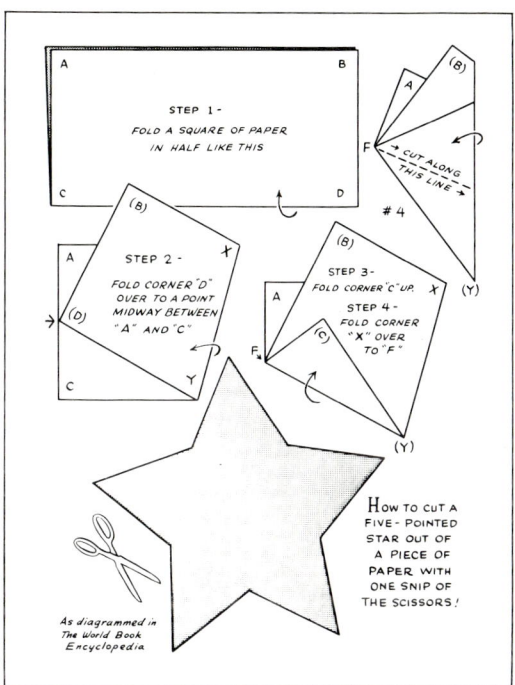

How to make a five-pointed star with one snip of the scissors.

Quaife did not believe the stars in a circle were found on early stars and stripes flags, and in his lack of objective research, said: [12]"The general public notion about the stars having been fixed in a circle on the early Stars and Stripes seems to have sprung mainly from wide circulation of two popular paintings made in the last quarter of the nineteenth century. About the year 1875 an Ohio carriage painter produced a humorous Fourth of July offering which he entitled 'Yankee Doodle.' Redrawn and renamed 'The Spirit of '76,'[13] it swept the country, becoming familiar to almost every American who lived in the decades immediately before and after 1900. The flag, prominently displayed in this picture, has the stars arranged in a circle. This conception of the original design became further fixed in the minds of millions of Americans following distribution, just at the close of the nineteenth century, of hundreds of thousands of copies of another painting, Charles H. Weisburger's (sic) [correctly - Weisgerber] 'Birth of Our National Flag,'

---

[12] Quaife, et al, op. cit. p. 107

[13] *The Spirit of '76*, by Archibald M. Willard, is at Abbot Hall, Marblehead, Massachusetts. A replica, gift to the Washington Crossing Foundation by the philanthropist and antiquarian, Russell W. Knight, hangs in Memorial Hall at Washington Crossing, Pennsylvania.

COURTESY WASHINGTON CROSSING FOUNDATION
"THE SPIRIT OF '76'"

A true Betsy Ross design of the flag, with 13 five-pointed white stars in a circle.

Archibald M. Willard's masterpiece which was introduced at the Centennial Exposition of 1876 "stirred the heart of the nation." The resurgence of patriotism following the dreadful carnage of the Civil War, and our pride of national accomplishment in 100 years of growth combined to instill new reverence in our hearts for what we held dear. This portrait seemed to epitomize the spirit we cherished.

Above is Robert B. Williams' rendition, after Willard. It was a gift in 1971 by the well known antiquarian and philanthropist, Russell W. Knight, to the Washington Crossing Foundation and it hangs in the State Park Memorial Building at Washington Crossing, Pennsylvania. The Willard original is owned by the Selectmen of Marblehead, Massachusetts and hangs in Abbot Hall at Marblehead.

which showed Betsy Ross in the act of displaying the mythical first Stars and Stripes made by her to George Washington and his companions. On the flag in Weisburger's (sic) picture, quite possibly in imitation of 'The Spirit of '76,' the stars are also arranged in a circle. Suffice it to say here that historical truth was dealt a crushing blow by these two paintings, the erroneous notion to which they gave birth having been perpetuated in uncounted illustrations appearing in school textbooks and other respectable publications. What actual evidence survives today all argues against a circular arrangement of the thirteen stars on the union."

How fortunate we are that history writing now has better foundations than the conjectures exhibited by some writers. What actual evidence survives today all argues for, not against, a circular arrangement. A number of such illustrations are cited in this work. Quaife does not give the contrary evidence against the circular arrangement which he writes about, he only gives his own surmises.

COURTESY AMERICAN FLAG HOUSE AND BETSY ROSS MEMORIAL

"THE BIRTH OF OUR NATION'S FLAG."
Charles H. Weisgerber's idealized depiction of Betsy Ross displaying her newly made flag of the United States to General George Washington, Colonel George Ross and Robert Morris. This popular picture was printed beginning in the 1890's in countless thousands of copies of books, framed displays, etc.

COURTESY PENNSYLVANIA ACADEMY OF THE FINE ARTS

WASHINGTON AT PRINCETON

In 1779 Charles Willson Peale was commissioned by the Supreme Executive Council of the State of Pennsylvania to make a portrait of General Washington. The artist chose a Princeton battle scene which he well knew as he had been there as captain of a company of foot soldiers with the General. The sittings were when the General was in Philadelphia that year, and in Washington's confident stance the victories of Trenton and Princeton were nobly portrayed. In the background is Nassau Hall and a file of prisoners being marched by their American captors. The prominent flag in the upper right is the General's own blue banner with a circle of 13 six-pointed white stars. The dexter blue sash was the insignia of the commander-in-chief from 1775 to 1780. He even had the captured Hessian flags at Washington's feet brought to him so he could be completely accurate as to flags, as well as accoutrements and uniform. The fallen British flag is at the General's right.

This portrait was immediately acclaimed as a masterpiece and the artist was asked for additional, similar works. The acting representative of Spain commissioned five replicas at once; French Ambassador Gerard ordered one for Louis XVI, and more were ordered for other courts, including Holland. Peale then chose different backgrounds, sometimes Trenton and later Yorktown; but always with appropriate flags, of which this one was repeated many times. In his *George Washington at the Battle of Princeton* (see frontis), he commemorated the American Flag, Betsy Ross style, on January 3, 1777, which was long after Betsy made the first one and prior to the Flag Resolution of Congress of June 14, 1777.

Even his own book refutes his conclusions against the circular arrangement of stars. There is a full page portrait[14] captioned,

> "Charles Willson Peale portrait of Washington at the battle of Trenton [December 26, 1776] showing an American flag in upper right background. . . ."

It is faithfully and precisely painted with 13 six-pointed, thin white stars on a blue field, which Washington used in his flag. The stars are unmistakably in a circle. Quaife says in his caption that Peale made the picture from life in 1779 and he allows that there are no red and white stripes. He might have mentioned another by Peale entitled, *George Washington at the Battle of Princeton*. That took place on January 3, 1777, eight days after Trenton and this painting has a true American flag, Betsy Ross style, with five-pointed white stars (not all showing) and red and white stripes (see frontis color plate). Peale distinguished himself militarily at Princeton as captain of a company of foot with Washington and was quite familiar with the General's flags.

The plain blue flag with a circle of white stars which is often pictured with Washington has more than one name, each with some reasonable logic but none with precise historical authority. Washington wrote a number of letters about flags but he never made a complete description of the components and colors of any of them. The Board of War and some of his officers also wrote about flags but with the single exception of Colonel Reed's letter of October 20, 1775 (Pine tree, white ground, An Appeal to Heaven) none of them gave specifics from which a flag could be made. It is apparent from his writings that Washington wanted, in addition to regimental identification flags, an army flag for the whole army; to be a sort of opposite number to our naval jack, and to the union jack of Great Britain. Some writers have concluded that the plain blue flag with stars was so intended for army use; other writers, observing that it was often pictured in Washington's presence have concluded that it was his own headquarters flag. There is favorable logic for both contentions but since nothing concrete can be determined from letters, orders or any other documentation perhaps the name for Washington's blue flag had better remain as another flag enigma.

All this should not be confused with the faded copen blue flag

---

[14] Quaife, et al, op. cit. p. 127.

at the museum of the Valley Forge Historical Society. This one has 13 six-pointed stars in rows and was retained in the Washington family until given in 1912 to the Society by a collateral descendant, Miss Frances B. Lovell. It is definitely believed to have been a Washington's Headquarters Flag. The stars in rows instead of a circle should not rule it out.

In the Library of Congress, Manuscript Department, there is a drawing containing a prominent Betsy Ross style American flag which was made for the diploma of the Society of the Cincinnati adopted by them on June 10, 1783. The banner is waving in the breeze and the circle of thirteen stars appears slightly oval, nevertheless it is rather positive documentary evidence of the early circular pattern.

The Cowpens Flag, also pictured in Quaife's book, has twelve white, five-pointed stars in a circle and one in the middle of the circle. They are on a blue union and there are seven red and six white stripes. He may have excepted it from his rule by terming it, as he did, a regimental banner,[15] though he had no authority for calling it such just because it was carried by the Third Maryland Regiment.[16,17] This stars in a circle flag is still in existence and is well documented; it is dear to Marylanders and is presently in the State House at Annapolis, where visitors are told it is the American flag which was carried by the Third Maryland Regiment.

Thus, it can be seen that our national flag has had throughout its early history many different forms and arrangements of stars, most of which were entirely in keeping with our Betsy Ross flag and that single sentence Flag Resolution of June 14, 1777. It is true that some were embellished with devices; such as, the numerals 76, eagles and scrolls, but the stars and stripes stayed with us firmly. Quaife freely stated that variations went on down to the year 1912 when the first official specifications were set forth in President Taft's executive order issued on June 24th of that year.

His book points out that at that time there were ".... no less than sixty-six different sizes and proportions currently in use by the

---

[15] Quaife, et al, op. cit. pp. 71 & 106.

[16] Morris, Robert, *The Truth About the Cowpens Flag*. Treatise in Maryland Hall of Records, Annapolis, and Enoch Pratt Library, Baltimore, 1978.

[17] The remnants of the Third Maryland Regiment, decimated earlier at the disastrous and ignominious Battle of Camden, South Carolina (where Major General Horatio Gates was defeated by British Lieutenant General Charles Cornwallis, our most crushing defeat of the entire war) were regrouped with a Delaware unit and, under the command of Lieutenant Colonel John Eager Howard, assisted in a successful and decisive battle at Cowpens, South Carolina on January 17, 1781. They were a part of the continentals and militia under General Daniel Morgan, left wing of General Nathanael Greene's Southern Army, and defeated a superior British force under Lieutenant Colonel Banastre Tarleton. The ensign carried by Howard's group was one of the many variations of our national flag of the time. It was nevertheless exactly in keeping with the Flag Resolution of Congress of June 14, 1777. This one became known as the Cowpens Flag.

several executive departments of the Federal Government."[18] In addition, he quotes Admiral Preble as saying that on July 4, 1857 in New York the flags flying on that Independence Day had stars in the form of a diamond, a lozenge, a large star made with a border of smaller stars, or a circle.[19] Quaife added to that quotation that, "Observations similar to the above could probably have been made in many other parts of the United States, more or less through the whole nineteenth century." He had no quarrel with artists who depicted the stars in rows but when there was a portrait with stars in a circle, and thus contrary to his own fixed notion, he either ignored it, or said the artist was not there at the time and hence was not accurate. History, and the Flag Resolution, are completely silent as to the arrangement of the stars in our flag during the Revolutionary War. Let us go by what artifacts we have, and the work of reliable contemporary artists with reputations for accuracy. Let not any modern day writer decide for us from his own conjectures what the form was.

A full two pages in Quaife's *The History of the United States Flag* are devoted to the Francis Hopkinson Flag, and Hopkinson as a possible designer of our first flag. At some unspecified time during the war, Hopkinson submitted to Congress a design for a flag, and a bill for same. After lengthy efforts to collect he was turned down by resolution of Congress August 23, 1781. The design was never described or even mentioned in correspondence or any other record that has survived; no one knows what it looked like nor is any such flag known to have ever been made. Nevertheless, Quaife illustrated in his book a "Conjectural Francis Hopkinson design for the Stars and Stripes."[20] Such a presumption serves no purpose but to confuse flag history. Writers have copied Hopkinson stories from one another and have given the amount of his invoice as £ 45, £ 2700 and $7200; they have also widely promulgated a Hopkinson Flag. Only by consulting original records can we make sense of it.[21]

On May 25, 1780 Hopkinson sent a letter to the Board of Admiralty, which was acting under Congress, listing therein a number of heraldic works which he had previously submitted; such as, ornamental borders for bills of exchange, devices for the Continental currency, a Great Seal of the United States of America,

[18] Quaife, et al, op. cit. p. 109.
[19] Ibid. p. 79.
[20] Ibid. p. 37.
[21] Papers of the Continental Congress. vol. IV, folio 685, no. 136. Washington: Library of Congress. Hastings, George Everett, *The Life and Works of Francis Hopkinson*. Chicago: University of Chicago Press, pp. 240-44, 254-57, 264, 466.

and among those items, the Flag of the United States of America. The closing paragraph of the letter contained:

"For these Services I have as yet made no Charge, nor received any Recompense. I now submit to your Honour's Consideration, whether a Quarter Cask of the public wine will not be a proper and reasonable Reward for these Labours of Fancy and a suitable Encouragement to further exertions of a like Nature?

Your very humble Servt
Fra^s Hopkinson."

On May 26 the Secretary of the Board of Admiralty sent Hopkinson's letter to the President of Congress. The letter was read to Congress and referred to the Board of Treasury, which on June 5, 1780 directed that he state his account and leave it with the Auditor.

Hopkinson then presented Congress with a bill for the same items of his previous letter, but this time he termed the flag "The Great Naval Flag of the United States." It was dated, Philadelphia, June 6, 1780 and the total amount of the invoice was £ 2700. In all ensuing invoices, at least two more, the flag item was termed a naval flag, not an American national flag.

Congress referred the bill to the Auditor-General, who registered it in his office records and forwarded it to the Commissioners of the Chamber of Accounts. On June 12, 1780 the commissioners returned it to the Auditor-General with this statement:

"The Commissioners Report —

"That they have examined the account of Francis Hopkinson, Esqr, for sundry Devices, Drawings, Mottoes & c^a for Public Use, amounting to seven thousand two hundred dollars and are of the opinion that the charge is reasonable and ought to be paid."

Hopkinson's £ 2700 was the equivalent of $7200 because the Continental dollar was then worth only 90d (7200 x 90 ÷ 240 pence in the pound = £ 2700)

The Auditor-General then sent the report to the Board of Treasury with his certification and presented same for allowance. The Board, however, noted that no vouchers to support the charges were attached, as required by a 1779 stipulation, so they sent it back to the Auditor-General together with a revised account in the amount of £ 45 and an explanatory note that, "£ 45 in hard money at 60 for one is £ 2700."

There followed correspondence over the months and continual rejection by the Board of Treasury. Hopkinson was at that time

Treasurer of loans and there was apparently friction between him and the Board of Treasury over this and other matters.

In a report to Congress dated October 27, 1780 the Board of Treasury said, "....it is within the knowledge of one of the Members of the Board, that... the said Francis Hopkinson was not the only person consulted on these exhibitions of Fancy, and therefore cannot claim the sole merit of them, and is not entitled in this respect to the full sum charged...."

Hopkinson, on July 23, 1781 sent to the President of Congress his resignation as Treasurer of Loans.

Congress closed the matter by stating in their minutes of August 23, 1781:

"The report of the committee on the reports before Congress previous to the 25 July was taken into consideration; and There upon,

"The committee appointed to revise the reports depending before Congress the 25th day of July 1781, and report which of them are fit to be acted upon, report that the following reports of the Board of War, to wit: [a list of money bills] ought to be acted upon...That the report relative —

"To the fancy work of F. Hopkinson bearing date of 27 October 1780...Ought not to be acted upon...."

Thus Hopkinson was never paid. He had long pursued a hobby of art in heraldry and his work was recognized, notably the Orrery Seal for the College of Philadelphia, now the University of Pennsylvania. His failure to wade through the red tape of our early congress and his difficulties with the Board of Treasury should not be allowed to denigrate his patriotic devotion and service to his country during the Revolution, for, in addition to his law practice; he served in the Continental Congress as a delegate from New Jersey, became a signer of the Declaration of Independence, was Chairman of the Navy Board, was Treasurer of Loans, and served as Judge of the Admiralty. Although while in the last named capacity he was impeached and tried, he was acquitted and continued in service, with the esteem of his many friends.

Quaife said he received a letter from a writer on behalf of the Historical Society of Pennsylvania stating that the address which William J. Canby read before that Society on March 14, 1870 was never published and is not known to be in existence.[22] That was

[22] Quaife, et al, op. cit. p. 184, Ch. II (1.).

the paper which first delineated the Betsy Ross Story. The story was indeed published and was soon well known in every corner of the country; it has since become an important element of American folklore. Moreover, it is in existence. It is at the Huntington Library, San Marino, California. It is in Canby's handsome Spencerian penmanship in the Rare Manuscripts Department and this researcher has read it there a number of times. An exact copy is at the Historical Society of Pennsylvania, Philadelphia.

CHAPTER XIII

Additional Flags

FRANK EARLE SCHERMERHORN
THE GENERAL PHILIP SCHUYLER FLAG
COWPENS FLAG - MURFIN CRITICISM

In the 1940's Frank Earle Schermerhorn wrote an accurate, authoritative and well researched book on Revolutionary War flags.[1] Although he did his work at the time Gottlieb's adverse comments were still fresh he took no sides in the Betsy Ross controversy. He was primarily interested in regimental and French flags but he described Major General Philip Schuyler's American flag in detail.[2] This is not the same as the Schuyler flag at Independence National Historical Park in Philadelphia but since it has become a disputed one seized upon by so called "flag historians" it is a good case in point illustrating their propensity to pick an argument in order to attract attention. Schermerhorn did not, himself, have that fault.

The flag, which has been referred to earlier as one of the few remaining stars and stripes flags from the Revolutionary War, is a true Betsy Ross ensign; 13 five-pointed white stars in a circle on a blue field, with a banner of seven red and six white alternate stripes. It measures two feet on the hoist and two and one-half feet on the fly. It was made by her for the General while he was stationed in Philadelphia; it was cherished by him and inherited by his daughter, Mrs. Alexander Hamilton. Being carefully preserved

---

[1] Schermerhorn, Frank Earle, *American and French Flags of the Revolution 1775-1783.* Philadelphia: Pennsylvania Society of Sons of the Revolution, 1948.
[2] Ibid. pp. 20-24.

it was handed down through succeeding generations and was only exhibited on special occasions. Shortly after Admiral Dewey's victory at Manila in 1898 it was reinforced with silk mesh, cross stitched with silk thread and mounted in a glass frame. It finally came to a great, great, great grandson, Schuyler Hamilton, Esq., who deposited it with the Fort Ticonderoga Museum in 1943.[3] This precious artifact of our history has an unbroken pedigree and is the earliest one that has come down to us in corpus from the Revolutionary War. No other national ensign has been claimed to date earlier, hence it has been confidently asserted to be the oldest American Flag in existence.

Some flag writers have set forth a possible anachronism in order to dispute the accuracy of the Schuyler flag story, pointing out that the donor had tied it in with the Flag Resolution of Congress when stating at the time of the gift to the museum that General Schuyler had it made while he was in Philadelphia and after the Flag Resolution. Actually the flag resolution was made a few days *after* the General had departed for Albany on a new assignment.

The facts are that Schuyler had been in New York State as Commander-in-Chief of the Northern Department of the Continental Army until relieved by resolutions of the Continental Congress dated March 25 and 31, 1777.[4,5] He left Kingston, New York, where the New York Convention was in session, on 30 March 1777 for Philadelphia, having been appointed a delegate of New York to the Continental Congress. On arrival in Philadelphia, he was appointed Commander-in-Chief of the military in Pennsylvania.[6] His army was encamped on the west bank of the Schuylkill River about two miles from the State House and the same distance from Betsy's shop. He formally assumed command on 14 April 1777. On 22 May the Board of War of the Continental Congress again appointed Schuyler to the Northern Department of the Continen-

[3] Fort Ticonderoga Museum Bulletin, Vol. VI, No. 6 July 1943, p. 184. Fort Ticonderoga is a gem of American antiquity for which we are indebted to one family. The well known Pell family, of New York, intensely patriotic and philanthropic, developed the area after its original purchase in 1820 by William Ferris Pell, and it has become a treasure for the American people. John H.G. Pell is at this time the President of Fort Ticonderoga. The connection with the Schuyler family is that they too are prominent patriots and married with the Alexander Hamilton family (first Secretary of the Treasury and New York commander of artillery) and also because General Schuyler had commanded troops in that area. It was Schuyler, ably assisted by Stark, Arnold, Morgan, Glover and others, who set up the forces and battle situation for our great victory at Saratoga. General Horatio Gates, who had recently succeeded him as commander of the Northern Army was naturally given credit and became a military hero, though not for long. He was mentioned to take over General George Washington's title as Washington was then doing badly in Pennsylvania (Brandywine and Germantown) but the plan (mostly Gates') failed. He later commanded the Southern Army and met ignominious defeat at Camden, South Carolina. He declined to oblivion after his shameful personal retreat from there.
[4] Tuckerman, Bayard, *Life of General Philip Schuyler*, 1905, p. 171.
[5] Lossing, Benj. J., *Life and Times of Philip Schuyler*. New York: Sheldon & Co. 1872, Vol. II, pp. 113,4; 154; 167,8.
[6] Morris, Robert, *The Truth About the American Flag*, op. cit. p. 63.

tal Army and he soon afterward departed Philadelphia for Albany, arriving there 3 June, or 8 June, 1777.[7]

We have seen abundant evidence that stars and stripes American flags were made long before the resolution of June 14, 1777 and not as a sudden invention from the floor of Congress on that busy Saturday. The General, being in the highest military echelon and a member of Congress was certainly close to Colonel Ross and knew what was going on at the State House. Ross was also a member of Congress and the Board of War; he was the previously mentioned uncle of John Ross, Betsy's late husband. It was logical for the General to ask her, a little more than four blocks away from the State House, to make one of her flags for him to fly at his headquarters on the Schuylkill. The Flag Resolution of June 14, 1777 had nothing to do with the matter and the dates which are involved are not to be confused with a reference to the Flag Resolution made five generations later.

The Cowpens Flag is another example of a Revolutionary War flag which has been wantonly maligned and deserves defense. The Baltimore Sunday Sun of December 14, 1975 published excerpts from an about to be published book, "From Lexington to Yorktown, a Guide to America's Revolutionary War Treasures," by James V. Murfin, of the National Park Service. Among the author's many questionable statements about the flag which are quoted in the Sun is this one:

". . . .The present day reactivated First Maryland Regiment made an exact copy of the flag, stitch for stitch, and tried to fly it. It was 5 feet long and 30 inches wide and it hung on the pole like a soaked dishrag. Strange! It was supposed to have been 'carried in battle.'"

The Cowpens flag now on exhibit at the Maryland State House is made of bunting, the same as present day flags. It is a common parade size, 30 inches on the hoist and 60 inches on the fly. The proportions, 1:2, are almost the same as those presently specified for our American Flag, which are 1:1.9.

Murfin goes on to say, ". . . .it had 13 stars just like Betsy Ross made them. But that was just it! Only 12 of the 13 stars were in a circle. The last one was stuck in the center. . .according to the books [which he does not name] there was no other flag quite like it from the Revolution."

---

[7]Lossing says June 3, Tuckerman says June 8.

It was in fact simply another of the many arrangements of stars which were common then and for more than a hundred years following, particularly during the Civil War.[8]

From the Murfin article we also find:

". . . .[the Cowpens Flag] was not carried at Cowpens by the Third Maryland Regiment or by any other regiment in any Revolutionary War battle. . .The Third Maryland Regiment of the Continental Line was not at the Battle of Cowpens. . .and one of Maryland's prized possessions, is a hoax." The author tells us that William Batchelor, a "color sergent" (sic) who was supposed to have carried the flag, was a private, not a color sergeant, and that he died in September 1780, at least three months before the battle.

So here was a family tradition about a flag that did not exist and could not have been carried by a member because he was dead! An incredible story to have ever been started and to have carried on so many years. This researcher's findings do not quite agree with Murfin's. There is ample documentation to show that the remnants of the Third Maryland Regiment were at the Battle of Cowpens.[9,10] The outfit did not lose its identity when it was combined with Delaware troops for command purposes. As to the charge that the flag was not carried at Cowpens, the time honored story says it was carried there by one William Batchelor, who was wounded and allowed to take it home with him. The family treasured it and 33 years later his son, Ensign Joshua Batchelor carried it in the Battle of Baltimore at North Point on September 12, 1814, during the War of 1812. Twenty-nine years later it was deposited with the Old Defenders' Association and has remained under competent care and responsible hands ever since. There is no reason to doubt the story and no fault has been found with it, only the contrary contentions of detractors who rely on their imagination, not facts. As to the charge that William Batchelor died in September 1780, before the battle, there are a number of records at the Maryland Hall of Records of Batchelors who served in Maryland companies. It seems that the name was a common one and there were various spellings. One record under the Third Maryland Regiment shows a William Bachilor, private, enlisted 27 April 1778, under *Remarks* the notation *Dead* and under *Discharged* there is the month, *September,* but not the year. As the roll goes to 1783 it could have

[8]Morris, Robert, *The Truth About the Cowpens Flag.* op. cit. pp. 11,12.

[9]See fn. re Third Maryland Regiment, supra.

[10] a. Berg, Fred Anderson, *Encyclopedia of Continental Army Units,* Harrisburg: Stackpole Books, 1972.
  b. Agniel, Lucien, *The American Revolution in the South, 1780-1781.* Riverside, Ct: The Chatham Press, 1972, pp. 84 & 92.
  c. Lossing, Benson J., *Pictorial Field Book of the Revolution,* New York: Harper & Bros., 1860.

been any year until then.[11] There were other Batchelor notations, some in faded handwriting almost illegible, and evidence within the register that not all of the original accounts survived in history.

The Sun article on Murfin's book quotes him as bringing in Betsy Ross, of whom he said, "And, of course, there's Betsy Ross, the biggest flag hoax of all. By now everyone must know that the story was just a figment of her grandson's imagination."

He wraps up the account of the Cowpens Flag by quoting from Grace Rogers Cooper's book[12] in which the flag is entirely ruled out as an eighteenth century product, and then generously inserts his own conjecture that, ". . . .it may well have been used as a banner celebrating Lafayette's return visit to the United States in 1824. . . ." He does not venture one shred of evidence that it was so used.

How sad it is that some writers will go to any lengths to be different no matter how destructive it may be for the many patriotic children and adults who feel just pride and inspiration in the stories of our flags.

---

[11] Archives of Maryland, Vol. XVIII, Muster Rolls and other Records of Service of Maryland Troops in the American Revolution, 1775 - 1783, p. 86. Annapolis: Hall of Records.

[12] Cooper, Grace Rogers, *Thirteen Star Flags*. Washington: Smithsonian Institution Press, 1973.

CHAPTER XIV

Critics Unlimited

THE TEXTILE ANGLE
THE COWPENS STORY
BENNINGTON FLAG
EMANUEL LEUTZE

Grace Rogers Cooper in her book, *Thirteen Star Flags,* attacks the authenticity of relic flags from the textile angle. She was at one time the curator of textiles in the Smithsonian Institution's National Museum of History and Technology. As this author has spent a good deal of his lifetime in the textile field and has some familiarity with fibres, yarns and weaving I will take the liberty of disputing some of her contentions.

She says of the Cowpens Flag that the stripes and union are of worsted bunting sewed with linen thread, but — "The cotton stars and the cotton thread used to stitch the stars would date this flag from the nineteenth century rather than the Revolutionary War...The circle of stars with one in the center does not date earlier than the nineteenth century."

Well, what did people use for clothing and other fabric uses before 1800? They used the same natural fibers we use today; mostly cotton, wool, flax (linen) and silk. Cotton can be grown in tropical and sub-tropical climates the world around and was produced by the Navajo Indians thousands of years ago. They spun yarns of it for weaving and for sewing. In colonial days we were exporters of raw materials and largely importers of manufactured goods. We got most of our fabrics and threads from England, some from France, and some of our silks came directly from China.

Calicut, a city on the coast of Malibar, in southwest India, exported cotton fabric (calico), much of which found its way here via England. Ireland, France and Belgium provided flax. We had some home spinning and weaving here and our first commercial manufacturing was in New England; Pawtucket, Rhode Island, at the head of Narragansett Bay, claims first honors. Spinning mules made good yarns and there are still some to be found in that area. The spinning jenny goes back to a time near the middle of the eighteenth century. Flax made a superior sewing thread. The fibers being longer and stronger than cotton, and in colonial times was easier to spin in the finer counts required for sewing. There was cotton sewing thread available however. Cotton can be identified today in finely tailored uniforms and other products that have been handed down through the generations.

How Cooper can be so positive about those stars and the thread used to sew them is something of a mystery. Cotton fabric viewed under a magnifying glass looks somewhat fuzzier on the surface than linen but that is hard to detect in the sewing thread. The flax fiber in linen thread is heavier by weight than cotton as well as longer and stronger, but to reveal all that would require scale and break tests involving skeins of thread. She could not have obtained such samples, from the flag, nevertheless let us assume that she did satisfy herself that those stars and the thread were of cotton; there was enough of it around to be used in the Cowpens Flag.

Her statement, quoted above, that the circle of stars with one in the center does not date earlier than the nineteenth century is indeed erroneous. She was looking at one, and of the many arrangements of stars this was as valid a variation as any. Flagmakers often had the stars in a square with one in the middle; this was easier to make than sewing them in a circle. As indicated earlier, contemporary artists who accurately painted for history what they had seen or what they knew to be correct, placed the stars in circles, rows and in squares, sometimes with one in the middle.[1]

Another flag she finds fault with is the well known and treasured Bennington Flag. Historian John Spargo wrote about the

[1] Amplifying Trumbull fn. supra - Colonel John Trumbull, in his *The Capture of the Hessians at Trenton, New Jersey, 26 December 1776*, Yale University Art Gallery, had the stars in a square with one in the middle; though in his *George Washington at the Battle of Trenton*, also at the Yale University Art Gallery, he had 13 in a circle. In *The Death of General Mercer at the Battle of Princeton*, Yale University Art Gallery the stars were prominent and were in squares with one in the middle. They were painted in squares of 12 with one in the middle in Trumbull's portraits in the Rotunda of the Capitol at Washington: *The Surrender of General Burgoyne at Saratoga, New York, 17 October 1777*, and *The Surrender of Lord Cornwallis at Yorktown, Virginia, 19 October 1781*.

COURTESY, THE BENNINGTON MUSEUM, BENNINGTON, VERMONT

BENNINGTON FLAG

A relic of the Battle of Bennington, August 16, 1777. It was present at the battle as a flag of the United States and is the earliest existing Stars and Stripes known to have been so used. Nathaniel Fillmore, who fought at that engagement, carefully preserved it and handed it down through his family, of which President Millard Fillmore was a descendant. It was presented to the Bennington Museum in 1926. It was one of the many variations of stars and stripes in the Revolutionary War.

This ensign is not to be confused with the regimental flag carried in the Battle of Bennington by men under Brigadier General John Stark. That banner was regimental, not United States, and was green (for the Green Mountain Rangers) with a blue field and 13 white stars scattered upon the field. The General cherished the flag and it too was handed down through descendants. Unfortunately, pieces have been cut for individual souvenirs, but a small section now reposes at the Bennington Museum.

Bennington Flag that,[2] after studying ". . . .the history of all the historic early flags of the United States. . .there is not one of them with a clearer record, better deserving of credence, and few indeed with a record of equal historic merit."

Nathaniel Fillmore, a member of a substantial Bennington family, fought with distinction in the Battle of Bennington on

---

[2] Spargo, John, *The Stars and Stripes in 1777*, Bennington, Vermont: Bennington Battle Monument and Historical Association, 1928, p. 38.

August 16, 1777.³ He was First Lieutenant of Captain Elijah Dewey's company. He cherished the flag which was present at that battle; and at the outbreak of the War of 1812, thirty-five years later, presented it to his nephew, Colonel Septa Fillmore. It was carefully preserved by succeeding generations and was presented to the Bennington Battle Monument and Historical Association in 1926. Nathaniel was a grandfather of President Millard Fillmore.

There are other convincing records cited in the above references but let us examine Cooper's statements. She says: ⁴"The flag appears to be of cotton rather than linen. . .The bottom or thirteenth stripe shows a selvedge along the full width of the flag. This definitely appears to be the selvedge of a cotton woven on a power loom...it can be concluded that the upper part of the union is approximately 27 inches. This was a fairly common power-woven cotton width during the nineteenth century...The stars are seven-pointed, which, although not conclusive, is not recorded as ever having been used in the eighteenth century...It [the flag] is not of the Revolutionary War period, but dates to sometime in the nineteenth century."

Persons who were able to handle the flag before it was framed said the material was linen. Cooper viewed it in a glass case. The selvage found on one of the stripes would hardly prove that it was cotton woven on a power-loom. Cooper apparently believes there were no power-looms in Revolutionary War times. Actually, the mechanical loom goes back to at least 1678 and the flying shuttle to 1733. Soon afterward, Edmund Cartwright successfully applied mechanical force and his invention was widely used, though he did not patent his power-loom until 1785.⁵ The same selvage (or selvedge, or self-edge) that was woven by hand was duplicated on the early power-looms and since the early power-looms were simply the application of mechanical force to the shuttle, reed and heddle, it would be most difficult to tell by a short length of fabric whether the weaving was by hand or power. As for the width of 27 inches, this was a common fabric width because it was easy for a single weaver to throw the shuttle back and forth that distance, also the width was practical for converting purposes. Of course, that same width was made on what few power-looms were available, though it was not the only width by any means. Hand loom widths went all the way from the requirements for great tapestries to narrow tapes and webbing, and when power-looms came along,

³Schermerhorn, Frank Earle, op. cit. pp. 45-47.
⁴Cooper, Grace Rogers, op. cit. p. 30.
⁵Encyclopedia Britannica, under Weaving.

they were built to produce the same widths, whether broadcloths, bed linen, tenting or whatever. As for the seven-pointed stars, there were five, six, seven and eight-pointed stars in flags of the Revolutionary War.[6]

Of the Navy Ensign of 1780 at the Germantown Historical Society, she says the fabric in the red and white stripes had a cotton warp and a wool weft, and that type would not have been used in the eighteenth century.

Remembering that we were importers of our principal fabrics in that century and for many years afterward, and remembering that wartime shortages necessitated substitutions by our handweavers, who is to say what combinations may or may not have been resorted to. A weave of wool on a cotton warp was doubtless not a popular fabric then and it is not today, but to make the flat statement that it "....would not have been used in the eighteenth century."[7] is preposterous.

Thus, Cooper has made almost a clean sweep of all the existing 13 star flags of the Revolutionary War period - telling us that none of them is authentic of the time. The only one she missed is the Schuyler Flag at the Fort Ticonderoga Museum, and she didn't see that one. Other writers have alleged faults with it, however, so all of our most precious flags from the birth of our nation have suffered from those so minded.

One more glaring example of our history being twisted to suit the purposes of those who might gain by taking a contrary stance is the beautiful portrait of Washington Crossing the Delaware, by Emanuel Leutze. This heroic painting; 21 feet, 4 inches wide and 12 feet, 5 inches tall, has been known to every school child for generations. The original is prominently displayed at the Metropolitan Museum in New York and the only existing exact copy on exhibition is at the Memorial Building in Washington Crossing Historical Park, Pennsylvania; a gift of Mrs. Ann Hawkes Hutton to the Washington Crossing Foundation. It portrays stalwart General George Washington leading his ragged army across the icy Delaware in the face of desperate odds to achieve the victory at Trenton which sustained our country and enabled us to carry on to final triumph at Yorktown. Of the many fine portraits of the Revolution this one seems to capture the entire war spirit on one inspiring canvas.

[6]Schermerhorn, Frank Earle, op. cit. illustrations of Revolutionary War flags, color plates 2, 3, 5 & 6.
[7]Cooper, Grace Rogers, op. cit. p. 31.

Its popularity has invited criticisms; two principal ones being our Betsy Ross flag being displayed in an event of December 25, 1776 although the stars and stripes were not officially adopted by the Continental Congress until June 14, 1777; the other being the charge that Leutze was a German, unfamiliar with our river scene or with our struggle.

The true facts are that Leutze came to America from Germany in 1825 at the age of nine. His father became a comb manufacturer in Philadelphia and Emanuel grew up on the banks of the Delaware. He became interested in painting and had initial success in this country before going in 1841 to Dusseldorf for further study. Then Dusseldorf was an art capital of Europe. In 1851 he completed his famous portrait and returned with it to America. The river landscape, the Durham boat and other components are accurate, as anyone visiting Washington Crossing, Pennsylvania can easily see today.

As for the Betsy Ross flag so proudly displayed, we have seen in previous chapters ample evidence that stars and stripes flags were with us at the time of the crossing. The Betsy Ross story was not made public until 1870, so in 1851 when the picture was completed, there was no controversy over our flag and Betsy was unknown. It was perfectly proper in 1851 for Leutze to paint a Betsy Ross flag as our national standard.

How to correct common misstatements about our history and how to avoid teaching them to our school children is a field of endeavor that could well be explored. Making sure that text books are correct and unbiased would be one way, another would be to see that guides at historic shrines are properly instructed. Experience has shown that persons in charge at historic tourist attractions often like to entertain visitors with their own versions of events and characters, which may not be correct. If they were educated to the facts they could be just as entertaining and would not leave lasting wrong impressions with their hearers. There will always be some who like to poke fun, but let us hope not where real damage can be done.

One more flag book unfavorable to Betsy came out in 1981. It was published by the Smithsonian Institution Press and titled "So Proudly We Hail" by Rear Admiral William Rea Furlong and Commodore Byron McCandless. Once more we have authors injecting their own opinions in substitution for facts which are missing in history.

The authors state, p. 116, "The story [Betsy Ross Story] has an enormous popularity. Yet the known facts do not substantiate it." Negative factors given are, "The subject of flags occurs in a postscript of a letter that he [General Washington] wrote on May 28 [1776] to Major General Putnam in New York. Washington wrote: 'I desire you'll speak to the several Colls. and hurry them to get their colours done.' "

The writers interpret Washington's failure to mention Betsy Ross in his postscript as meaning that Washington probably did not meet with her at all in respect for a design for national colors. Well, the absence of mention of her does not prove that he did not see her, or did not accompany Colonel George Ross and Robert Morris to call on her then or a few days later. Further, on p. 117 they make the statement that "It is illogical to assume that Washington was present at the alleged meeting with Betsy Ross [of late May or early June, 1776] on the design when it is known that he wanted a national standard for the use of the army in 1779." They then quote from a letter (op. cit.) of the Board of War to Washington dated May 10, 1779 requesting guidance, " '....on the Subject of Drums and Colours for the several regiments...[and] a Plan as to the Colours.' " The writers further comment: "Thus the board states that the design of the United States flag for use by the army was not yet established in May 1779, or nearly two years after the passage of the flag resolution [June 14, 1777] by the Continental Congress."

The troubles the army had with colors went on for another 75 years, as alluded to earlier, but what does all this have to do with Betsy? Are we to conclude that this nation did not have a national flag by 1779, notwithstanding the Flag Resolution of June 14, 1777, and notwithstanding the Betsy Ross Story just before July 4, 1776? Such shallow conclusions as stated in the book are not derived from the words of the letters, but are obviously slanted toward preconceived notions.

There is also an interjection in the book with regard to the famous portrait entitled *Birth of Our Nation's Flag* by Charles H. Weisgerber. Of this inspiring picture, with its 13 stars in a circle, Furlong and McCandless said on p. 117, "The artist took liberties with history by painting the stars in a circle...and the Weisberger (sic) painting was reproduced in school history textbooks throughout the United States."

We have seen ample reasons hitherto that Weisgerber had every right to paint 13 stars in a circle, as did Leutze, Trumbull, Peale and others, moreover no historian has yet produced facts to show that they were inappropriate or non-existent — except in his own undocumented opinion.

There are more examples in the book wherein the Admiral and the Commodore speculate on what was in the minds of the Board of War. Such a hodgepodge of latter day thinking two hundred years after the events is of little service to the reader today and serves largely to confuse. The "logical" deductions of those naval officers remind one of the logic of the admiral in "H.M.S. Pinafore!"

Our nation needs to inculcate patriotism in our present trying days as much as ever before and one effective way is to correctly teach the known facts and not guess, where facts are missing. If the known facts are properly presented the reader should have enough to make his own conjectures without prodding from the author; the unknown should be left unknown until proven otherwise. The events of our history speak for themselves and well founded traditions help us enjoy their memory.

INDEPENDENCE HALL, Philadelphia 1876
Lithograph published by Thomas Hunter in Philadelphia 1875
from a painting by Theodore Poleni entitled as above.

Originally the State House of the Province of Pennsylvania. Construction began in 1732 to provide a meeting place for the Pennsylvania Assembly, which had hitherto met in private dwellings and at the old City Hall, Second and Market (High) Streets. A Supreme Court Chamber was provided and small wing buildings along both sides were included in the project. The structures were not completed until about 1748 and the tower was finished in 1753. A bell, now known as the Liberty Bell, was ordered in 1751 and was hung in the tower in 1753. Various county and city offices, records storage and the Library Company of Philadelphia were accommodated during construction or just after final completion. The population of Philadelphia was only 11,500 persons when this ambitious project was begun in 1732 and the location was on what was then the outskirts of the city. The first use by the Continental Congress came on May 10, 1775 when the Second Continental Congress was formed and convened there.

The care and skill in the architecture and building have left us one of the most beautiful colonial structures our nation now enjoys. Edmund Wooley was the architect, master carpenter and builder under the supervision of Andrew Hamilton, Speaker of the State Assembly.

This view is along Chestnut Street, foreground left to upper right. Fifth Street intersects from the left, Sixth Street is at the extreme right, not shown, where the ornate Public Ledger Building stands in the far background. The end building on the left along Chestnut Street was built in 1790 and 1791 to be City Hall; but with the establishment of Philadelphia as the temporary Federal Capital of the United States for the decade 1790 to 1800, it became the U.S. Supreme Court from 1791 to 1800. The twin at the extreme right was completed in 1789 as the County Courthouse, but it became the Hall of the United States Congress from 1790 to 1800. Both buildings were later connected to the State House (main building, center) by the modern office buildings shown in this lithograph. The Federal Constitutional Convention, composed of 55 delegates chosen by the legislatures of the States, wrote the Constitution of the United States in the State House from May 25 to September 17 of 1787.

The visit of the Marquis de Lafayette in 1824 awakened interest in the State House as a national shrine and inspired construction of the beautiful steeple, designed by William Strickland and built in 1828, replacing the original one which had been taken down in 1781. By 1852, the State House became known as Independence Hall, the building at the left foreground was called the Supreme Court and at the far right Congress Hall, as the three are known today. They are referred to collectively as Independence Hall.

The building on the extreme left, facing Fifth Street is Philosophical Hall of the American Philosophical Society. Founded in 1743 by Benjamin Franklin the hall was erected between 1785 and 1789 and is still standing.

The Pennsylvania Legislature, by an act of March 11, 1816, ordered the Independence Hall buildings and the square sold and divided into lots suitable for building. The funds realized were to be applied toward the building of the new capitol at Harrisburg. However, there was a proviso that the city might purchase the entirety from the state for $70,000, which the city did, taking title March 23, 1818. The old State House tower bell, being cracked and useless, was forgotten for many years and had been relegated to remote storage with other unused items in a lower hideaway of the Hall. There is a story, now disproved, that it was offered for scrap metal in 1828; but it may have been its cumbersome weight that actually kept it from the scrap heap. By 1839 however, someone discovered its biblical inscription "....to proclaim liberty...." and wrote a pamphlet entitled "The Liberty Bell." From then on it became so known. As with many of our early flags, veneration came only with the passage of time and many items were lost in the process. By good fortune the Liberty Bell and the State House were saved and remain as priceless relics of our national heritage.

The Independence Hall group has had architectural and structural changes during its history but was finally restored to its colonial grandeur in 1896 to 1898 when the connecting modern office buildings were changed to resemble the former colonial wings and arcades, which is the way it remains today.

Since 1777 the Liberty Bell has been moved a number of times; there were several locations within the Hall and it has traveled as far away as San Francisco in 1915. Its last move was on New Year's Eve of the Bicentennial year 1976 when it was placed in a new structure across Chestnut Street in Independence Mall where increased space was available to permit viewing by large crowds, many of whom are moved to tears by the awesome sight.

-excerpts from *Independence,* National Park Service Historical Handbook Series No. 17, by Edward M. Riley, 1956 U.S. Government Printing Office, Washington 20402.

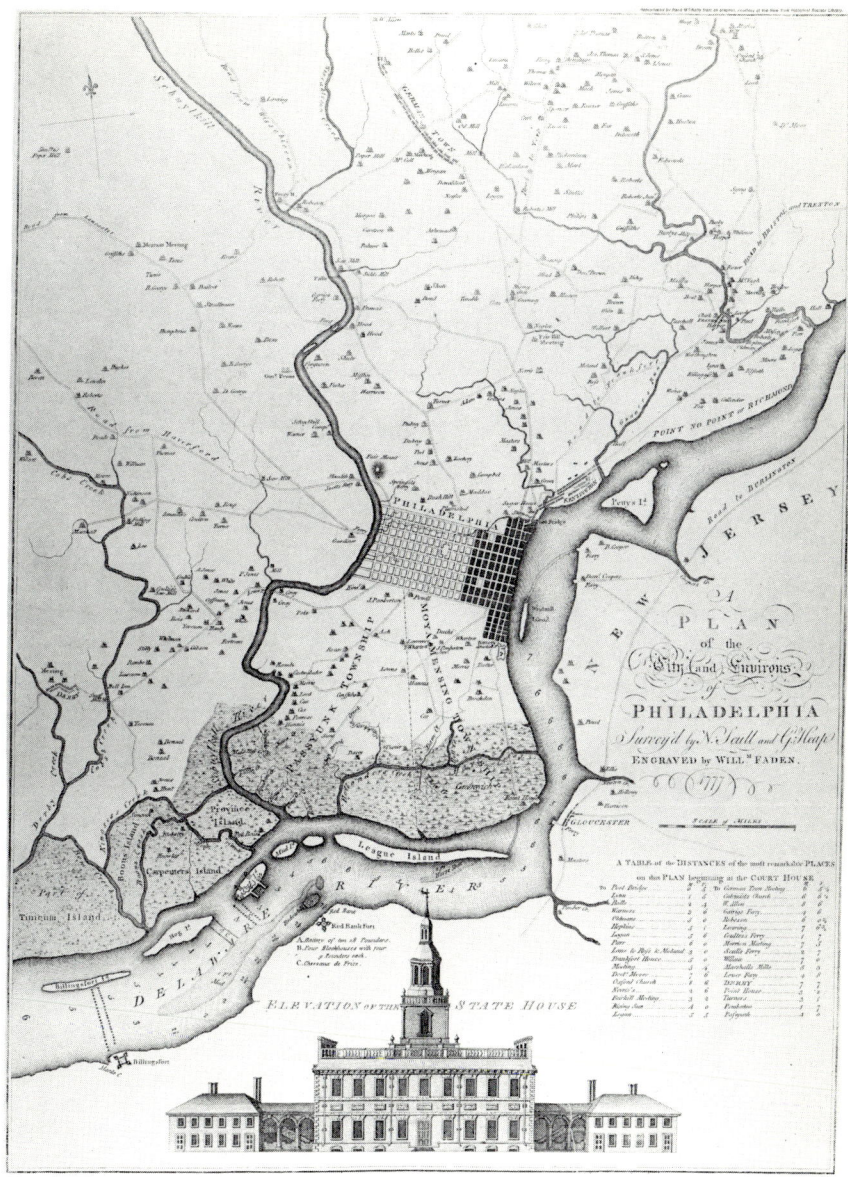

COURTESY RAND McNALLY AND COMPANY

Surveying, cartography and drawings of the mid-eighteenth century by Nicholas Scull and George Heap have contributed greatly to our knowledge of history of Philadelphia and the surrounding area. Martin P. Snyder has brought a number of their works together in his book, *City of Independence*. This popular map is dated 1777 and was engraved by William Faden after a map by Scull and Heap published in 1752. The elevation of the State House shows the first tower and wing buildings. The river fortifications were apparently added by Faden.

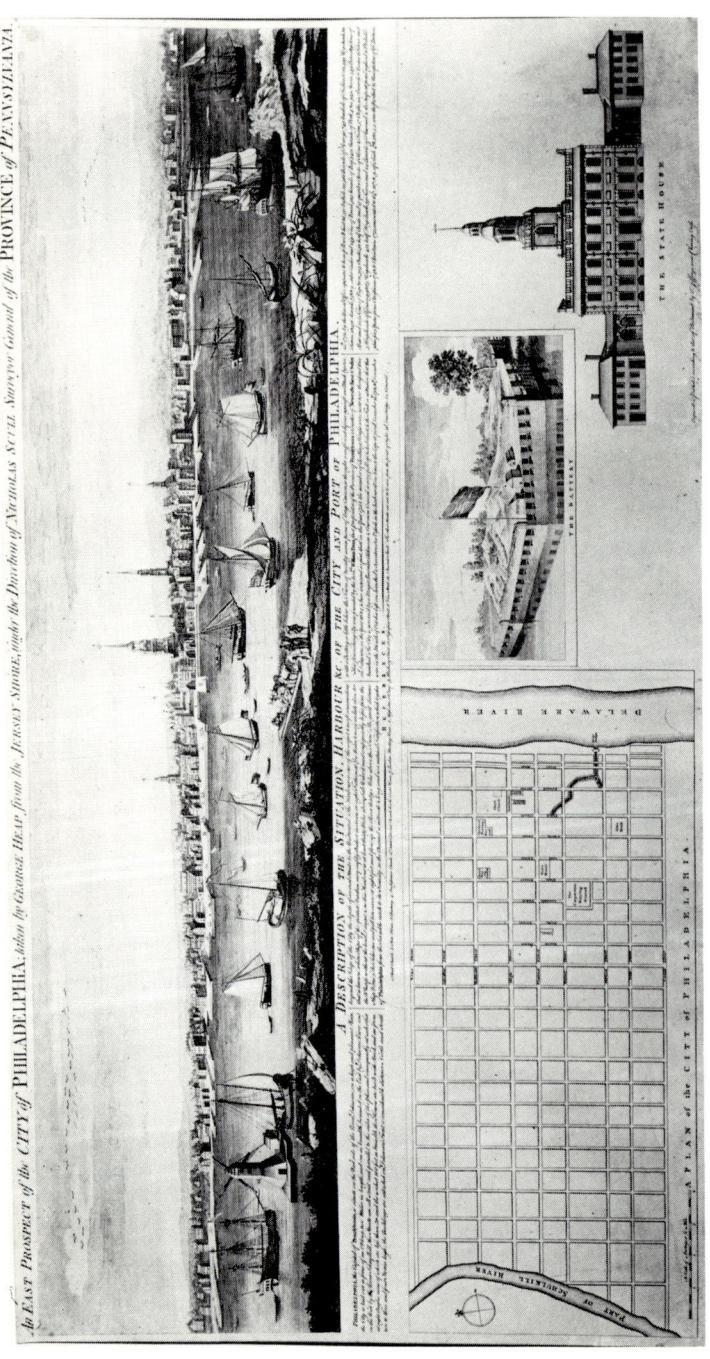

"AN EAST PROSPECT OF THE CITY OF PHILADELPHIA," Scull and Heap
This work by George Heap is nearly like the 1752 illustration on p. 38 and was done at about the same time. The similarity has confused historians and has not solved the flag enigma referred to on p. 40.

Chronology of Important Dates of Flag Changes

Appendix - A

Autumn 1775 (or earlier)	The Grand Union Flag, which was the familiar British Red Ensign with six white stripes added across the red banner, making thirteen alternate red and white stripes. It stood for the unity of the thirteen colonies under the British Union (The British Union Jack in the upper left corner).
Early June, 1776	The Betsy Ross flag. According to well founded tradition, thirteen five-pointed white stars on a blue ground replacing the British Union Jack in the canton of the Grand Union.
June 14, 1777	The Continental Congress passed the Flag Resolution, affirming the stars and stripes flag as the flag of the United States. The date, June 14th, now celebrated annually as Flag Day.
January 13, 1794	The fifteen stars and fifteen stripes flag adopted effective May 1, 1795.
April 4, 1818	Effective July 4, 1818 the flag to be thirteen alternate red and white stripes and twenty stars, white in a blue field. Upon admission of every new State into the Union one star to be added effective the next fourth of July. These provisions — retaining thirteen stripes and adding one star for each new State have remained in effect ever since.
June 24, 1912	President Taft, in an executive order, set forth certain dimensions and proportions of the elements of the flag and the arrangements of the stars. This was the first time this had been done in the long history of our flag.
August 21, 1959	President Eisenhower, in Executive Order 10834, prescribed the exact dimensions and proportions of the constituent parts of the flag and the positioning of the stars of the new fifty star ensign. The order has been published in full in the Federal Register, Vol. 24, No. 166, pp. 6865-6867, issued August 29, 1959.

Chronology of Important Dates in Betsy Ross' Life

Appendix - B

January 1, 1752	Born. Daughter of Samuel and Rebecca Griscom, Quakers, who were married on February 6, 1741 and had seventeen children. Betsy was the eighth born.
November 4, 1773	Married John Ross, son of Eneas and Sarah Leech Ross. Eneas had been Assistant Rector of Christ Church, Philadelphia and was presently the rector of the churches of Oxford (Old Trinity) and White-Marsh, both north of the city and organized by Christ Church. They eloped to Gloucester, New Jersey and were married by a Justice of the Peace at Hugg's Tavern.
May 24, 1774	Betsy was disowned by the Philadelphia Monthly Meeting of Friends, Northern District, whose Minute book records as follows: 24th 5th Mo. 1774. A Testimony having been prepared as directed last month in the case of Elizabeth Ross; John Parrish, and John Thomson in company with such Women Friends as may be appointed at their Meeting, are desired to deliver to her a copy of said Testimony and acquaint her with her right of appealing, it being as follows: Elizabeth Ross, late Griscom of the Northern District of this City, having had her education and made profession with us, the people called Quakers, but for want of taking heed to the dictates of Truth in her mind, hath so far deviated therefrom as to be married to a man of another religious persuasion — without consent of her parents, — for which disorderly and undutiful conduct she hath been treated with, But our labors of love not having the desired effect, we hereby testify that she hath disunited herself from Religious Fellowship with us, until through Repentance and amendment of Life, she seeks to make such acknowledgment to this Meeting as the nature of her case requires, which we desire she may be enabled to do through the assistance of Divine Grace.
January 21, 1776	John Ross had been injured while on military guard duty as a civilian. He died, and was buried at Christ Church on this date. Betsy became a widow at age 24.

Early June, 1776 (or end of May)	General Washington, Colonel George Ross (uncle of her late husband) and Robert Morris called at the Betsy Ross upholstery shop. Washington submitted a rough sketch of a stars and stripes flag. Betsy completed a flag and it was accepted at the State House. She was ordered to produce as many flags as she could make. She did so and her shop continued to make flags until 1857, when operations ceased.
June 5, 1776	Washington departed Philadelphia hurriedly for the defense of New York. He probably took the new flag with him, though there is no such written record.
June 15, 1777	Betsy married Joseph Ashburn at Gloria Dei Church, Philadelphia.
September 15, 1779	First child born to Betsy, Zilla Ashburn. Died at age 2.
February 25, 1781	Second child born, Eliza Ashburn.
July 6, 1781	John Claypoole, a long time friend of Joseph and Betsy Ashburn had been captured at sea April 4, 1781 and was convicted in England of high treason. Soon after this date he was incarcerated in Old Mill Prison, Plymouth, England, and later found Joseph Ashburn there.
Early 1782	John Claypoole and Joseph Ashburn met in Old Mill Prison. Ashburn had been there for some time, probably longer than Claypoole. Ashburn had not been heard from for over a year.
March 3, 1782	Joseph Ashburn died at Old Mill Prison, Plymouth, England.
August, 1782	John Claypoole, released from prison, was returned to Philadelphia. He confirmed to Betsy the rumors that her husband had died at Old Mill Prison.
May 8, 1783	Betsy married John Claypoole. They worshiped at Christ Church, Philadelphia. Five daughters were born to this marriage: Clarissa Sidney, 1785; Susannah, 1786; Rachel, 1789; Jane, 1792; Harriet, December 20, 1795, who died at nine months. The Claypooles joined the Society of Free Quakers, probably shortly after their marriage.
August 3, 1817	John Claypoole died at age 64. He had been born at Mount Holly, New Jersey on August 15, 1752.
1834	Free Quakers Society terminated meetings for worship.
January 30, 1836	Elizabeth Griscom Ross, Ashburn, Claypoole died. She is now buried adjacent to her original shop at 239 Arch Street, Philadelphia.

Affidavits Affirming That Betsy Made Our First Stars and Stripes Flag

Appendix - C

No. 1 Affidavit of Sophia B. Hildebrandt, granddaughter of Betsy, 27 May 1870.

> Affidavit of Sophia B. Hildebrant,
> Daughter of Clarissa S. Wilson and Granddaughter
> of Elizabeth Claypoole (Betsy Ross)
>
> I remember to have heard my grandmother Elizabeth Claypoole frequently narrate the circumstance of her having made the first Star Spangled Banner; that it was a speciman flag made to the order of the committee of Congress, acting in conjunction with General Washington, who called upon her personally at her store in Arch Street, below Third Street, Philadelphia, shortly before the Declaration of Independence; that she said that General Washington made a redrawing of the design with his own hands after some suggestions made by her; and that this specimen flag was exhibited in Congress by the committee, with a report, and the flag and report were approved and adopted by the Congress; and she received an unlimited order from the committee to make flags for the government, and to my knowledge she continued to manufacture the government flags for about fifty years, when my mother succeeded her in the business, in which I assisted. I believe the facts stated in the foregoing article, entitled "The First American Flag, and Who Made It," are all strictly true.
>
> Witness my hand at Philadelphia the Twenty-seventh day of May A.D. 1870.
>
> Witnesses present.
> Isaac R. Oakford
> Charles H. Evans   S.B. Hildebrandt.
>
> State of Pennsylvania,
> City of Philadelphia   SS
>
> On the Twenty-seventh day of May A.D. 1870, Before me Charles H. Evans, a Notary Public in and for the Common-wealth of Pennsylvania, duly commissioned, residing in the said City of Philadelphia personally appeared the within named Sophia B. Hildebrandt, who being duly affirmed did depose and say that the statements within certified to by her are all strictly true, according to the best of her knowledge and belief, and that she is a daughter of Clarissa S. Wilson, who was a daughter of Elizabeth Claypoole.
>
> Affirmed and subscribed before
> me, this day and year aforesaid.
> Witness my hand and Notarial seal.
> Charles H. Evans   S.B. Hildebrant
> Notary Public.

No. 2 Affidavit of Margaret Boggs, niece of Betsy, 3 June 1870

Affidavit of Margaret Donaldson Boggs, Daughter of Sarah Donaldson, who was a Sister of Elizabeth Claypoole (Betsy Ross)

I, Margaret Boggs, of the City of Philadelphia, Widow, do hereby certify that I have heard my aunt, Elizabeth Claypoole say many times, that she made the first Star Spangled Banner that ever was made with her own hands; that she made it on the order of General Washington and a committee of the Continental Congress, who together called personally upon her at her house on the North side Arch Street below Third Street, Philadelphia, some time previously to the Declaration of Independence. That they brought with them a drawing, roughly made, of the proposed flag; that she said it was wrong, and proposed alterations, which Washington and the Committee approved; that one of these alterations was in regard to the number of points of the star; that she said it should be five-pointed, and showed them how to fold a piece of paper in the proper manner, and with one cut of the scissors, to make a five-pointed star; that General Washington sat at a table in her back parlor, where they were, and made a drawing of the flag embodying her suggestions, and that she made the flag according to this drawing, and the committee carried it before Congress, by whom it was approved and adopted. That she then received orders to make flags for the government as fast as possible; and from that time forward, for upwards of fifty years she made all the flags made for the United States in Philadelphia, and largely for the other naval stations. I was for many years a member of her family, and aided her in the business. I believe the facts stated in the foregoing article entitled "The First American Flag and Who Made It," which has now been read to me are all strictly true.

Witness my hand at Germantown in the City of Philadelphia, this Third day of June A.D. 1870.

Witnesses present.
Charles B. Engle
Stephen T. Beale   Margaret Boggs.

State of Pennsylvania
City of Philadelphia   SS.

On the Third day of June A.D. 1870, before me Charles B. Engle a Notary Public in and for the Commonwealth of Pennsylvania, duly commissioned, residing in the said City of Philadelphia, personally appeared the within named Margaret Boggs, who being duly affirmed did depose and say that the statements within certified to by her are all strictly true, according to the best of her knowledge and belief, and that she is a daughter of Sarah Donaldson, who was a sister of Elizabeth Claypoole.

Affirmed and subscribed before me
day and year aforesaid.
Witness my hand and Notarial Seal   M. Boggs
Charles B. Engle, Notary Public.

No. 3 Affidavit of Rachel Fletcher, daughter of Betsy, 31 July 1871

Affidavit of Rachel Fletcher, a daughter of Elizabeth Claypoole (Betsy Ross)

I remember having heard my mother Elizabeth Claypoole say frequently that she, with her own hands, (while she was the widow of John Ross,) made the first Star-spangled Banner that ever was made. I remember to have heard her also say that it was made on the order of a Committee, of whom Col. Ross was one, and that Robert Morris was also one of the Committee. That General Washington, acting in conference with the committee, called with them at her house. This house was on the North side of Arch Street a few doors below Third Street, above Bread Street,-a two story house, with attic and a dormer window, now standing, the only one of the row left, the old number being 89; it was formerly occupied by Daniel Niles, Shoemaker. Mother at first lived in the house next East, and when the war came, she moved into the house of Daniel Niles. That it was in the month of June 1776, or shortly before the Declaration of Independence that the committee called on her. That the member of the committee named Ross was an uncle of her deceased husband. That she was previously well acquainted with Washington, and that he had often been in her house in friendly visits, as well as on business. That she had embroidered ruffles for his shirt bosoms and cuffs, and that it was partly owing to his friendship for her that she was chosen to make the flag. That when the committee (with General Washington) came into her store she showed them into her parlor, back of her store; and one of them asked her if she could make a flag and that she replied that she did not know but she could try. That they then showed her a drawing roughly executed, of the flag as it was proposed to be made by the committee, and that she saw in it some defects in its proportions and the arrangement and shape of the stars. That she said it was square and a flag should be one third longer than its width, that the stars were scattered promiscuously over the field, and she said they should be either in lines or in some adopted form as a circle, or a star, and that the stars were six-pointed in the drawing, and she said they should be five pointed. That the gentlemen of the committee and General Washington very respectfully considered the suggestions and acted upon them, General Washington seating himself at a table with a pencil and paper, altered the drawing and then made a new one according to the suggestions of my mother. That General Washington seemed to her to be the active one in making the design, the others having little or nothing to do with it. That the committee then requested her to call on one of their number, a shipping merchant on the wharf, and then adjourned. That she was punctual to her appointment, and then the gentlemen drew out of a chest an old ship's color which he loaned her to show her how the sewing was done; and also gave her the drawing finished according to her suggestions. That this drawing was done in water colors by William Barrett, an artist, who lived on the North side of Cherry Street above Third Street, a large three story brick house on the West side of an alley which ran back to the

Pennsylvania Academy for Young Ladies," kept by James A. Neal, the best school of the kind in the city at that time. That Barrett only did the painting, and had nothing to do with the design. He was often employed by mother afterwards to paint the coats of arms of the United States and of the States on silk flags. That other designs had also been made by the committee and given to other seamstresses to make, but that they were not approved. That mother went diligently to work upon her flag and soon finished it, and returned it, the first star-spangled banner that ever was made, to her employers, that it was run up to the peak of one of the vessels belonging to one of the committee then lying at the wharf, and was received with shouts of applause by the few bystanders who happened to be looking on. That the committee on the same day carried the flag into the Congress sitting in the State House, and made a report presenting the flag and the drawing and that Congress unamimously approved and accepted the report. That the next day Col. Ross called upon my mother and informed her that her work had been approved and her flag adopted, and he gave orders for the purchase of all the materials and the manufacture of as many flags as she could make. And that from that time forward, for over fifty years she continued to make flags for the United States Government.

I believe the facts stated in the foregoing Article entitled "The First American Flag and Who Made It," are all strictly true.

  This affidavit having been signed by Rachel Fletcher with violet ink, the signature has faded, but is at this time, Seventh Month 24th, 1908, still plainly legible.

Rachel Fletcher

I, Mary Fletcher Wigert, daughter of the said Rachel Fletcher, recognize the signature in the rectangular space outlined in black above, as the signature of my mother Rachel Fletcher.

Mary Fletcher Wigert

Signed in the presence of Mary W. Miller
Philadelphia Seventh Mo. 24th, 1908

State of New York
City of New York   SS
  On the 31st day of July A.D. 1871. Before me the subscriber a Notary Public in and for the Commonwealth of New York, duly commissioned, residing in the said City of New York, personally appeared the above named Rachel Fletcher, who being duly affirmed did depose and say that the statements above certified to by her are all strictly true according to the best of her knowledge and belief, and that she is a daughter of Elizabeth Claypoole. Affirmed and subscribed before me the day and year aforesaid. Witness my hand and Notarial Seal.   Th. J. McEvily
Notary Public
City & Co. New York

Signature of Rachel Fletcher, above, can still be faintly seen on the original affidavit at the Huntington Library, San Marino, California. See Index and Folio I of Section H. HM41760.   Robert Morris 1978

Dates the States Entered the Union, Flag Dates, Number of Stars in Our Flags

Appendix - D

Order of States and Dates of Ratification of the Constitution		Number of Stars	Dates Effective on Flag
1 Delaware	December 7, 1787	13	From June 1776,
2 Pennsylvania	December 12, 1787	13	officially adopted
3 New Jersey	December 18, 1787	13	June 14, 1777
4 Georgia	January 2, 1788	13	
5 Connecticut	January 9, 1788	13	
6 Massachusetts	February 6, 1788	13	
7 Maryland	April 28, 1788	13	
8 South Carolina	May 23, 1788	13	
9 New Hampshire	June 21, 1788	13	
10 Virginia	June 25, 1788	13	
11 New York	July 26, 1788	13	
12 North Carolina	November 21, 1789	13	
13 Rhode Island	May 29, 1790	13	

Order of States and Dates of Admission to the Union			
14 Vermont	March 4, 1791	13	
15 Kentucky	June 1, 1792	13	

By Congressional Act of January 13, 1794, flag of 15 stars and 15 stripes effective May 1, 1795.

16 Tennessee	June 1, 1796	15	(& 15 stripes)
17 Ohio	March 1, 1803	15	(& 15 stripes)
18 Louisiana	April 30, 1812	15	(& 15 stripes)
19 Indiana	December 11, 1816	15	(& 15 stripes)
20 Mississippi	December 10, 1817	15	(& 15 stripes)

By Congressional Act of April 4, 1818, flag changed to 20 stars and 13 stripes effective July 4, 1818, and one star to be added for each new state effective the next July 4th after admission. This Act has remained in effect ever since.

Order of States and Dates of Ratification of the Constitution		Number of Stars	Dates Effective on Flag
21 Illinois	December 3, 1818	21	July 4, 1819
22 Alabama	December 14, 1819		
23 Maine	March 15, 1820	23	July 4, 1820
24 Missouri	August 10, 1821	24	July 4, 1822
25 Arkansas	June 15, 1836	25	July 4, 1836
26 Michigan	January 26, 1837	26	July 4, 1837
27 Florida	March 3, 1845	27	July 4, 1845
28 Texas	December 29, 1845	28	July 4, 1846
29 Iowa	December 28, 1846	29	July 4, 1847
30 Wisconsin	May 29, 1848	30	July 4, 1848
31 California	September 9, 1850	31	July 4, 1851
32 Minnesota	May 11, 1858	32	July 4, 1858
33 Oregon	February 14, 1859	33	July 4, 1859
34 Kansas	January 29, 1861	34	July 4, 1861
35 West Virginia	June 20, 1863	35	July 4, 1863
36 Nevada	October 31, 1864	36	July 4, 1865
37 Nebraska	March 1, 1867	37	July 4, 1867
38 Colorado	August 1, 1876	38	July 4, 1877
39 North Dakota	November 2, 1889		
40 South Dakota	November 2, 1889		
41 Montana	November 8, 1889		
42 Washington	November 11, 1889		
43 Idaho	July 3, 1890	43	July 4, 1890
44 Wyoming	July 10, 1890	44	July 4, 1891
45 Utah	January 4, 1896	45	July 4, 1896
46 Oklahoma	November 16, 1907	46	July 4, 1908
47 New Mexico	January 6, 1912		
48 Arizona	February 14, 1912	48	July 4, 1912
49 Alaska	January 3, 1959	49	July 4, 1959
50 Hawaii	August 21, 1959	50	July 4, 1960

How to Display Our Flag, Laws, Regulations

Appendix - E

FLAG LAWS AND REGULATIONS

The following codification of existing rules and customs pertaining to the display and use of the flag of the United States of America be, and it is hereby, established for the use of such civilians or civilian groups or organizations as may not be required to conform with regulations promulgated by one or more executive departments of the Government of the United States. The flag of the United States for the purpose of this chapter shall be defined according to title 4, United States Code, Chapter 1, Section 1 and Section 2 and Executive Order 10834 issued pursuant thereto.

Sec. 2. (a) It is the universal custom to display the flag only from sunrise to sunset on buildings and on stationary flagstaffs in the open. However, when a patriotic effect is desired, the flag may be displayed twenty-four hours a day if properly illuminated during the hours of darkness.

(b) The flag should be hoisted briskly and lowered ceremoniously.

(c) The flag should not be displayed on days when the weather is inclement, except when an all weather flag is displayed.

(d) The flag should be displayed on all days, especially on New Year's Day, January 1; Inauguration Day, January 20; Lincoln's Birthday, February 12; Washington's Birthday, third Monday in February; Easter Sunday (variable); Mother's Day, second Sunday in May; Armed Forces Day, third Saturday in May; Memorial Day (half-staff until noon), the last Monday in May; Flag Day, June 14; Independence Day, July 4; Labor Day, first Monday in September; Constitution Day, September 17; Columbus Day, second Monday in October; Navy Day, October 27; Veterans Day, November 11; Thanksgiving Day, fourth Thursday in November; Christmas Day, December 25; and such other days as may be proclaimed by the President of the United States; the birthdays of States (date of admission); and on State holidays.

(e) The flag should be displayed daily on or near the main administration building of every public institution.

(f) The flag should be displayed in or near every polling place on election days.

(g) The flag should be displayed during school days in or near every schoolhouse.

Sec. 3. That the flag, when carried in a procession with another flag or flags, should be either on the marching right; that is, the flag's own right, or, if there is a line of other flags, in front of the center of that line.

(a) The flag should not be displayed on a float in a parade except from a staff, or as provided in subsection (i).

(b) The flag should not be draped over the hood, top, sides, or back of a vehicle or of a railroad train or a boat. When the flag is displayed on a motorcar, the staff shall be fixed firmly to the chassis or clamped to the right fender.

(c) No other flag or pennant should be placed above or, if on the same level, to the right of the flag of the United States of America, except during church services conducted by naval chaplains at sea, when the church pennant may be flown above the flag during church services for the personnel of the Navy.

(d) The flag of the United States of America, when it is displayed with another flag against a wall from crossed staffs, should be on the right, the flag's own right, and its staff should be in front of the staff of the other flag.

(e) The flag of the United States of America should be at the center and at the highest point of the group when a number of flags of States or localities or pennants of societies are grouped and displayed from staffs.

(f) When flags of States, cities, or localities, or pennants of societies are flown on the same halyard with the flag of the United States, the latter should always be at the peak. When the flags are flown from adjacent staffs, the flag of the United States should be hoisted first and lowered last. No such flag or pennant may be placed above the flag of the United States or to the United States flag's right.

(g) When flags of two or more nations are displayed, they are to be flown from separate staffs of the same height. The flags should be of approximately equal size. International usage forbids the display of the flag of one nation above that of another nation in time of peace.

(h) When the flag of the United States is displayed from a staff projecting horizontally or at an angle from the window sill, balcony, or front of a building, the union of the flag should be placed at the peak of the staff unless the flag is at half-staff. When the flag is suspended over a sidewalk from a rope extending from a house to a pole at the edge of the sidewalk, the flag should be hoisted out, union first, from the building.

(i) When displayed either horizontally or vertically against a wall, the union should be uppermost and to the flag's own right, that is, to the observer's left. When displayed in a window, the flag should be displayed in the same way, with the union or blue field to the left of the observer in the street.

(j) When the flag is displayed over the middle of the street, it should be suspended vertically with the union to the north in an east and west street or to the east in a north and south street.

(k) When used on a speaker's platform, the flag, if displayed flat, should be displayed above and behind the speaker. When displayed from a staff in a church or public auditorium, the flag of the United States of America should hold the position of superior prominence, in advance of the audience, and in the position of honor at the clergyman's or speaker's right as he faces the audience. Any other flag so displayed should be placed on the left of the clergyman or speaker or to the right of the audience.

(l) The flag should form a distinctive feature of the ceremony of unveiling a statue or monument, but it should never be used as the covering for the statue or monument.

(m) The flag, when flown at half-staff, should be first hoisted to the peak for an instant and then lowered to the half-staff position. The flag should be again raised to the peak before it is lowered for the day. On Memorial Day the flag should be displayed at half-staff until noon only, then raised to the top of the staff. By order of the President, the flag shall be flown at half-staff upon the death of principal figures of the United States Government and the Governor of a State, territory or possession, as a mark of respect to their memory. In the event of the death of other officials or foreign dignitaries, the flag is to be displayed at half-staff according to Presidential instructions or orders, or in accordance with recognized customs or practices not inconsistent with law. In the event of the death of a present or former official of the government of any State, territory, or possession of the United States, the Governor of that State, territory, or possession may proclaim that the National flag shall be flown at half-staff. The flag shall be flown at half-staff thirty days from the death of the President or a former President; ten days from the day of death of the Vice President, the Chief Justice or a retired Chief Justice of the United States, or the Speaker of the House of Representatives; from the day of death until interment of an Associate Justice of the Supreme Court, a Secretary of an executive or military department, a former Vice President, or the Governor of a State, territory, or possession; and on the day of death and the following day for a Member of Congress. As used in this subsection —

(1) the term "half-staff" means the position of the flag when it is one-half the distance between the top and bottom of the staff;

(2) the term "executive or military department" means any agency listed under sections 101 and 102 of title 5, United States Code; and

(3) the term "Member of Congress" means a Senator, a Representative, a Delegate, or the Resident Commissioner from Puerto Rico.

(n) When the flag is used to cover a casket, it should be so placed that the union is at the head and over the left shoulder. The flag should not be lowered into the grave or allowed to touch the ground.

(o) When the flag is suspended across a corridor or lobby in a building with only one main entrance, it should be suspended vertically with the union of the flag to the observer's left upon entering. If the building has more than one main entrance, the flag should be suspended vertically near the center of the corridor or lobby with the union to the north, when entrances are to the east and west or to the east when entrances are to the north and south. If there are entrances in more than two directions, the union should be to the east.

Sec. 4. That no disrespect should be shown to the flag of the United States of America; the flag should not be dipped to any person or thing. Regimental colors, State flags, and organization or institutional flags are to be dipped as a mark of honor.

(a) The flag should never be displayed with the union down, except as a signal of dire distress in instances of extreme danger to life or property.

(b) The flag should never touch anything beneath it, such as the ground, the floor, water, or merchandise.

(c) The flag should never be carried flat or horizontally, but always aloft and free.

(d) The flag should never be used as wearing apparel, bedding, or drapery. It should never be festooned, drawn back, nor up, in folds, but always allowed to fall free. Bunting of blue, white and red, always arranged with the blue above, the white in the middle, and the red below, should be used for covering a speaker's desk, draping the front of the platform, and for decoration in general.

(e) The flag should never be fastened, displayed, used, or stored in such a manner as to permit it to be easily torn, soiled, or damaged in any way.

(f) The flag should never be used as a covering for a ceiling.

(g) The flag should never have placed upon it, nor on any part of it, nor attached to it any mark, insignia, letter, word, figure, design, picture, or drawing of any nature.

(h) The flag should never be used as a receptacle for receiving, holding, carrying, or delivering anything.

(i) The flag should never be used for advertising purposes in any manner whatsoever. It should not be embroidered on such articles as cushions or handkerchiefs and the like, printed or otherwise impressed on paper napkins or boxes or anything that is designed for temporary use and discard. Advertising signs should not be fastened to a staff or halyard from which the flag is flown.

(j) No part of the flag should ever be used as a costume or athletic uniform. However, a flag patch may be affixed to the uniform of military personnel, firemen, policemen, and members of patriotic organizations. The flag represents a living country and is itself considered a living thing. Therefore, the lapel flag pin being a replica, should be worn on the left lapel near the heart.

(k) The flag, when it is in such condition that it is no longer a fitting emblem for display, should be destroyed in a dignified way, preferably by burning.

Sec. 5. During the ceremony of hoisting or lowering the flag or when the flag is passing in a parade or in review, all persons present except those in uniform should face the flag and stand at attention with the right hand over the heart. Those present in uniform should render the military salute. When not in uniform, men should remove their headdress with their right hand and hold it at the left shoulder, the hand being over the heart. Aliens should stand at attention. The salute to the flag in a moving column should be rendered at the moment the flag passes.

Sec. 6. During rendition of the national anthem when the flag is displayed, all present except those in uniform should stand at attention facing the flag with the right hand over the heart. Men not in uniform should remove their headdress with their right hand and hold it at the left shoulder, the hand being over the heart. Persons in uniform should render the military salute at the first note of the anthem and retain this position until the last note. When the flag is not displayed, those present should face toward the music and act in the same manner they would if the flag were displayed there.

Sec. 7. The Pledge of Allegiance to the Flag, "I pledge allegiance to the Flag of the United States of America, and to the Republic for which it stands, one Nation under God, indivisible, with liberty and justice for all", should be rendered by standing at attention facing the flag with the right hand over the heart. When not in uniform men should remove their headdress with their right hand and hold it at the left shoulder, the hand being over the heart. Persons in uniform should remain silent, face the flag, and render the military salute.

Sec. 8. Any rule or custom pertaining to the display of the flag of the United States of America, set forth herein, may be altered, modified, or repealed, or additional rules with respect thereto may be prescribed, by the Commander in

Chief of the Armed Forces of the United States, whenever he deems it to be appropriate or desirable; and any such alteration or additional rule shall be set forth in a proclamation.

No person shall display the flag of the United Nations or any other national or international flag equal, above, or in a position of superior prominence or honor to, or in place of, the flag of the United States at any place within the United States or any Territory or possession thereof; Provided, That nothing in this section shall make unlawful the continuance of the practice heretofore followed of displaying the flag of the United Nations in a position of superior prominence or honor, and other national flags in positions of equal prominence or honor, with that of the flag of the United States at the headquarters of the United Nations.

HOW TO DISPLAY THE FLAG

1. When the flag is displayed over the middle of the street, it should be suspended vertically with the union to the north in an east and west street or to the east in a north and south street.

2. The flag of the United States of America, when it is displayed with another flag against a wall from crossed staffs, should be on the right, the flag's own right, and its staff should be in front of the staff of the other flag.

3. The flag, when flown at half-staff, should be first hoisted to the peak for an instant and then lowered to the half-staff position. The flag should be again raised to the peak before it is lowered for the day. By "half-staff" is meant lowering the flag to one-half the distance between the top and bottom of the staff. Crepe streamers may be affixed to spear heads or flagstaffs in a parade only by order of the President of the United States.

4. When flags of States, cities, or localities, or pennants of societies are flown on the same halyard with the flag of the United States, the latter should always be at the peak. When the flags are flown from adjacent staffs, the flag of the United States should be hoisted first and lowered last. No such flag or pennant may be placed above the flag of the United States or to the right of the flag of the United States.

5. When the flag is suspended over a sidewalk from a rope extending from a house to a pole at the edge of the sidewalk, the flag should be hoisted out, union first, from the building.

6. When the flag of the United States is displayed from a staff projecting horizontally or at an angle from the window sill, balcony, or front of a building, the union of the flag should be placed at the peak of the staff unless the flag is at half-staff.

7. When the flag is used to cover a casket, it should be so placed that the union is at the head and over the left shoulder. The flag should not be lowered into the grave or allowed to touch the ground.

8. When the flag is displayed in a manner other than by being flown from a staff, it should be displayed flat, whether indoors or out. When displayed either horizontally or vertically against a wall, the union should be uppermost and to the flag's own right, that is, to the observer's left. When displayed in a window it should be displayed in the same way, that is with the union or blue field to the left of the observer in the street. When festoons, rosettes or drapings are desired, bunting of blue, white and red should be used, but never the flag.

9. That the flag, when carried in a procession with another flag, or flags, should be either on the marching right; that is, the flag's own right, or, if there is a line of other flags, in front of the center of that line.

10. The flag of the United States of America should be at the center and at the highest point of the group when a number of flags of States or localities or pennants of societies are grouped and displayed from staffs.

11. When flags of two or more nations are displayed, they are to be flown from separate staffs of the same height. The flags should be of approximately equal size. International usage forbids the display of the flag of one nation above that of another nation in time of peace.

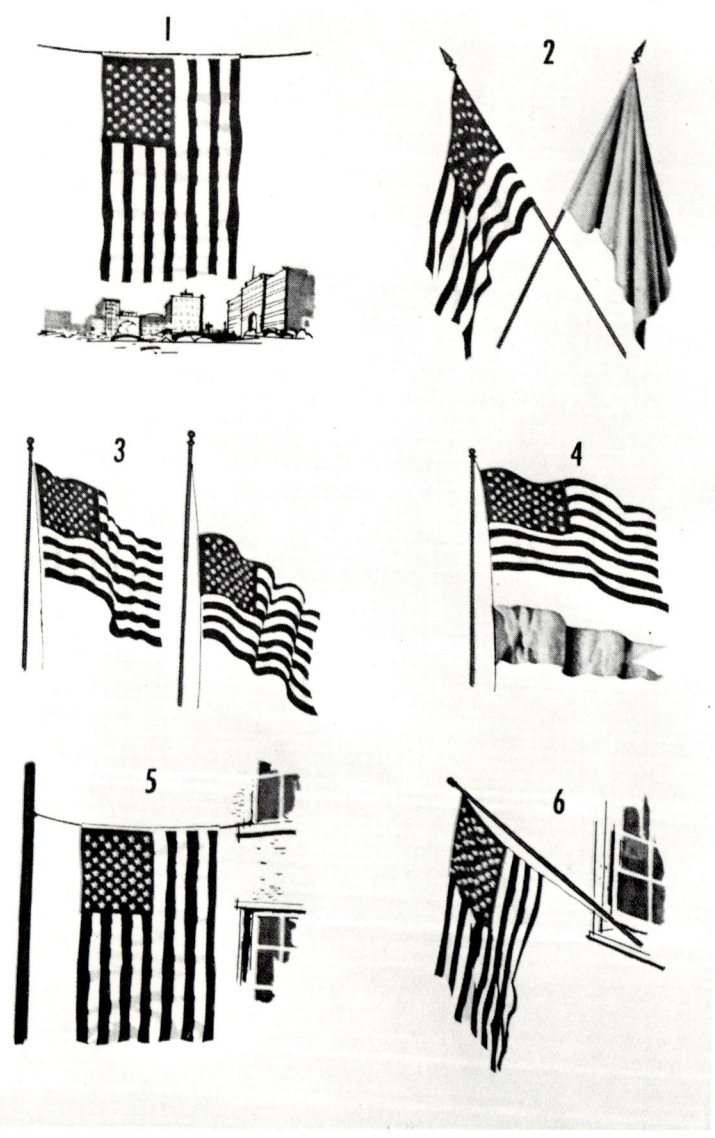

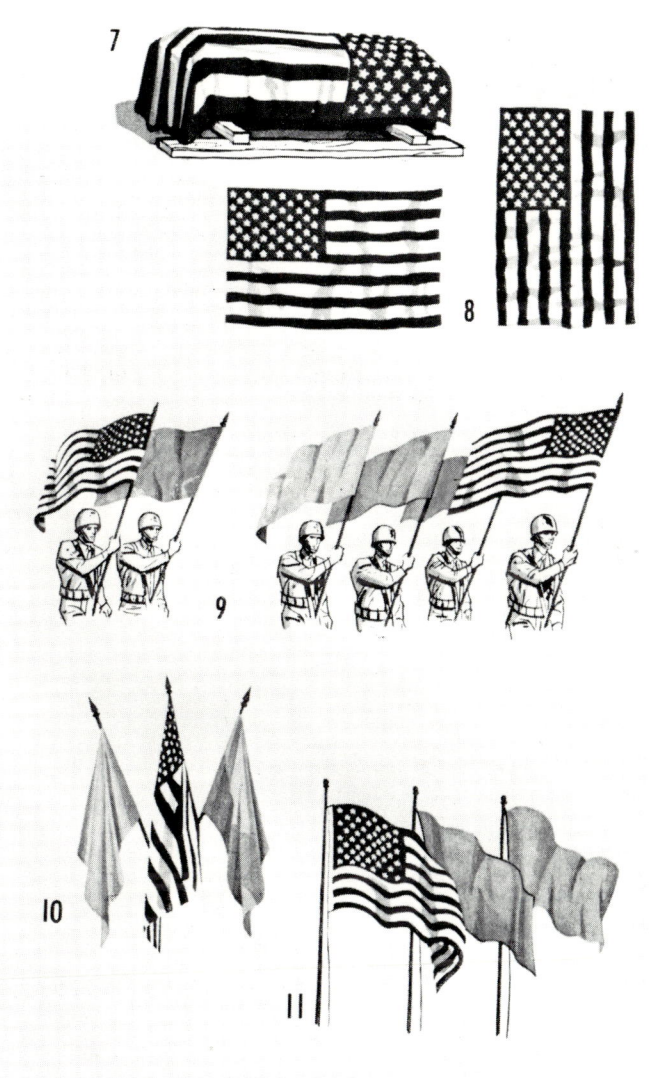

General Greene's Letters

Appendix - F

Some letters of Major General Nathanael Greene which were written at a low point of the war just before Washington's crossing of the Delaware and the Battle of Trenton, may be of passing interest to scholars. They reveal intimately a military command situation which was critical and tend to indicate that the behavior of men in the heat of war has not changed materially in the past two centuries.

At the Huntington Library, in San Marino, California, originals and handwritten copies of letters which were written by General Greene were found in the Rare Manuscript Department by this researcher. They show first hand not only the desperate situation we found ourselves in during December of 1776, but also that the depredations by invaders at war were not unlike those of today.

The Hessian troops had been told by their ruler, the Landgrave of Hesse-Cassell, who leased their services to his cousin, King George III, that this was a rich land and that much looting would be available to them. Nearly 30,000 Hessians were provided. Their depredations and scavenging at this stage of the war, particularly around Princeton and Nassau Hall, are well known.

Princeton Dec. 7 [1776]

To General Washington

Lord Stirling will write by the same express that this comes by, and enclose your Excellency several pieces of intelligence obtained of different people yesterday. His Lordship thinks the enemy are making a Disposition to advance; for my part I am at a loss to determine whether their Disposition is to advance or for defence. The enemy have got to a party advanced about seven miles this side of Brunswick; another at Boundbrook. . . .

Major Clarke reports General Lee is at the heels of the enemy. I should think he had better keep upon the flanks. . . .
[Note: Greene did not like Lee. General Lee turned in a sordid performance at several points during the war].

Our retreat should not be neglected, for fear of consequences. The bottom of the river [Delaware] should be examined, and see if the boats can be anchored in the ferry way. . . .

This moment a captain has returned...and it is beyond a doubt the enemy are advancing, and my Lord Stirling thinks they will be up here by twelve o'clock.

I shall make the best Disposition I can to oppose them.

I am, Dear Sir, your most obedient servant.
Nath. Greene

Corell's Ferry, Dec. 21, 1776.

To   The President of Congress.

Although I am far from thinking the American cause desperate, yet I conceive it to be in a critical situation. The enemy is at the heart of the country, the disaffected daily increasing; the time for which the troops stand engaged almost ready to expire; very few inlisted upon the new establishment; the tide of publick sentiment at a stand, and ready to run through different channels; the people refusing to supply the army, under various pretenses, but evidently from a disaffection to the cause and to the currency, are combined evils. . . .

Nath. Greene

Coryell's Ferry December 21, 1776

To   Weston (?) Nicholas Cooke, Jr.

By your letter to General Washington — I find the British Troops have landed on Rhode Island. Although I am sorry my own Country should be subject to their ravages yet I rejoice that they are surrounded by a people who are united and firmly determined in opposition...We are now in the West side of the Delaware our force tho small...I hope to give the enemy a stroke in a few days should fortune favor the attack perhaps it may put a stop to General Howe's progress. His ravages in the Jersey's exceeds all description. Men slaughtered, Women ravisht, and Houses plundered, little girls not ten years old ravisht, Mother and Daughters ravished in the presence of the Husband and Sons — who were obliged to be spectators — to their brutal conduct.

I think notwithstanding the General disaffection of a certain order of people, [referred to Quakers earlier in the letter] the army will fill up — should that be the case nothing is to be feared.

French war is inevitable. . .Short enlistments has been in a great measure the source of all the misfortunes that we labor under. . .the Congress in the infancy of Politicks could not be brought to believe many serious truths. . . .

I am told some melicious reports propergated industriously about me, about the loss of the Baggage and Stores at Fort Lee — they are as malecious as they are untrue. . . .

Everything was got off. . .that could be with the Roads and Waggons we had to move the Stores with. The Evacuation of Fort Lee was determined upon several days before the Enemy landed above us — and happily the most valuable stores were away. . .not an article of Military Stores was left there or nothing worth mentioning.[1]

. . . .The Congress have moved to Baltimore. . . .

Nath Greene

Head Quarters Dec. 24, 1776

Dear Sir

If your business [as Quartermaster] will permit. I should like to see you here. There is some business of importance to communicate to you which I wish to do today. No butter, no cheese - no cyder - this is not for the honor of Pennsylvania. Col Griffin is at Mount Holly collecting great numbers of Jersey troops. They have drove the Hessians & Highlanders many miles. Yesterday a great firing was heard there. The consequence I have not learnt.

Yours sincerely, N. Greene

To   Col Clemment Biddle

---

[1] Historians and contemporary writers do not quite agree with General Greene about the losses at Fort Lee. They relate that upon our withdrawal from Fort Lee on November 20, 1776 the Americans were over-run by the British and Hessians. Prisoners were taken and considerable stores were lost. Captain Levin Friedrich Ernst von Muenchhausen, aide to General Howe, reported taking 7 mortars, 32 cannon, 432 tents, 400,000 rounds of ammunition, provisions for 3 months for 5,000 men and 73 invalids. See Samuel Stelle Smith, At General Howe's Side. Monmouth Beach, NJ: Philip Freneau Press, 1974, p. 5.

Betsy's Family - Children

Appendix - G

Children of Samuel and Rebecca Griscom

		Born	Died
1	Deborah	April 1743	1793
2	Susanna	July 1744	
3	Sarah	October 1745	March 25, 1747
4	Rebecca	January 1746/7	
5	William	April 1748	August 18, 1749
6	Sarah (2nd)	July 1749	
7	Mary	October 1750	
8	ELIZABETH	January 1, 1752	January 30, 1836
9	Samuel	April 1753	September 9, 1756
10	Martha	July 1754	July 28, 1757
11	Hannah	November 1755	December 21, 1836
12	Ann	March 1757	August 25, 1759
13	Samuel (2nd)	July 1758	July 23, 1761
14	Joseph	November 1759	October 10, 1762
15	Abigail	November 1759	November 15, 1762
16	George	April 1761	
17	Rachel	November 1762	November 15, 1825

From The Huntington Library: HM 41760 Canby Papers, Box 2, Folio 19 A.

CHILDREN OF JOHN AND BETSY ROSS
None

CHILDREN OF JOSEPH AND BETSY ASHBURN

1 Zilla   September 15, 1779   Aged 2
2 Eliza   February 25, 1781
m. Captain Isaac Silliman

CHILDREN OF JOHN AND BETSY CLAYPOOLE

	Born	Died
1 Clarissa Sidney m. Jacob Wilson	April 3, 1785	
2 Susannah m. Abel Satterthwaite	1786	
3 Rachel m. Richard Fletcher	1789	
4 Jane m. Caleb H. Canby	1792	
5 Harriet	December 20, 1795	Aged 9 months

Biographical Notes on Principal Characters

Appendix - H

In writing about Betsy, her family, her husbands, and the principal military figures of the early Revolutionary War days it became necessary to obtain biographical data about them. Such information was required in order to follow the military men through their various ranks and titles, and genealogical data was needed from various sources for Betsy and her family. For the former a number of biographies were consulted, the principal one being the National Cyclopaedia of American Biography. Minor differences in dates and ranks were found between some of the sources but none of significant consequence.

The data is reproduced here in the belief that it will save time for future scholars seeking to develop further the subjects contained herein.

Alexander, William. (Lord Stirling) Born 1726, Colonel 1775; brigadier general 1776. At Long Island was taken prisoner by the British August 26, 1776, later exchanged and was commissioned Major General. At Washington Crossing, Trenton and Princeton Dec. 25, 1776 to Jan. 8, 1777 he was a brigadier general. Lossing says he was commissioned Major General February 19, 1777. He fought at Brandywine and at Germantown. He was at Valley Forge and was engaged at Monmouth.

Arnold, Benedict. Born January 14, 1741 at Norwich, Connecticut. Arrived at Cambridge as a captain April 29, 1775 and was at once commissioned a colonel. Wounded at Quebec December 1, 1775 and made brigadier general. In April, 1777 (or in October after Saratoga) was made major general. Arnold resented Congress failing to promote him to major general on February 19, 1777 when they so appointed Lincoln, Stirling, St. Clair, Stephen and Mifflin. In 1780 he was in command of the fort at West Point, New York. He communicated with British General Sir Henry Clinton who was then in command at New York City and on September 23, 1780 British Major John Andre was captured carrying criminal evidence from Arnold to Clinton. Arnold escaped to a British ship in the Hudson. He was commissioned a brigadier general in the British army and then led British raids in the Chesapeake December, 1780 and April 1781, during which Richmond was burned. Raided New London, Connecticut September 6, 1781. He had received money grants from Clinton and during late 1781 Arnold went to England where he received more money grants for himself, annuities for his wife and children, and 13,400 acres in Canada. After the war he was a merchant in the West Indies trade.

Cadwalader, John. Became a colonel of a Philadelphia militia battalion. At Bristol, Pennsylvania, General Washington brevetted him brigadier general on December 24, 1776 the day prior to Cadwalader's attempt to cross the Delaware just below Bristol. On April 5, 1777 he was made a brigadier general in the Pennsylvania militia.

Cornwallis, Charles. First Marquis and Second Earl Cornwallis. (succeeded to title of Earl in 1762). Was made major general in Royal Army in 1775. After Battle of Princeton, and before his departure for England that month, General Howe appointed him on January 8, 1777 as Lt. General in America. He returned to America and after the capture of Philadelphia in October 1777 he went back to England and was made permanent lieutenant general. On April 21, 1778 sailed again for America to be second in command of his majesty's forces in America under C-in-C Sir Henry Clinton. Major John Andre, in his diary under date of November 27, 1777 at Philadelphia, addressed him as Lord. Apparently, being a marquis and Earl, he was properly addressed as Lord.

de Fermoy, Roche. French officer serving as a brigadier general in American forces. Crossed with Washington and led a brigade in the left column in the Battle of Trenton.

Dickinson, Philemon. Born April 5, 1739. Colonel 1775; brigadier general October, 1775; major general June 6, 1777.

Ewing, James. Born August 3, 1736. Became brigadier general of Pennsylvania militia July 4, 1776.

Gates, Horatio. Born 1728 (?). Joined Continental Army as Adjutant General in 1775; major general 1776.

Glover, John. Born November 5, 1732. Was a colonel in 1776. Promoted to brigadier general February 21, 1777.

Greene, Nathanael. Born August 7, 1742. Was made brigadier general in Continental Army June 22, 1775; major general August 9, 1776; Quartermaster General of the Continental Army March 2, 1778, succeeding Major General Thomas Mifflin; succeeded Gates as Commander-in-Chief of the Southern Army on October 14, 1780. Died June 19, 1786.

Hamilton, Alexander. Born January 11, 1757. January 1776 joined an artillery company in New York State, then joined General Washington's staff as a captain. Was at Washington Crossing, Trenton, Princeton, Brandywine and Germantown. Was made a lieutenant colonel in the spring of 1777.

Howe, Richard. Born 1726. Succeeded, by death of his brother Lord Howe at Ticonderoga on July 5, 1758, as 4th Viscount Howe. Was made rear admiral on October 18, 1770; vice admiral December 7, 1775. On October 30, 1778 gave over his command in American waters to Rear Admiral Gambier. Became admiral in 1782. In January 1783 appointed First Lord of the Admiralty. On 19 August, 1788 appointed Earl Howe and Baron of Langar; in 1790 appointed Admiral of the Fleet — temporary. In March 1796 was made permanent Admiral of the Fleet. Was knighted June 1797.

Howe, William. Born August 10, 1729, 5th Viscount Howe. Became major general in 1772. Shortly after Bunker Hill on June 17, 1775 became lieutenant general and was knighted. On October 10, 1775 Lt. Gen. Sir William Howe succeeded General Thomas Gage with the rank of General in America. In 1793 he was appointed a full General of the Royal Army. While at winter quarters in New York in 1776-1777 some of his officers wrote that he engaged in "dissipation and high play." Biographer Bancroft wrote of his excessive pleasantries in Philadelphia in 1777-1778.

Knox, Henry. Born July 25, 1750, Boston. Joined Continental Army in Cambridge in 1775 and was commissioned a colonel of artillery there. During the winter of 1775-1776 was in charge of transportation of 55 pieces of artillery from Ticonderoga to Boston. Promoted to brigadier general at Newtown, Pennsylvania on December 27, 1776. Was at Washington Crossing, Trenton, Princeton, Morristown, Germantown. Was made a major general November 15, 1781. Was a founder of the Society of the Cincinnati. Was Secretary of War under the Articles of Confederation and in Washington's cabinet. Died October 25, 1806.

Lafayette, Marquis de, Marie Joseph Paul Yves Roch Gilbert Motier. Born September 6, 1757. Arrived at Charleston summer 1777. Appointed major general by Congress on July 31, 1777. Died 1834.

Lee, Charles. Born 1731. Appointed major general by Congress on June 17, 1775.

Lincoln, Benjamin. Born January 24, 1733. Brigadier general in militia February, 1776; major general, militia, May, 1776. Major general Continental Army February 19, 1777.

MacDougall, Alexander. Born 1731(?) Brigadier general 1776; major general 1777. Took command at West Point after Benedict Arnold's defection late 1780. Member Continental Congress 1781, 1782, 1784, 1785.

Mercer, Hugh. Born 1720. Colonel of 3rd Virginia Regiment in 1776. Commissioned brigadier general in Continental Army 1776. Died Jan., 1777.

Mifflin, Thomas. Born 1744. Major general, Continental Army, February 19, 1777. Died January 20, 1800.

Monroe, James. Born April 28, 1758. Enlisted in New York in 1776. Was a lieutenant at Washington Crossing and Trenton; major at Brandywine and Germantown. During War of 1812 became Secretary of War after the British incendiary raid on the capital in 1814. Inaugurated 5th President of the United States in 1817, served two terms. Died July 4, 1831 — the third President to die on a July 4th.

Putnam, Israel. Born January 7, 1718. Lieutenant colonel in Connecticut militia October 1774; in 1775 brigadier general in Connecticut militia. Became major general in Continental Army on June 17, 1775.

Rall, Johan Gottlieb. Born 1726(?). Colonel. Commanded Hessian garrison at Trenton.

St. Clair, Arthur. Born March 23, 1736. Colonel December 1775; brigadier general August 9, 1776; major general February 19, 1777.

Sargent, Winthrop. Born May 1, 1753. January to March 16, 1776 was naval agent at Gloucester, Mass. and a captain in Henry Knox' regiment of artillery. By end of war was a major.

Schuyler, Philip John. Born November 11, 1733. Was a delegate from New York to the Continental Congress. Appointed by Congress as one of the four major generals under George Washington June 17, 1775 (others were Artemus Ward, Charles Lee and Israel Putnam). On June 25, 1775 Washington appointed Schuyler Commander of the Northern Army. On August 4, 1777 Congress appointed Horatio Gates to that post and he relieved Schuyler August 19. Schuyler resigned his commission during the spring of 1779.

Stark, John. Born August 28, 1728. Colonel of New Hampshire militia at Bunker Hill and at Cambridge. Was at Washington Crossing, Trenton and Princeton. Resigned commission March 1777. In July 1777 appointed brigadier general of New Hampshire militia. On October 4, 1777 appointed brigadier general of Continental Army; major general September 1783.

Stephen, Adam. Born 1730. Colonel 1775; brigadier general September 4, 1776; major general February 19, 1777.

Stirling, Lord. See Alexander, William.

Sullivan, John. Born February 17, 1740. Appointed by Congress brigadier general June 22, 1775; major general August 9, 1776.

Tilghman, Tench. Born December 25, 1744. Military secretary to General Washington 1776 - 1783. Lieutenant colonel April 1, 1777.

von Donop, Carl Emil Ulrich. Colonel in Hessian forces in western New Jersey and at the fight for the Delaware.

Wayne, Anthony. Born January 1, 1745. Appointed colonel in Chester County, Pennsylvania militia January 3, 1776. On February 21, 1777 appointed brigadier general commanding the Pennsylvania Line. Was at Stony Point, New York, Paoli Massacre, Germantown. Brevetted to major general before retiring in 1783.

BIBLIOGRAPHY

Agniel, Lucien. "The American Revolution in the South." Riverside, Ct.: Chatham Press. 1972

"The American Flag in the Art of Our Country." Allentown Art Museum, Allentown, PA 1976.

Andre, John, Major. "Major Andre's Journal, 1777-1778." Boston: The Bibliophile Society, 1903. Vols. I & II, Limited Ed., Manuscript No. 7604. Huntington Library.

Archives of Maryland, Vol. XVIII. "Muster Rolls and Other Records of Service of Maryland Troops in the American Revolution, 1775-1783." Annapolis: Hall of Records.

Baker, Wm. S., ed. "Itinerary of General Washington from June 15, 1775 to Dec. 23, 1783." Philadelphia: 1892.

Barclay, Charles B., Mrs., Research Notebook in Historical Society of Pennsylvania. Philadelphia. Reference shelves TJ/573.

Beck, Alverda S., ed. "The Correspondence of Esek Hopkins, C-in-C, U.S. Navy." Providence: Rhode Island Historical Society. 1933.

Berg, Fred Anderson. "Encyclopedia of Continental Army Units." Harrisburg: Stackpole Books. 1972.

Betsy Ross Historical Papers. Doylestown, PA: Bucks County Historical Society Library.

Betsy Ross Papers. Philadelphia: American Philosophical Society.

Bill, Alfred Hoyt. "The Campaign of Princeton, 1776-1777." Princeton, NJ: 1948.

Boatner, Mark M. Encyclopedia of the American Rev.: New York. 1958.

Boldt, David R., and Randall, Willard S. "The Founding City, Bicentennial Journal, Philadelphia Inquirer." Radnor, PA: Chilton Book Co. 1976.

Bowie, Oden, Ch., et al, "In Grateful Remembrance." Annapolis: Maryland Comm. on Artistic Property. 1976.

Brewington, M.V. & Dorothy. "The Marine Paintings and Drawings in the Peabody Museum of Salem, Mass." Salem: Peabody Museum. 1968.

Callahan, North, "Henry Knox." New York: Rinehart & Co. 1958.

Canby, George, and Balderston, Lloyd, "The Evolution of the American Flag." Philadelphia: Ferris & Leach. 1917.

Canby, William J., Mss. and misc. papers. Balderston donation. The Huntington Library, San Marino, Calif. HM41760, case 33 and uncatalogued envelopes 60 and 122.

Chappelle, Howard I. "The History of the American Sailing Navy." New York: W.W. Norton & Co. 1949.

Chapin, Howard M., "The Artistic Motives in the United States Flag." Providence: Rhode Island Historical Society. 1930.

Chapin, Howard M., "Roger Williams and the King's Colors." Providence: Society of Colonial Wars, E.L. Freeman Co., Printers. 1928.

Christ Church in Philadelphia. Burial Record Book. Marriage Record Book, 1709-1800. "The Story of Christ Church." Pub. 1959. Philadelphia: Archives of Christ Church.

Chunn, Calvin Ellsworth, "Not by Bread Alone." Valley Forge, Pa.: Society of the Descendants of Washington's Army at Valley Forge. 1981.

Clark, Wm. Bell, et al, eds. "Naval Documents of the American Revolutions." Washington: Naval History Dept. United States Navy, Vols. I, II, II, IV (of 8 vols.). 1964.

Clinton Papers. William L. Clements Library, Univ. of Michigan, Ann Arbor, Mich.

Coakley, Robert W. & Conn, Stetson. "The War of the American Revolution." Washington: Center of Military History, United States Army. 1975.

Commager, Henry Steele, and Morris, Richard B., eds. "The Spirit of Seventy-Six." Vol. I. New York and Indianapolis: Bobbs Merrill Co. 1958.

Company of Military Historians, Col. John R. Elting, Ed., "Military Uniforms in America." San Rafael, Calif.: The Presido Press. 1974.

Continuing Education Institute. "The Story of Old Glory." Boy Scouts of America. 1971.

Cooper, Grace Rogers, "Thirteen Star Flags." Washington: Smithsonian Institution Press. 1973.

Cunningham, John T., "This is New Jersey." New Brunswick, NJ: Rutgers University Press. 1976.

Cutler, Alfred H. "The Continental 'Great Union' Flag." Somerville, Mass.: Somerville School Committee. 1929.

Davis, Gherardi. "Regimental Colors in the War of the Revolution." New York: Gillis Press. 1907.

Dorr, The Rev. Benj. D.D. "History of Christ Church in Philadelphia." Philadelphia: Christ Church. 1841.

Eggenberger, David. "Flags of the U.S.A." New York: Thomas Y. Crowell Co. 1959.

Elting, John R. "The Battles of Saratoga." Monmouth Beach, NJ: Philip Freneau Press. 1977.

Encyclopedia Britannica. Listings under "Flags."

Fast, Howard, "The Crossing." New York: Morrow & Co. 1971.

Fisher, Linda A. and Kingsley, Wm. A. "Authenticity of the Betsy Ross House." Philadelphia: Betsy Ross House. 1975.

Force, Peter, ed., "American Archives: Consisting of a Collection of Authentic Records." 9 vols. Washington: 1837-53.

Fow, John H. "The True Story of the American Flag." Philadelphia. Wm. J. Campbell. 1908.

Freeman, Douglas Southall. "George Washington, Leader of the Revolution." Vol. IV, New York: Charles Scribner's Sons. 1951. (5 vols.).

Furlong, Wm. R. & McCandless, Byron. "So Proudly We Hail." Washington: Smithsonian Institution Press. 1981.

Gifford, Edward S., Jr., "The American Revolution in the Delaware Valley." Philadelphia: Pennsylvania Soc. of Sons of the Revolution. 1976.

Gloucester County Historical Society, Bulletin. Gloucester, NJ: Vol. 14, No. 1, Sept. 1973.

Hamilton, Schuyler, "The History of the National Flag of the United States of America." Philadelphia. Lippincott, Grambo & Co. 1852.

Hastings, George E., "The Life and Works of Francis Hopkinson." Chicago: University of Chicago Press. 1926.

Heitman, Francis B., "Historical Register of Officers of the Continental Army During the War of the American Revolution, April 1775 to December 1783." Washington: Gov't. Printing Office. 1893.

Hutton, Ann Hawkes. "House of Decision." Philadelphia. 1956.

Hutton, Ann Hawkes. "George Washington Crossed Here." Radnor, PA: Chilton Book Co. 1976.

Hutton, Ann Hawkes. "Portrait of Patriotism." Radnor, PA: Chilton Book Co. 1959.

Hutton, Ann Hawkes. "The Year and The Spirit of '76." Radnor, PA: Chilton Book Co. 1972.

Jenkins, Charles Francis. "John Claypoole's Memorandum Book." Philadelphia: Historical Society of PA: Penna. Mag. of History & Biography, Vol. 16.

Journal of The Company of Military Historians, Vol. XXVI, No. 4, 1974. Washington, D.C.

Lebegern, George F., Jr. "Episodes in Bucks County History." Fallsington, Penna.: Bucks County Historical-Tourist Commission. 1975.

Lord, Walter. "The Dawn's Early Light." New York: Norton & Co. 1972.

Lossing, Benson J. "Lossing's New History of the United States." New York: Gay Bros. & Co., Vol. II. 1889.

Lossing, Benson J. "Pictorial Field Book of the Revolution." New York: Harper & Bros. Vol. II (30 vols. @ 25¢ bound into two vols.). 1852.

Mastai, Boleslaw & Marie Louise d'Outrange. "The Stars and Stripes." New York: Alfred A. Knopf, Inc. 1973.

Miller, Lillian B. et. al. "The Dye Is Now Cast." Washington: National Portrait Gallery, Smithsonian Institution Press. 1975.

Miller, Nathan. "U.S. Navy, an Illustrated History." Annapolis: U.S. Naval Institute Press. 1977.

Mitchell, Broadus. "Alexander Hamilton, The Revolutionary Years." New York: Thomas Y. Crowell Co. 1970.

Moore, John M., ed. "Friends in the Delaware Valley: Phila. Yearly Meeting 1681-1981." Haverford, PA: Friends Historical Assn. 1981.

Morris, Richard B. "Encyclopedia of American History." New York: Harper & Bros. 1953.

Morris, Robert. "Betsy Ross Papers." Philadelphia: Microfilm in American Philosophical Society, Historical Society of Penna., Library of Congress, Huntington Library, etc.

Morris, Robert. "The Truth About the American Flag." Beach Haven, NJ: Wynnehaven Publishing Co. 1976.

Morris, Robert. "The Truth About the Cowpens Flag." Beach Haven, NJ: Wynnehaven Publishing Co. 1978.

National Geographic Society, Magazine, Vol. XXXII, p. 288.

Naval Documents of the American Revolution. Wm. Bell Clark, et. al. eds. Washington: Naval History Dept., United States Navy, Vols. I, II, III, IV (of 8 vols.) 1964 -

Newman, Eric P. "The Early Paper Money of America." Racine, Wisc.: Whitman Publ. Co. 1967.

Parry, Edwin S. "Betsy Ross, Quaker Rebel." Philadelphia: John C. Winston Co. 1930.

Pedersen, Christian Fogd, et. al. "The International Flag Book." New York: Wm. Morrow & Co. 1971.

Pennsylvania Magazine of History and Biography. Vol. XCVIII, July 1974. p. 324. Philadelphia: Historical Society of Pennsylvania.

Pennsylvania Magazine of History and Biography. Vol. XCIX, April 1975, Dunlap. Philadelphia: Historical Society of Pennsylvania.

Pennsylvania Magazine of History and Biography. Vol. XCIX, July 1975, p. 366. Philadelphia: Historical Society of Pennsylvania.

Preble, Geo. Henry, U.S.N. "History of the Flag of the United States of America." Boston: A. Williams & Co. 1880.

Preble, Geo. Henry, U.S.N. "The Story of the United States Flag." Albany: Joel Munsell, Printer. 1872.

Pennsylvania Archives, Second Series, A(2)1, Minutes of Board of War, 1777. Harrisburg: Commonwealth of Pennsylvania Pubs., see Historical and Museum Commission, Harrisburg.

Philadelphia Monthly Meeting, Minutes of, 1715-1744. Friends Historical Library, Swarthmore College.

Philadelphia Monthly Meeting, Minutes of, 1772-1781. Haverford College, Quaker Collections.

Perrin, William G. "British Flags, Their Early History and Their Development at Sea." Cambridge, England: Cambridge Press. 1922.

Quaife, Milo M., Weig & Appleman. "The History of the United States Flag." New York: Harper & Row. 1961.

Reede, Arthur H. "America's Revolution: How it was Financed." Ch. 2 Foreign Aid, the Secret Phase." Loretto, PA: St. Francis College. 1975.

Richardson, Edward W., "Standards and Colors of the American Revolution." Philadelphia: Pa. Soc. of Sons of the Revolution - The Color Guard, and Univ. of Pa. Press, 1982.

Roberts, Kenneth Lewis, "The Battle of Cowpens: The Great Morale Builder." New York: 1958.

Schermerhorn, Frank Earle. "American and French Flags of The Revolution, 1775-1783." Philadelphia: Pennsylvania Society of Sons of the Revolution. 1948.

Sellers, Charles Coleman. "Portraits and Miniatures by Charles Willson Peale." Philadelphia: American Philosophical Society. 1952.

Shankle, George Earlie, "State Names, Flags, Seals, etc." New York: H. W. Wilson Co. 1934.

Sizer, Theodore. "The Works of Colonel John Trumbull." New Haven: Yale University Press. 1967.

Smith, Samuel Stelle. "At General Howe's Side 1776-1778." Monmouth Beach, NJ: Philip Freneau Press. 1974.

Smith, Samuel Stelle. "The Battle of Princeton." Monmouth Beach, NJ: Philip Freneau Press. 1967.

Smith, Samuel Stelle. "The Battle of Trenton." Monmouth Beach, NJ: Philip Freneau Press. 1965.

Smith, Samuel Stelle. "Fight for the Delaware, 1777." Monmouth Beach, NJ: Philip Freneau Press. 1970.

Smith, Whitney. "The Flag Book of The United States." New York: William Morrow & Co. 1970.

Snyder, Martin P. "City of Independence." New York: Praeger Publishers. 1975.

Spargo, John. "The Stars and Stripes in 1777." Bennington, VT: Bennington Battle Monument and Historical Association. 1928.

Stryker, Wm. S. "The Battles of Trenton and Princeton." Boston: 1898.

Thompson, Ray, "Betsy Ross, Last of Philadelphia's Free Quakers." Fort Washington, PA: Bicentennial Press. 1972.

Thompson, Ray. "Washington Along the Delaware." Ft. Washington, PA: Bicentennial Press, 1970.

Thompson, Ray. "Washington at Germantown." Ft. Washington: Bicentennial Press. 1971.

Thompson, Ray. "Washington at Whitemarsh." Ft. Washington, PA: Bicentennial Press. 1974.

Thruston, Ballard. "Origin and Evolution of the U.S. Flag" House Document 258, 69th Congress, 1st Session, 1926. Washington: U.S. Gov't Printing Office. 1926.

Tower, Lawrence Phelps. "The Untold Story of Our Flag." United States Flag Foundation. New York. 1956.

Trevelyan, Sir Geo. Otto, "The American Revolution." London and New York. 4 Vols. 1899-1913.

Tuckerman, Bayard, "Life of General Philip Schuyler." 1905.

Turp, Ralph K. "West Jersey Under Four Flags." Philadelphia: Dorrance & Co. 1975.

Wannamaker, W. W., Jr., Capt. USNR, "A Story of American Flags." Columbia, SC: State Printing Co. 1971.

Ward, Christopher. "The War of the Revolution." New York: Macmillan Co. 1952.

Wilson, Robert H. "Philadelphia Quakers." Philadelphia: Yearly Meeting of the Religious Society of Friends. 1981.

Wolf, Edwin II. "Philadelphia, Portrait of an American City." Harrisburg: Stackpole Books. 1975.

U.S. Department of Defense. "Our Flag." Washington: Supt. of Documents. NAVMC 6915, Rev. 1960.

U.S. Naval Institute. Proceedings, Vol. 101, No. 10/872, Oct. 1975. Annapolis, Md: The Naval Institute Press. 1975.

U.S. Naval Institute. Proceedings Vol. 101, No. 11/873. Nov. 1975. Annapolis, Md: The Naval Institute Press. 1975.

Webster Encyclopedic Dictionary. p. 953. Chicago: The English Language Institute of America. 1971.

INDEX

Abbot Hall, Marblehead, Mass., *vii*, 151fn, 152

Abington, PA, *117*

Academy of The Fine Arts, Pennsylvania, *vii*

Adams, John, *43fn, 44, 92, 123*

Adams, Sam, *89*

Albany, N.Y., *66*

Alexander, Wm. (Lord Stirling) See Stirling, Lord

Alfred, Ship, *30*

Allen, Ethan, *29*

American Crisis, Tom Paine pamphlet, *55*

American Flag House and Betsy Ross Memorial Assn., *118, 140, 146*

American Philosophical Soc., *vii, xii, 137fn*

American Philosophical Soc. Library, *115*

Annapolis, State House, *vii, 157*

Appleman, Roy E., *150*

Army and Navy Museum, *vii, 132*

Army, U.S., Birth of, *29*

Arnold, Benedict, Col., *29, 43, 46, 163fn*

Articles of Confederation *124*

Ashburn, Eliza (Aunt), *98*

Ashburn, Eliza (Daughter), *103, 104*

Ashburn, Elizabeth (Mrs. Joseph) *100, 101, 102, 103, 105, 141, 143*
also see Ross, Betsy
also see Claypoole, Elizabeth

Ashburn, Joseph,*66, 98, 100, 101, 102, 104, 141, 141fn, 143*

Ashburn, Zilla, *101, 104*

Assunpink Creek, *61*

Atlantic City, N.J., *88*

Atwater Kent Museum, *116*
also see Kent, A. Atwater

Augusta, British Frigate, *81, 82, 83, 84, 84fn, 85*

Ayres, Captain of the *Polly, 27, 28, 29*

Balderston, Lloyd, Ph.D., *92*

Baltimore, MD., *48, 62, 64*

Baltimore Sunday Sun, newspaper, *164, 166*

Barclay, Charles B., Mr. & Mrs., *vi, 140, 145, 146*

Barkly, Gilbert, *37fn*

Barrett, William, *128*

Basking Ridge, N.J., *49*

Batchelor, Joshua, Ensign, *165*

Batchelor, William, *165*

Baylor, Regimental Cmdr., *70, 71*

Beggarstown, PA, *76*

Bennington Battle Monument and Historical Assn., *170*

Bennington, Battle of, *169*

Bennington Flag, *96, 132, 168, 169*

Bennington Historical Museum and Library, *vii, 132*

Berkeley, Lord John, *8*

Betsy Ross - see Ross, Betsy

Biddle, Clement Col., *74, 107, 139, 143*

Billing, Edward (Billinge, Byllynge), *8*

Billings Island, *67*

Billingsport, N.J., *67, 78*

"Birth of Our Nation's Flag," portrait, *151, 153*

Black Horse, N.J., *62*

Black Prince, Ship, 30
Bland, Theodore, Regimental Commander, 70, 71
Board of Admiralty, 158, 159
Board of Treasury, 159
Board of War, 97, 99, 130, 156, 160, 163, 164, 173, 174
Boggs, Margaret Donaldson, 117, 122, 127, 128, 145
Bon Homme Richard, Ship, 90
Boon's Island, 79
Bordentown, N.J., 48, 50, 58, 61, 62
Boston Gazette, 92
Boston, Mass., 29, 36, 129
Boston Massacre, 26
Boston, Siege of, 1775, 42
Bowman, James, 1, 2, 3, 5
Bradford, Colonel, 78
Brandywine, Battle of, 72, 102
Brandywine Creek, PA., 72
Brennan, Thomas G., 41
Brigantine Shoals, N.J., 88
Bristol, PA., 50, 57, 58
British East India Co., 36, 37, 40, 149
British Museum Library, 92
British Red Ensign, 35, 36
British Union Jack, 35, 36
Brooklyn Heights, 46
Brunswick, New Jersey, 48, 50
Bucks County Historical Society and Spruance Library, *vii*
Bunker (Bunker's) Hill, Boston, 30, 41, 137, 145
Burgoyne, John Maj. Gen., 66, 68, 78
Burlington, N.J., 50, 58, 62
Burnham, Smith, 92, 93

Byllynge, Edward, 8
Cadwalader, John, Col., 50, Brig. Gen., 57
Calendar, Gregorian, *fn6*
Calendar, Julian, *fn6*
Calendar Act of Parliament, *fn6*
Cambridge, Mass., 29, 30, 36, 56
Camden, N.J., 48
Camden, S.C., Battle, 157fn
Canada, 34, 43, 46, 49, 66, 68, 118
Canby, Caleb H., 106
Canby, Jane Claypoole, 117, 118
Canby, Wm. J., *xii*, 118, 119, 120, 121, 126, 127, 128, 160, 161
Cape Charles, 68
Cape Henlopen, 104
Carpenters' Hall, Phila., 8
Carpenter's Island, 79, 81
Carteret, Sir George, 8
Cartwright, Edmund, 170
Center Point, PA., 76
Chadd's Ford, PA., 72
Champlain, Lake, 29, 43, 46, 66
Charleston, S.C., 43, 68
Charlestown, Mass., 36
Chesapeake Bay, 46, 69
Chester, PA., 8, 68, 79
Chestnut Hill, PA., 114
Chestnut Neck, N.J., 88
Cheveaux de frise, 66, 67, 78, 79
Chew Mansion, Germantown, 76, 77
Chisholm, Caroline, *vi*
Christ Church, Phila., *vii*, 6, 23, 24, 30, 33, 98, 105, 109, 147
Christiana River, Del., 72

Christina Swedish Settlement, 99

Churchill, Sir Winston, 63

City Tavern, 66

Civil War, xi, 93, 122

Claypoole, Clarissa Sidney, 106

Claypoole, Elizabeth, (Mrs. John), 105, 115, 117, 118, 119, 120, 127, 141
also see, Ross, Betsy
also see, Ashburn, Elizabeth

Claypoole, Harriet, 106

Claypoole, Jane, 106

Claypoole, John, 98, 102, 103, 104, 105, 115, 116, 118, 140

Claypoole, Rachel, 106

Claypoole, Susannah, 106

Clements Library, vii

Clymer, George, 49

College of Philadelphia, 160

Colonial Dames of America, 69

Committee of Correspondence, 125

Committee of Safety of Penna., 43, 99

Concord, Mass., 145

Continental Army, 30, 36, 46, 72, 114, 145, 148, 163

Continental Congress, 26, 29, 30, 37, 43, 46, 48, 49, 62, 64, 72, 74, 90, 119, 145, 149, 158, 163
flag resolution, see Flag Resolution of Congress

Continental Navy, 30, 36, 145

Cooch's Bridge, Del., 72, 96

Cooper's Ferry, 1, 48, 79, 88

Cooper, Grace Rogers, 166, 167, 170, 171

Cornwallis, Galley, 81

Cornwallis, Lord Earl Charles,
Major Gen., 46, 47, 48
Lt. Gen., 48, 62, 63, 72, 74, 75, 76, 78, 96, 114

Coryell's Ferry, 48, 50, 51, 69

Council of Safety of PA., 35, 47

Cowpens Flag, 96, 131, 157, 164, 167, 168

Cowpens, S.C., 132, 157fn

Cowperthwaite, Col., 58

Craig, Lt. Col. Thomas, 114

Crown Point, N.Y., 29, 43, 145

Cummings, The Rev., 5

Daily Advertiser, 66

Darragh, Charles, 109

Darragh, Lydia, 109

Darragh, Susanna, 109

Darragh, William, 109

Daughters of the American Rev., Library, vi

Deane, Silas, 46

Declaration of Independence, 24fn, 26, 26fn, 29, 35, 43, 44, 89, 90, 126, 127, 150

de Fermoy, Mathieu Alexis Roche, Brig. Gen., 51, 54, 59

Delaware Bay, 66, 88
Capes, 69, 105
Pilots, warnings, 27, 28, 29

Delaware River,
1773 - 1776, 1, 27, 28, 29, 30, 31, 36, 48, 50, 145
Washington Crossing, 48, 51, 54, 63, 172
1777 and after, 68, 74, 76, 78, 99, 103

Dewey, Elijah, Capt., 170

Dickinson, Philemon, Brig. Gen., 51, 55

Digby, Wm., Lt., 93, 96

Dock Ward, Phila., 145

Dole, Sarah, 8

Donaldson, Sarah, 104, 127

Donaldson, Wm., Capt., *104*

Drinker, Tory, *29*

Dunk's Ferry, PA., *50, 58*

Dunlap's Pennsylvania Packet or General Advertiser, *92*

Dunmore, Governor Lord, *46*

Durham boats, *48, 51, 172*

Durham Furnace, *48*

du Portail, Louise, Col., *72*

Dusseldorf, Germany, *172*

East Jersey, *8, 88*

Eisenhower, Dwight D., Pres., *63*

Elkton (Head of Elk),MD., *68*

Elting, John R., Col., *vi, 95*

Enoch Pratt Library, *vii*

Enterprize (sic), Ship, *103*

Ewing, Brig. Gen. James, *50, 58, 61*

Eyre, Col. Jehu, *102*

Fenwick, John, *8*

Fight for the Delaware, *78 - 87*

Fillmore, Millard, President, *170*

Fillmore, Nathaniel, *169*

Fillmore, Septa, *170*

Fisher, Henry, *68*

Fisher, Linda A., Esq., *140, 140fn*

Five-pointed star, how to make, *151*

"Flag Committee" of Congress, *123, 124, 147, 148*

Flag Day, *89, 91, 149*

Flag Resolution of Congress, *89, 90, 91, 93, 132, 137, 149, 158, 163, 164*

Fletcher, Rachel, *127, 128, 140, 145*

Fletcher, Richard, *106*

Fort Ann, N.Y., *93*

Fort Island, *79*

Fort Lee, N.J., *46*

Fort Mercer, *66, 67, 79, 81, 84, 87*

Fort Mifflin, *66, 67, 78, 81, 84, 85, 87*

Fort Ticonderoga, *29, 56, 66, 145*

Fort Ticonderoga, Museum and Library, *vii, 163*

Fort Washington, N.Y., *46*

Frankford, PA., *109*

Franklin, Benjamin, *3, 24fn, 36, 43fn, 44, 46, 73, 92*

Franklin, Schooner, *125fn*

Franklin, Wm., Esq., *2, 3, 4*

Free Quakers, see Society of Free Quakers

Freeman, Douglas Southall, *42, 148*

Friends Historical Library of Swarthmore College, *vii*

Friends Meeting House, Phila., *9*

Friends Public School, *16*

Furlong, Wm. Rea, Rear Admiral, *172*

Fury, Galley, *85*

Gabitis, Debora, *8*

Gaspee, Schooner, *26*

Gates, Maj. Gen. Horatio, *49, 51, 78, 96*

Genealogical Society of Penna., *vi, 137*

George, Lake, N.Y., *66*

Germain, Lord George, *63, 74*

Germantown Academy, *29fn*

Germantown, Battle of, *74-78 incl., 102, 109*

Germantown Historical Society, *vii, 136, 171*

Germantown, PA., *68, 69, 70, 74, 76, 77*

Giannini, Robert L. III, *132*

216

Glassboro State College, 5

Gloria Dei Church, *vii,* 99

Gloucester County Historical Society, *vi, vii,* 2, 3, *3fn,* 67

Gloucester, New Jersey, *1,* 3

Glover, John Col., *36fn,* 54, 56, 59, 61 Major Gen., *163fn*

Gordon's Ford, PA., 74

Gottlieb, Theodore J., *123, 126, 127, 129, 138, 140, 162*

Grand Union Flag, *30, 35, 36, 37, 40, 89, 90, 130, 149, 150*

Grant, Major General James, 48, 50

Great Bay, N.J., 88

Green Mountain Boys, 41

Greene, Nathanael, Maj. Gen., *51,* 54, *59, 63, 68, 70, 72, 76, 77, 79, 107fn*

Gregory III, Pope, 6

Griscom, Andrew, 6, 8

Griscom, condemnation, Samuel & Rebecca, 9

Griscom, Deborah, 10

Griscom, Elizabeth, *1,* 5, 6, 16

Griscom, Family, 6

Griscom, Genealogical, 6, 8

Griscom, Marriage, Samuel & and Rebecca, 9, 10

Griscom, Rebecca, 6

Griscom, Samuel, 6, 8

Griscom, Tobias, 8

Griscom, unchaste intimacy, *10, 11, 12, 13*

Haddonfield, N.J., 79

Hallinan, Laurence, *136fn*

Hall of Records, Annapolis, MD., *vii,* 165, *166fn*

Hamilton, Alexander, Captain, *51,* 74

Hamilton, Alexander, Mrs., *162*

Hamilton, Schuyler, Esq., *163*

Hancock, John, 44

Hartsville, PA., 69

Haussegger, Nicholas, Col., 48

Haverford College Library, *vii, 19fn*

Hazelwood, Commodore John, *84, 87*

Head of Elk, MD., 68

Heap, George, 40

Hewes, Joseph, 24

Hildebrandt, Sophia B., *117, 127, 128, 145*

Historical Society of Penna., *vi, xii,* 34, *118, 122, 126, 160, 161*

Hitchcock, Daniel, Col., 57, 58

Hoelle, Edith, *vi, 84fn*

Hog Island, 79

Hopkins, Esek, Commodore, 30, 90

Hopkinson, Francis, 24, *158, 159, 160*

Hortalez, Et Cie., 43

Howard, John Eager, *157fn*

Howe, Elias, 31

Howe, Richard, Lord Admiral, 66, 76, 81

Howe, Sir William, Gen., 34, 42, 48, 62, 66, 67, 71, 72, 73, 74, 76, 77, 79, 81, 109

Hudson River, 46, 66, 68, 69

Hugg, William, *1,* 3

Hugg's Tavern, *1,* 3, 5

Huntington Library, *vi, vii, xii, 123, 126, 161*

Hutton, Ann Hawkes, *vi, 148, 171*

Hyder Ally, ship, 105

Independence Hall, *xi, 174, 175, 176*

Independence National Historical Park, *132*

Peace Treaty, Revolutionary War, *136*

Peale, Charles Willson, *96, 136, 137, 148, 149, 149fn, 156*

Peale, Titian R., *137, 150fn*

Pearl, 5th rate ship, *81*

Pearson's Mill, *109, 114*

Pelham, N.Y., military action, *46*

Pell, John H.G., *163fn*

Pell, William Ferris, *163fn*

Penn, William, *8, 16, 69*

Pennington, N.J., *48*

Penn's Manor, PA., *50*

Pennsylvania, Academy of the Fine Arts, *vii*
 Archives, *99*
 Charter, *8*
 Evening Post, *92*
 Gazette, *44, 66*
 Journal, *55*
 Map, SE Cor., Holme, *32*
 Packet, Dunlap's, *92*
 Post War, *116, 118, 171*
 State Navy Board, *99*
 University of, *140, 160*

Perkiomen Creek, *76*

Philadelphia Contributionship Insurance Company, *146*

Philadelphia, Pennsylvania
 1741-1773, *1, 2, 3, 4, 5, 6, 6fn, 7, 8, 25, 26, 29*
 1774-1776, *18, 29, 30, 34, 36, 48, 50, 62, 64*
 1777 and after, *10, 66, 67, 68, 69, 70, 71, 72, 78, 81, 87, 88, 98, 99, 104, 105, 123, 125, 146*
 Associators, *64*
 Junior League, *116*
 Light Horse, *71*
 Main Line, *74*

Philosophical Hall, *125*

Philosophical Society Library, *115*

Phoenixville, PA., *74*

Plymouth, England, *103*

Polly, tea ship, *26, 27*

Port Republic, N.J., *88*

Portraits
 Peale, Charles Willson, *96, 136, 137, 148, 149, 149fn, 156*
 Trumbull, John, Col., *96, 136, 137, 138, 149, 149fn, 168fn*
 Weisgerber, Charles H., *151, 153*
 Willard, Archibald M., *151, 151fn, 152*

Potts Grove, PA., *76*

Pottstown, PA., *74*

Preble, George Henry, Rear Admiral *36, 37, 126, 158*

Princeton, N.J., *48, 50, 61, 62, 63, 66, 76, 96, 137, 156*

Princeton University, *29fn, 150fn*

Printz, Johann, Gov., *99fn*

Province Island, *79, 81*

Putnam, Israel, Maj. Gen., *37, 50, 173*

Quaife, Milo M., *96, 97, 150, 153, 156, 157, 158, 160*

Quebec, Canada, *43, 145*

Rall, Johann Gottlieb, Col, *48, 50, 51, 59, 61*

Reading, PA., *62, 67, 74*

Reed, Joseph, Col., *37fn, 57, 156*

Red Bank, N.J., *66, 67, 81*

Remington, Frederic, *138*

Rhode Island, First and Second Regiments, *41, 42*

Rhode Island Historical Society,
 Library, *vii*
 Museum, *41*

Rhode Island, State Capitol, Library, *vii*

Richards, William, *99*

Richardson, Edward West, *vi*

Richelieu River, Canada, *66*
Ritzema, Colonel, *37*
Rodney, Caesar, *44*
Rodney, Thomas Col., *57*
Roebuck, ship, *81*
Rosenthal, Joseph, *96*
Ross, Betsy, Griscom, Ashburn, Claypoole, *vi, xi, xii, 1, 2, 3, 4, 5, 6, 7, 23, 33, 49, 62, 64, 69, 73, 87, 103, 141, 146*
   Christ Church, *23, 24, 30, 33, 98, 105, 109, 147*
   Free Quakers, *107, 109, 115, 116*
   Marriage, Ashburn, *99*
   Marriage, Claypoole, *105*
   Story, *121, 122, 123, 125, 126, 130, 147, 148, 150, 153, 166, 173*
   see also, Ashburn, Elizabeth
   see also, Claypoole, Elizabeth
Ross, Eneas, *5, 6*
Ross, George, Col., *24, 35, 42, 123, 127, 147, 148, 164*
Ross, John, *1, 2, 3, 4, 5, 7, 23, 30, 33, 35, 141, 143, 164*
Rush, Benjamin, Dr., *24fn, 117, 117fn*
Ryerson, William Alan, *8fn*
St. Clair, Arthur, Brig. Gen., *51, 54, 59*
St. Johns, Quebec, *66*
St. Michaels, West Indies, *104*
Salem, New Jersey, *8*
San Diego Museum of Art, *vi*
Sandy Hook, N.J., *43, 66*
Saratoga, N.Y., *78*
Sargent, Paul, Col., *54, 59*
Satterthwaite, Abel, *106, 118*
Satterthwaite, Susan, *117*
Savannah, Georgia, *29*
Savitz Library, N.J., *3*
Scattergood, Thomas, *19*

Schermerhorn, Frank Earle, *162*
Schiffli, Embroidery, *31*
Schuyler, Elizabeth, *136*
Schuyler Flag (Ft. Ticonderoga), *131, 162, 171*
Schuyler Flag (Philadelphia), *132*
Schuyler, Philip John, Maj. Gen., *96, 136, 162, 163, 164*
Schuylkill River, *33, 68, 69, 74, 76, 79, 163, 164*
Schwenksville, PA., *76, 78*
Scull, Nicholas, *40*
Sellers, Charles Coleman, *137fn*
Serapis, ship, *90*
Seven Years War, *25, 40*
Shannon, River, Ireland, *103*
Sheldon, Regimental Cmdr., *70*
Sherman, Roger, *43fn, 44*
Sizer, Theodore, *137*
Smith, Samuel Stelle, *vi, 46fn*
Smith, Whitney, *147, 148, 149, 150*
Smithsonian Institution, *167, 172*
Snyder, Martin P., *40fn, 177cap.*
Society of Free Quakers, *107, 109, 114, 115, 118*
Society of the Cincinnati, *157*
Somerville, Mass., *36*
Sons of Liberty, *26*
South Amboy, N.J., *62*
Spargo, John, *129, 168*
"Spirit of '76" portrait, *151*
Stamp Act, *26*
Stark, John, Col., *41, 54*
State House, Annapolis, *vii, 131, 157, 164*
State House, Philadelphia, *8, 8fn, 29, 69, 71, 149, 163, 164*

State House, Rhode Island, *41*

State House, Trenton, *3*

Stenton Mansion, *69, 70, 77*

Stephen, Adam, Brig. Gen., *51, 54, 59, 70, 77*

Stewart, Frank H., *3*

Stirling, Brig. Gen. Lord (Wm. Alexander), *51, 54, 59, 60, 61, 62, 70*

Stony Point, N.Y., *68*

Suffolk Resolves, *26*

Sugar Act, *26*

Sullivan, John, Maj. Gen., *43, 49, 51, 54, 59, 68, 69, 72, 76, 77*

Swallow, Brig, *98, 101, 102*

Taft, William Howard, President, *157*

Tarleton, Banastre, Col., *157fn*

Tea cargoes, *26*

Thayer, Simeon, Major, *87*

Third Maryland Regiment, *132, 165*

Thompson-Neely House, *51*

Thomson, Charles, *44, 89, 123*

Thomson, John, *19*

Three Rivers, Quebec, *43*

Throgs Neck, N.Y., *46*

Thruston, Ballard, *130*

Tilghman, Tench, *71*

Tinicum, PA., *99, 99fn*

Tokyo Bay, *xi*

Townshend Acts, *26, 40*

Trenton, N.J., *46, 48, 50, 55, 57, 58, 59, 63, 66, 68, 76, 137, 156, 171*
  Attack on - maps, *60, 61*
  State House, *3*

Trevelyan, Rt. Hon. Sir George Otto, *62, 63*

Wrightstown Road, PA., *55*

Yale University Art Gallery, *vii, 137*

Yardley, PA., *55*

Yarrington, Robert W., *8fn*

York, PA., *72*

Yorktown, VA., *51, 63, 96, 137, 171*

Truman, Harry, President, *149*

Trumbull, John, Col., *96, 136, 137, 138, 149, 149fn, 168fn*

Trumbull, Jonathan, *137*

Tuckerton, N.J., *88*

Tullytown, PA., *50*

Turner, Susan McCord, *104*

United Company of the Train of Artillery of Providence, *41*

United States Capitol, *vi, xifn, 138*

United States Navy Ensign, *136, 171*

University of Pennsylvania, *140, 160*

Upland, PA., *8*

Upper Darby School, *118*

Valcour Island, *46*

Valley Forge Historical Society and Museum, *137, 157*

Valley Forge, PA., *107*

Varnum, James, Brig. Gen., *85, 87*

Vigilant, Galley, *81, 85*

Von Donop, Carl Emil Ulrich, Col. *48, 58, 79, 81*

Von Knyphausen, Gen., *61, 72*

Walton, George, Esq., *49*

Warminster, PA., *69*

Warren, Joseph, Maj. Gen., *26fn*

Washington Crossing, PA., *50, 76*
  Foundation, *171*
  Historic Park, *171*
  Library of the American Revolution *vii*

"Washington Crossing the Delaware," Leutze portrait, *54, 171*

Washington, George, Gen., *30, 34, 36, 42, 44, 46, 48, 63*
   Flags, *xii, 35, 37, 41, 42, 89, 147, 148, 150, 156, 157, 171, 173*
   At and near Brandywine, Germantown, Philadelphia, *69, 70, 71, 72, 73, 74, 77, 78, 85, 102, 123, 125, 126, 127*
   At McKonkey's Ferry, Trenton, Princeton, *49, 50, 51, 56, 59, 61, 62, 96, 137, 171*
   At Whitemarsh and Valley Forge, *109, 114*

Washington, John Augustine, *49, 68*

Washington, Martha, *23, 35, 125, 147*

Wayne, Anthony, Brig. Gen., *68, 70, 72, 76*

Webster, William, *5, 23, 141*

Weig, Melvin J., *150*

Weisgerber, Charles H., *151, 153*

Wentz, Peter, farm, *76*

West Jersey, *7, 8, 88*

Wetherill, George D., *115*

Wetherill, John Price, *115*

Wetherill, Reeves, *115, 116*

Wetherill, Samuel, *107, 115, 116*

Wetherill, Sarah, *107*

Wetherill, William, Dr., *115*

White, Frances, *140*

"White House," first, *77cap.*

White-Marsh, Church, *6*

Whitemarsh, PA., *69*

White Plains, N.Y., military action, *46*

Williamsburg, Colonial, Governor's Palace, *vii*

Williamson's, Duncan, Ferry, *50*

Wilmington, Delaware, *99*

Wilson, Clarissa, *115, 117, 122, 127, 128*

Wilson, Jacob, *106*

Wilson, James, *24fn*

Wilson, Robert H., *8fn*

Wilson, Woodrow, President, *149*

Wolf, Edwin 2nd, *vi, 29fn*

Woodbury Creek, N.J., *81*

Woodruff, Mrs., *136*

Worcester P.O., PA., *76*

World Wars I & II, *xi*

Resolved That the Flag of the united states consist of 13 stripes alternate red and white, that the union be 13 stars white in a blue field representing a new constellation. —

The Council of the state of Massachusetts bay having represented by letter to the president of Congress that capt John Roach some time since appointed to command the continental ship of war the Ranger is a person of doubt-